YOUTH IN SOCIETY

contemporary theory, policy and practice
second edition

edited by
Jeremy Roche, Stanley Tucker,
Rachel Thomson and Ronny Flynn

SAGE
Los Angeles • London • New Delhi • Singapore

in association with

The Open University

SAGE Publications Ltd
1 Oliver's Yard
55 City Road
London EC1Y 1SP

SAGE Publications Inc
2455 Teller Road
Thousand Oaks
California 91320

SAGE Publications India Pvt. Ltd
B 1/I 1 Mohan Cooperative Industrial Area
Mathura Road, New Delhi 110 044
India

SAGE Publications Asia-Pacific Pte Ltd
33 Pekin Street #02-01
Far East Square
Singapore 048763

British Library Cataloguing in Publication Data

A catalogue record for this book is available from the British Library

ISBN 978-1-4129-0023-2 (hbk)
ISBN 978-1-4129-0024-9 (pbk)

Library of Congress Control Number: 2003112198

Typeset by M Rules, Southwark, London
Printed and bound in Great Britain by Cpod, Trowbridge, Wiltshire
Printed on paper from sustainable resources

£20-99

YOUTH IN SOCIETY

Contents

List of contributors

Les Back works at the Department of Sociology, Goldsmiths College, University of London. His current research focuses on politics, racism and urban culture. He is author of *New Ethnicities and Urban Culture* (1996) and co-author of *Out of Whiteness: Color, Politics and Culture* (2002) and *The Changing Face of Football: Racism and Multiculture in the English Game* (2001).

Sarah Banks is Senior Lecturer in Community and Youth Work at the University of Durham. Her current research interests lie in the fields of professional ethics and community development. She is the author of *Ethics Values in Social Work* (Second edition 2001) and *Ethics, Accountability and the Social Professions* (2004); editor of *Ethical Issues in Youth Work* (1999); and co-editor of *Teaching Practical Ethics for the Social Professions* (2003) and *Managing Community Practice* (2003).

Gargi Bhattacharyya teaches in the Department of Theology at the University of Birmingham. She is the author of a number of articles on issues of race, ethnicity, sexuality and global cultures. Her publications include *Tales of Dark-Skinned Women* (UCL Press, 1988),.with John Gabriel and Stephen Small *Race and Power* (Routledge, 2001) and *Sexuality and Society* (Routledge, 2002).

Simon Bradford is at the Department of Education, Brunel University. His research interests are professional education, managing services for young people and services for young people.

Harriet Bradley is Professor of Sociology and Dean of Social Sciences at Bristol University. Her research interests and publications are in the areas of work, trade unions, gender, young people and class. Among her books are *Fractured Identities* (1996) and *Gender and Power in the Workplace* (2000).

Liza Catan is Director of the Economic and Social Research Council's programme of research on *Youth, Citizenship and Social Change*, and is based at the Trust for the Study of Adolescence. Her interests are communication in adolescence, transition to adulthood and social inequalities. She also has a deep interest in making research relevant to policy makers and practitioners through dissemination.

John Coleman is a development psychologist, and Director of the Trust for the Study of Adolescence. His most recent books are *The Nature of Adolescence*, 3rd Edn (2000) and *Key Data on Adolescence* (2003). He was appointed OBE in 2001 for his services to youth justice.

Bob Coles is at the Department of Social Policy and Social Work at the University of York where his major interest is youth research and youth policy. He is the author of *Youth and Social Policy: Youth Citizenship and Youth Careers* (1995) and *Joining-Up Youth Research, Policy and Practice: a New Agenda for Change?*, Leicester, Youth Work Press-Barnardos (2000).

Brian Corby is Professor of Social Work Studies at the University of Central Lancashire. His main interests are child protection studies, child care policy and practice and social work practice. He is author of *Child Abuse: Towards a Knowledge*, 2nd edition (2000) and co-author of *Public Inquiries into the Abuse of Children in Residential Care* (2001).

*Catherine Dennison is at the Trust for the Study of Adolescence. Her major areas of interest are adolescent health behaviours, teenage parenthood and communication in adolescence.

Brian Dimmock is Principal Lecturer in Social Work at Gloucestershire University. His research and publishing covers family change following separation, divorce or death, remarriage and stepfamilies and inter-generational relations. He was formerly co-chair of the National Open Learning DipSW Partnership (NOLP).

Tim Edwards lectures in Sociology at the University of Leicester. He is currently writing a book on masculinities, editing a collection of essays on cultural theory and joint holder of an ESRC award to look at children and fashion. Major previous works include *Contradictions of Consumption* (OUP 2000), *Erotics and Politics* (Routledge, 1994) and *Men in the Mirror* (Cassell, 1997).

Sally French is Senior Lecturer in the Faculty of Health and Social Science at the University of Hertfordshire. She is co-editor of *Disability Discourse* (Open University Press, 1999) and author of *Disability and Employment* (Ashgate, 2001).

Ronny Flynn is a black woman Lecturer in the School of Health and Social Welfare at The Open University. Her interests are in anti-oppressive practice, kinship care, user participation and services for black disabled children and their families.

*John Gabriel is at the Department of Cultural Studies, University of Birmingham. His main areas of interest are racism, ethnicity and media. He is author of *Racism Culture Markets* (1994).

*Daren Garratt is a freelance writer, musician and researcher. He works with young people in the creative arts and is actively involved in promoting young people's rights and users of services within the community.

Christine Griffin is at the Department of Psychology at the University of Bath. She is particularly interested in the relation between consumption and identity for young people, especially for young women. Her book *Representations of Youth: The Study of Youth and Adolescence in Britain and America* was published in 1993.

Claire Hackett worked at Save the Children. She is the author of 'Out of our mouths not out of our heads' an article which appeared in a Report on drugs and drug use in West Belfast, published in 1996.

Paul Hickman worked for WMEB Consultants (a division of West Midlands Enterprise Board). He contributed to a national report on adult literacy and basic skills training in the workplace and also to a research project into approaches to meeting the special training needs of young people. He died in 2003 as a result of a car accident.

*Ladislav Lovás is at the Institute of Social Sciences in Košice, Eastern Slovakia and is a member of the Presidium of the Slovac Academy of Science. His main research interest is in human aggression, and most recently he has been studying bullying.

Harriette Marshall is at the Department of Psychology at Staffordshire University. Her major research interests lie with recent developments in cultural, and especially, feminist social science. Most recently she has focused her interests on young people's relationships.

John Muncie is at the Department of Social Science at the Open University. His major research is on contemporary reforms of the youth justice system in England and Wales. He is the author of *Youth and Crime: A Critical Introduction* (Sage, 1999) and editor of *The Sage Dictionary of Criminology* (Sage, 2001) and *Youth Justice: Criminal Readings* (Sage, 2002).

Joe Oldman is a housing campaigner who has worked for both Shelter and National Homeless Alliance and helped the development of resettlement services for young people when he was the Policy and Development Officer at CHAR. He is now the Older Homelessness and Housing Needs Manager for Help the Aged.

Mara Pini (Dr) lectures in the Media and Communications Department of Goldsmiths College, University of London. She is author of numerous articles on femininity and British dance cultures and in 2001 she published her first book, *Club Cultures and Female Subjectivity: The Move from Home to House*. She has recently started a new research project looking at femininity and diaspora.

*Lena Robinson is at the Department of Social Policy and Social Work at the University of Birmingham. Her research interests include racial/ethnic identity, inter-racial communication and black child development. She is the author of *Psychology for Social Workers: Black Perspectives* (1995).

Jeremy Roche is Senior Lecturer in law in the School of Health and Social Welfare at the Open University. He has written widely on children and the law, and on children's rights. He is co-editor of *Changing Experiences of Youth* (Sage, 1997).

Rex Stainton Rogers was a Lecturer in the Department of Psychology at the University of Reading up until his death in 1999. His best known work in his field is *Stories of Childhood*, published by Harvester Wheatsheaf in 1992.

Wendy Stainton Rogers currently heads the Open University's Research School. She has written extensively around child protection and child welfare work, and images of childhood and youth. Her interests in this field now centre around issues of young people's sexuality.

Paul Stenner is at the Department of Psychology, University College, London. His research interests include the social construction of personal relationships, the psychology of emotion and the history and philosophy of psychology. He is co-author of *Social Psychology: A Critical Agenda* (1995) and *Textuality and Tectonics: Troubling Social and Psychological Science* (1994).

Tom Storrie, formerly Principal of Colleges of Further and Higher Education, is a consultant for the Open University. His major area of research is the nature and potential of citizenship within the fields of the environment and of the local development of democracy in intercultural contexts.

John Swain is Professor of Disability and Inclusion at the University of Northumbria. He is co-author of *Controversial Issues in a Disabling Society* (Open University Press, 2003) and of *Disabling Barriers – Enabling Environment* (Sage, forthcoming).

Rachel Thomson is a Lecturer in the School of Health and Social Welfare at the Open University. Her research interests focus on young people, intimacy, gender and social change and she has published widely in these areas.

Stanley Tucker is Head of the School of Community and Professional Development at Newman College of Higher Education. He has researched and published widely in the area of young people and social policy.

*Josef Výrost is at the Institute of Social Sciences in Košice, Eastern Slovakia. His research interests include people's responses to 'hard times'.

Steve Walker is Reader in Education at Newman CHE, Birmingham. His research interests include education policy, action research in education and school democratisation. He is the author of *Democrazia a Scuola e Ricerca-Azione* (2000).

Adrian Ward is in the School of Social Work and Psychosocial Science at the University of East Anglia, Norwich. His major research interests are child care, therapeutic work with children and young people, and education and training for residential staff.

*Ron Westerby is an educational consultant. He was formerly Chief Education Officer in Dudley, West Midlands. His current research is for a PhD on the introduction of comprehensive schools, nationally and in Dudley, comparing the aspirations and outcomes.

* these entries are unchanged from the first edition of this book.

Introduction to the second edition

Rachel Thomson, Ronny Flynn, Jeremy Roche and Stanley Tucker

Generally 'youth' tends to be seen as a problem: young people are beset by predominantly negative images, are seen as either a source *of* trouble or *in* trouble. In bringing together this collection one of our main goals has been to challenge this 'problematising' perspective on youth. We also want to promote critical reflection on the position of young people in the UK today and in so doing we have sought to capture and analyse the changing images and experiences of young people as well as the complexity of the transitions they go through. We perceive a need to rethink youth in terms of acknowledging and respecting the many positive contributions young people can and do make to their communities and how adults can provide young people with both effective support and positive criticism. We believe that adults and young people alike can learn and benefit from such a refashioned public dialogue. Thus this reader, along with its companion anthology *Changing Experiences of Youth* (Garratt, Roche and Tucker, 1997), is presented as a positive contribution towards promoting the rights, and acknowledging the responsibilities, of young people in contemporary society. Yet a great deal has changed since this reader was first published in terms of young people's everyday lives: the policies directed towards them and the practice issues affecting those that work with them. In this new introduction we will provide an overview of some of the main changes that have taken place, and comment on the new material included in this second edition.

The changing face of youth

Many of the trends that shaped the transitions of young people in the late 1990s have become more pronounced over recent years. It is increasingly the case that young people remain in education and in the family home beyond the age of 16. The dramatic expansion of higher education, the removal of independent benefits to young people and the introduction of student loans mean that young people continue to be economically dependent on their families for much longer. Such 'extended dependency' is consistent with a wider European picture. However the effective privatisation of higher education in the UK means that a disproportionate number of students in the UK are engaged in high levels of part and full time work as well as generating significant debts.

The expansion of higher education and the promotion of lifelong learning has been associated with a powerful 'can do' ethos amongst the young. This is the idea that 'anyone can make it as long as they try hard enough', with young people tending to blame failure on their individual faults rather than on wider economic conditions or social policies (Evans et al., 2001). Yet evidence from panel studies (that follow the same people over an extended period of time) suggests that opportunities for young people are in fact *less* than they were 20 years ago, and that the expansion in higher education has benefited the 'not so bright middle classes' rather than industrious working class youth (Schoon et al., 2001). In many ways the UK is a more diverse, polarised and less meritocratic society than it was a generation ago. The majority of white, non-disabled and middle class young people face a relatively smooth and predictable (if highly demanding) pathway through initial and higher education into professional employment. However, less privileged young people may struggle to find a clear and linear path from dependence to independence – going through a range of short term vocational courses and training schemes, and periods of unemployment. Moreover, the goal of independence as a model of adulthood has to be questioned with a growing recognition of the interdependence of members of families and households. So for example, the costs of young people's further education may be offset by the wages of mothers, and the care provided by older siblings may in turn facilitate the employment and training of other family members (Irwin, 1995).

Commentators have described this picture in terms of *uneven* and *fragmented transitions*. Uneven, because different groups of young people have very different experiences of the transition to adulthood. Fragmented, because the different markers of adulthood are increasingly uncoupled from each other. So for example, although young people may have to wait longer before they are economically independent, evidence suggests that other markers of adulthood such as sexual activity and consumption are practised at increasingly young ages. In the past for example, a young person may have begun work, left home and established an intimate relationship at roughly the same time. Today we may find that a young person becomes sexually active at the age of 15, continues to live at home until 25 and spends the money from their part-time employment on paying their way and supporting a social life.

The material world has also changed since 1997. One of the most dramatic changes has been the rapid expansion of information and communication technologies, and in particular the near saturation of the mobile phone youth market in the UK. While access to computer skills and the internet continue to be constrained by material factors, the overwhelming majority of young people from a range of backgrounds now have mobile telephones. In a longitudinal study of young people's lives begun in 1996 Henderson et al. (2003) found ownership of mobile telephones by young people exploding. New practices of sociability emerged, through which young people increasingly became the mobile centre of their social worlds, freed from the surveillance of parents and other gatekeepers. So although young people may be staying at home longer, they are able to carve out a new more autonomous way of living within the home. They thus find themselves at greater freedom to pursue work and leisure opportunities by virtue of being contactable whilst mobile. Young people are also targeted as independent consumers. The 'pesterpower' of young children is understood by advertisers to be a powerful influence on family expenditure. The high level of school and college students in part-time work provides an important market for a range of products and services that are marketed aggressively at both boys and girls. And of course, you no longer have to be young to enjoy youth culture, as the music, styles, games and gossip of the teenager are made available to all those with the money and inclination to acquire them.

Thinking through transitions

One way of thinking about the changing conditions of young people's lives is to recognise that in becoming adult, young people are pursuing the experience and recognition of *competence*. This is the feeling that you are good at doing or being something. There are rewards gained from the ways in which others react to this such as greater freedom, responsibility, privacy and respect. In the past competence came as a package, and was founded on economic independence. Increasingly, the process of becoming competent is a piece-meal affair. Different forms of competence may be available in different areas of young people's lives. So for example, a young person may develop a sense of competence by being a valued worker, a parent, a successful student, musician, sportsperson, sexual partner, popular or even feared member of a social scene. Failure to be recognised as competent in one area may encourage young people to invest and seek recognition in other areas. So for example, young people who struggle as students may seek competence and recognition from work, consumption and parenthood.

This perspective makes visible two themes that underlie the contemporary policy agenda on youth. First, a concern with *social exclusion*. We are familiar with the notion that young people's experiences are shaped by economic inequality. However, there is also a cultural dimension to inequality. This is where an initial disadvantage creates the conditions through which it makes sense to young people at the time to make choices and pursue lifestyles that in turn can reduce their life chances and those of their children. This is particularly clear in the area of teenage pregnancy where associations are made between deprivation and educational failure and peer, class or family cultures in which early parenthood 'makes sense' and is valued within local terms.

The second theme that this perspective makes visible is a more nuanced understanding of the role of *timing* in the processes of social inclusion and exclusion, highlighting the potential for *targeting* resources and interventions. Not all young people from disadvantaged backgrounds fall into the stigmatised policy categories of 'teenage parents', 'problematic drug users' or 'young offenders'. The increasingly fluid and diverse character of modern UK society means that outcomes are determined by a particular combination of circumstances and conditions in conjunction with an individual's resources. So for example, the experience of parental illness or family disruption near to the time of examinations may be decisive in terms of the qualifications that a young person is able to gain. This in turn may be decisive in terms of the ways they subsequently invest their energies. Increasingly, policy makers are seeking to understand the ways in which *risk* and *resilience* operate in young people's lives, enabling the targeting of resources on those most in need, at the times they are most needed. This brings with it a new commitment to prevention which takes two forms. First, there is an investment to reduce child poverty, most clearly expressed in the Sure Start initiative, but also a range of health, education and neighbourhood renewal schemes targeted at disadvantaged communities. Second we find a move to identify 'vulnerable' children and young people' deemed to be 'at risk' (of offending, taking drugs, dropping out of education, becoming teenage parents, etc). The emergent policy agenda signalled by the 'Every Child Matters' green paper is an approach which 'identifies, refers and tracks', drawing on individualised support in the form of mentors/ personal advisers as well as more material support such as grants and special allowances. It is also an approach where services work together, sharing information in order to ensure that young people do not fall between the cracks which mark professional boundaries.

A new youth policy?

There are a number of chapters that have been fully revised for this second edition, and which reflect those areas of youth policy that have been subject to most dramatic change in recent years:

In Chapter 10 'Welfare Services for Young People' Bob Coles leads us through an array of new initiatives, spearheaded by a series of reports from the Social Exclusion Unit and culminating in what he describes as the closest thing that we have had to 'a coherent youth policy' – including, in England, a Minister for Youth, a Children and Young People's Unit and, most recently, a Minister for Children and a Directorate which draws together children's services under one departmental brief. In many ways youth policy can be seen as heralding a new way of working in which disciplinary, sectoral and professional boundaries are crossed in the pursuit of 'joined up' working and service delivery. Thus we find local interdisciplinary teams delivering drugs policy, teenage pregnancy prevention and criminal justice referrals. We also find the development of new hybrid professionals such as Connexions Personal Advisors and Learning Mentors, drawn from a range of backgrounds and providing one-to-one support to young people. The drive to keep a greater number of less privileged young people in full-time education and training has been central to government strategy with key policy developments including the launching of Connexions (a universal careers service for 13–19 year olds) and New Deal (a welfare to work initiative for 18–24 year olds). In Chapter 11 Stanley Tucker and Steve Walker provide a history of the split between academic and vocational training that characterises the British education system, including proposals for a new 14–19 curriculum. In Chapter 13 Harriet Bradley and Paul Hickman update the reader on changes to the youth labour market and associated policy initiatives.

Important questions remain as to how services for children and young people will be integrated when they have been developed separately and when some of the most crucial ones have been left out of the new vision of joined up government – namely youth justice which will stay within the Home Office. This leads us to the second area in which New Labour youth policy has distinguished itself. While the welfare agenda has been focused on understanding and meeting the needs of socially excluded young people, the youth justice agenda has pursued a more controversial and punitive approach. Ironically, the same young people are treated very differently within these two policy areas, with young offenders barraged with a range of initiatives that not only infringe their human rights but also fail to recognise them as simultaneously children 'in need' (Goldson, 2002). In Chapter 14 John Muncie describes the many changes that have been enacted in the field of youth justice in recent years. He argues that a 'discourse of responsibility' lies at the heart of New Labour's reforming programme, in which criminal justice policy is being turned to for the resolution of social problems. Communities are held responsible for crime prevention, individuals for their own behaviour and parents for their children. Despite a rhetoric of restorative justice, Muncie argues that a growing trend towards the incarceration of young offenders undermines principles of crime prevention, rehabilitation and human rights.

The third area in which youth policy has developed concerns the treatment of young people in local authority care. Coles (Chapter 10) describes the background to the policy initiative known as 'Quality Protects' which, amongst other things, sets local authorities targets to improve the educational attainment of young people in care and to provide personal advisors to support them when leaving the care system after the age of 16. Evidence of repressive and/or abusive regimes in several highly-publicised court cases in the early 1990s led to a number of official reports cataloguing the evidence of bad practice and prescribing ways in which better practice could be planned and delivered. The impact of these developments on working with young people in residential settings is discussed by Adrian Ward in Chapter 26. In Chapter 23 Brian Corby discusses current policy requirements and understandings of good practice in what he defines as the mistreatment of young people. He draws examples of mistreatment from families, state institutions, schools and the streets, and in doing so draws attention to the *unevenness* of the provision of rights and protection for young people across these different locations.

These new contributions reframe those chapters which stand as originally

published. In most cases these contributions provide insights that have stood the
test of time. For example, chapters by Rex Stainton-Rogers (Chapter 1) and
Christine Griffin (Chapter 2) encourage us to understand youth as a historically
specific constructed category – an important point to understand as we witness
the economic foundations of youth refiguring. Chapters which explore youth
cultures of the past (Daren Garratt, Chapter 15) and present (Maria Pini, Chapter
17, Les Back, Chapter 4) as important sites of creativity and expression are all the
more important as youth culture becomes a big business in its own right. The
mutually constructing/constraining relationship between social policy categories
and the identities that they make available is the subject of a number of chapters.
Tim Edwards (chapter 18) explores tensions between policy attempts to proscribe
teenage sexuality and the social and economic conditions that make sexuality one
of the most accessible forms of 'feeling adult' available to young people. Similarly
Gargi Battacharyya and John Gabriel (Chapter 7) document how social policy has
constructed racialised identities, and Lena Robinson (Chapter 16) explores the
ways in which young people may struggle to inhabit identities that do not feel
like they belong to them.

There are four overlapping themes which structure the reader. First, there is
the issue of how young people are seen, or socially constructed, and how they see
themselves. This is a critical agenda in the sense that it seeks both to displace the
dominant images of young people, which see them as problems, and to take
seriously the varied ways in which young people tell us in symbolic and practical
social activity who they are and what their interests are. Second, there are the
emerging demands for rights for young people and their claims to citizenship.
Central here is the emphasis on their participation not just in disputes which
concern them but also in the life of the communities in which they live. Allied to
this are the mechanisms by which their interests are represented by others and
how these representatives are held accountable. Third, there is the issue of social
difference. Young people are not a homogeneous group in this society. While they
are unified by the fact of their age they are differently located socially on the basis
of class, gender, ethnicity, impairment and sexuality. Any serious study of the
lives of young people must deal with the politics of their social place and identity.
Finally, the services that society provides for young people and the practical
issues raised by different service delivery strategies in different settings are
explored.

There is still a long way to go in developing policies and practices that address
the real needs of young people and which build the capacity of workers and
professionals to this end. We hope that this collection will stimulate those who
work with young people, in a variety of different settings, to examine their day-
to-day practices and service delivery strategies. At the same time the collection
has an agenda that extends beyond the directly practical. It is not a 'rough guide'
to good practice, though we hope that improved practice will be an outcome.
Rather we are concerned to challenge the solidity of the category of youth in
order to open up new possibilities of thinking about young people and their

relations with adult society. Youth is historically varied and significant, it is also a social process and not a fixed life stage. The contributions to this collection reflect a paradox: the lives led by young people are as varied and as divided as those of adults, and at the same time what unites youth is the reactions of adult society. If young people are to become effective social actors then social practices and attitudes will have to undergo change.

References

Department for Education and Skills (2003) *Every Child Matters*, London: The Stationery Office, and at www.dfes.gov.uk/everychildmatters

Evans, K., Rudd, P., Behrens, M., Kaluza, J. and Wooley, C. (2001) 'Reconstructing fate as choice? Initial findings from the comparative study "Taking control?: personal agency and social structures in young adult transitions in England and the new Germany"', *Young*, 9 (3): 2–29.

Garratt, D., Roche, J. and Tucker, S. (eds) (1997) *Changing Experiences of Youth*, London: Sage.

Goldson, B. (2002) 'New Labour, social justice and children: Political calculation and the deserving-undeserving schism', *British Journal of Social Work*, 32: 683–95.

Henderson, S., Taylor, R. and Thomson, R. (2003) 'In touch: Young people, communication and technologies', *Information, Communication and Society*, 5 (4): 494–512.

Irwin, S. (1995) *Rites of Passage: Social Change and the Transition From Youth to Adulthood*, London: UCL Press.

Schoon, I., McCulloch, A., Joshi, H., Wiggins, D. and Bynner, J. (2001) 'Transitions from school to work in a changing social context', *Young*, 9: 4–22.

I

The Making and Moulding of Modern Youth: a Short History

Rex Stainton Rogers

Modern times

What do we mean by 'modern times'? As I am using the term, they began around 1770, as a result of two processes which had a profound effect upon the ways in which we now live our lives. The first of these was the introduction of humanistic forms of governance which stemmed from the writings of people like Thomas Paine on *The Rights of Man* from the constitutions of revolutionary France and the American ex-colonies. The second was the process set in train by industrialisation, in which technological progress (for example in engineering) was paralleled by a social regime of 'humaneering' (Stainton Rogers et al., 1995). Both were intended for the betterment of humankind, but they also brought about (in part in order to achieve this betterment) a regime of regulation and social control.

To regulate their peoples, the new industrial societies needed social and economic data, such as the first UK census, taken in 1801, which revealed a population of about 10 million (a sixth of the current figure). However, the *proportion* of young people in 1801 was markedly greater than it is in the ageing population of Britain today. Such crude data alone, of course, give us little idea of what lives were like then compared with now, but we can flesh out the picture by looking at contrasts. On the material front, 1801 was a world without railways, but where macadamised roads had begun to be built for the stage-coaches beloved of nostalgic Christmas cards. Health care was dire, infectious disease was rife, surgery proceeded without anaesthetics and death in childbirth, childhood and youth was commonplace. It was also a community without a police force or a health and social security system (as we understand them); without probation officers, youth and social workers, psychologists or counsellors.

Being young in the 'Bleak Age'

At the beginnings of modernism, as industrialisation and urbanisation grew, so too did population. Along with a falling death rate, early (uncontracepted) marriages produced rapid population growth (to around 14 million by 1821) and big families. At this time, the legal 'age of consent' was 12 for young women and

14 for young men. The historians Hammond and Hammond (1947) dubbed this 'the Bleak Age' to convey how dire a time it was for most people. This was especially so for the young. It was a period of *laissez-faire* economics and social policies, in which much that marks our contemporary boundaries between child, youth and adult either did not exist or was constituted differently. For example in 1818 rather less than a third of children were at school, and consequently illiteracy was widespread (particularly amongst females).

Of course, behind those statistics lay an enormous diversity in young people's lives. For example, while working class young men and young women laboured together in coal-mines and mills and received the same beatings for laziness or mistakes, they were subject (where they got any at all) to varying regimes of moral and formal education. Lives were also becoming ever more strongly divided by income and by class. A considerable gap was emerging between the genteel recreations of the bourgeois young people of the world of Jane Austen, and the drinking, fornicating and brawling of both working class young people and those in the public schools and universities. If Britain ever was a land of near 'anarchic' social life, it was so for the workers and the aristocrats of this time.

Meanwhile, back at the Queen Vic . . .

However, by the time Victoria came to the throne in 1837 there had begun a very different period. Young (1960) argues that a profound evangelical turn in British Christianity led to little short of a moral revolution. A project was set in place – in working class non-conformist communities and among the middle classes and even in the newly reformed public schools – to bring an external moral gaze to, and to foster an internal self-surveillance upon, the many faces of evil. As Young observes, family discipline was set within the new ethic: 'becoming milder . . . it was, perhaps for the same reason, more vigilant; and moral, or social, anxiety made it for girls at least more oppressive' (1960: 2). Victorian moral 'double standards' and their stigmatisation of 'fallen women' were crushingly real to their victims (cf. Pearsall, 1971; Fowles, 1977).

At the same time, society itself, in both private and public sectors, entered into a massive reform movement. Charities and a whole gamut of 'philanthropic' ventures abounded. A campaign was afoot to turn out a morally upright and educated cohort of young workers, professionals and (in that very gendered world) wives and mothers. Young people found themselves the target of a spectrum of moral entrepreneurs. As the century closed, this army of regulators came to include a new breed of doctors and academics who specialised (or at least claimed to specialise) in a new 'science' of youth. However, it would be as much of a mistake to see the Victorian young as living universally regulated lives as it would be to see today's young people living a global 'youth culture'. Improvements in living standards brought their own possibilities for independence. For example, 'living in digs' became commonplace for young people, while the new resorts like Blackpool and access to popular entertainment (such as the music halls) gave a subterranean world of fun beneath the stern face of Victorian morality.

Young as the century

Compared with a century before, the young people of 1900 were better educated and legally protected, more disciplined and, one suspects, vastly more prone to the regulatory emotions: guilt and shame. Yet they lived in a reality which was profoundly removed from our own. For example, in 1897 there were just 844 women in all the English universities and women doctors numbered a mere 87 (Showalter, 1992). On wages and salaries (where employed at all) of around 50% the male rate, young women were far from living in an egalitarian society. One of the profound events (for heterosexuals and gays alike) of around the turn of the century was the trial of Oscar Wilde (1895). At the time the very idea of being a 'nancy-boy' induced deep worries in most young men, yet the typical youth of that time was hardly a macho model of 'manly' muscles. Both the Boer War and social research revealed young men to be a pretty weedy bunch, many in pretty poor health. In the context of another reforming phase in society (this time the Liberal government of 1905–14), the outcomes were a school meals service and a school medical inspection scheme. Medical attention for minors became a 'right' in the Children Act 1908. The result was a fitter upcoming generation of young people. It is also possible to see in changes around that time the drawing of boundaries (and the drawing-out of lines of dispute) between youth and the adult world which have clear resonances with our own times. Specifically, it saw the setting up of juvenile courts and of 'borstals' for juvenile offenders. Young mothers (at least those that were decently married) found in Edwardian Britain charitable child welfare clinics which gained government funding in 1914, though for the 'unmarried mother', life was not so charitable. But, diversity is the key to grasping these times, for alongside the Grundyism of sending unmarried mothers away to 'homes' to have their babies in secret, others were beginning to promote contraception among young people (albeit against strong opposition).

The 'Great War' and its aftermath

As something which wiped out a major segment of Britain's young men in the mud of Flanders, the impact of World War I can hardly be over-estimated. In addition to the slaughter itself, the 'Great War' proved fatal to Britain's pretentions to 'greatness', and to the values (such as nationalism) which underpinned them. Just to put one mark upon that, World War I validated (in both legal and moral terms) conscientious objection. As well as the 'angels' who worked in the field hospitals, it revealed a set of less stereotypic young women.

From Mata Hari to the yellow-stained workers in the munitions factories, women became not only more visible, but also visibly different from the delicate maidens of Victorian sensibilities. At the same time, the horrors and disillusionment of a four-year war brought back to Britain a surviving generation of young men who were, quite literally, transformed.

Much has been made of the 'roaring twenties' that followed. Dramatic in style, particularly in clothing, the period was perhaps the first since Regency days when fashion was for (and only really worked for) the young. The body politics of the 1920s were – as both statistics and personal accounts bear out – more than superficial. No doubt sexual guilt (in the Victorian sense) was on the wane, but that is only a small part of the story. At least as important were technical innovations that brought the sexes together, inventions as diverse as the typewriter, the motor car and charabanc, and the latex from which 'rubbers' were made.

Depression and social therapy

What was also true of those times was that unemployment was, by pre-war standards, high (around a million), and welfare benefits were, at best, limited and haphazardly targeted. For many young people (it was true of my own mother) illness or death in the family meant the end of schooling at 13 or 14 and early entry into a world of work (if you could find a job) in which protection for the employee was minimal. As the world entered the Great Depression (1926), a pattern very typical of our own times emerged. Faced with rising outgoings and falling income, government could find little else to do beyond cutting expenditure. Even where welfare measures were promoted and passed in Parliament (such as the raising of the school leaving age to 15) they were not enacted.

Nevertheless the inter-war years did see some major changes in young people's lives. Perhaps the most important was the growth of popular cinema that took audiences 'out of themselves'. Along with dance halls, cinemas became places to meet other young people and to start and develop relationships. Both innovations were possible only because Britain gradually became a generally electrified country, making, for example, the lights of Piccadilly Circus into an icon of a 'good time'. Radio (as 'wireless') also came into homes, although probably more important to the young was the gramophone – particularly after electric recording brought a new sound quality, often of bands spun off from the new popular (talking) movies of the time.

Salient also to lifestyle changes was a movement into suburban 'little boxes'. Arguably it led to some recontainment of women as the controllers of new home technology (refrigerators, vacuum cleaners and the like) – though no doubt, for those few pre-war homes that had a television, the man took charge! The new television service, along with much that remained of the 'old Britain', was to disappear in 1939 as Britain entered World War II. The domestic politics of the 1930s had been marked for several years by the shadow of fascism and Nazism (cast most heavily upon the Jewish community). Both those extremes and the counter-pole of communism had attracted their followers among young people. With war, virtually all were mobilised (both literally and figuratively) into what was a largely consensual national venture.

Their finest hour?

As the bombs began to fall, many early teenagers (along with their younger brothers and sisters) were evacuated from their urban homes. Their experiences were often far from happy ones (Wicks, 1988). For young men of conscription age, the role of that war is generally well known. Not quite so familiar is the considerable place of young women in the forces and also their 'conscription' into arms factories and as 'Land Girls'. A Britain 'fighting for her life' proved highly liberating for the young. Many moved to live away from their parents, and their active heterosexuality was tacitly (and sometimes quite explicitly) accepted. So too was smoking, and the new, wonder drug to combat fatigue amphetamine. At the same time the war led to a growing 'Americanisation' of British culture. Military personnel from the USA – 'over-paid over-sexed and over here' – had a variety of effects upon young people, from the cultural (such as bebop and the new experience for many of encountering black people as a coherent group) to the personal (the considerable quantity of war brides and the even greater number of war babies). And it needs to be remembered that the end of World War II was the start of the nuclear age.

Living by the ration book

Britain in World War II was permeated by propaganda making much of the peace to come, a time of social change verging on social revolution. Young voters in particular were moved by the Labour party's immediate post-war programme, and in the election of July 1945 Attlee gained a majority of 186 seats. Despite economic times of great hardship, of food, clothes and petrol rationing, Attlee's government, in a series of measures produced the nearest any country has come to a socialist-welfarist state. From antenatal care to funeral payments, a basic safety-net was put in place for all. Young people, on the whole fit and able either to study or to work, gained few unique benefits from many of these measures directly. What was, however, fostered for them was a belief in a future which would see them not only employed on a progressive wage but also protected from being arbitrarily undercut by illness or unemployment. This ethos was equally clear within the post-demobilisation family, where family allowances and sickness and maternity benefits helped to create stability of income.

The social reality of Attlee's Britain was not one where 'fun' had much of a priority. While younger children often enjoyed what family privileges there were (for example, a banana!), little was directed at their older siblings except perhaps as a reward for passing the 11+. Relatively few new consumer goods were produced for the home market, and there was little by way of clothes, music or other resources around which a thoroughgoing youth culture could have consolidated. A considerable respect-for-cum-fear-of authority still pervaded, backed up by a legal system in which 'approved schools', borstals and judicial birchings awaited young offenders. Conscription continued along with its associated 'short back and sides' mentality.

New Elizabethans

By the 1950s, the electorate (that is, those over 21) had become disenchanted with austerity, and the October of 1951 saw the election of a Conservative government. Two visible symbols of changing times attracted young and old alike, The Festival of Britain (1951) and the Coronation of the 'young' Queen Elizabeth (1953), which many watched on newly acquired, nine-inch, black-and-white, one-channel televisions, where 'interludes' of angel-fish and potter's wheels were used to cover camera moves! However, youth and changing times were soon to liven up social consciousness by quantum leaps.

Movies and music are crucial to narrating the next part of our story, which is (I think unavoidably) androcentric. In 1954, a balding former country and western singer called Bill Haley cut a track called 'Rock around the Clock'. It proved a 'sleeper'. What woke it up was its use as the title music to a 'youth angst' film *The Blackboard Jungle* (1955). Popular music for the young (that which was hated by their elders) had arrived. To contextualise this in terms of international events which left a mark upon the young, 1956 was the year of the Suez invasion (reactions to which often exposed a 'generation gap' within families) and of the Soviet crushing of the Hungarian uprising. When Haley's own film *Rock around the Clock* was released (1956), in the words of the *NME Book of Rock*, 'cinema seats were ripped up from San Francisco to Scunthorpe' (Logan, 1975: 163). A new image of the young, moulded and refined in the USA (by professors of sociology as much as by Hollywood), had arrived. As a role model, Haley was a joke; that site was much more easily filled by the likes of Elvis Presley. The quintessential 'youth angst' movie of this time, *Rebel without a Cause* (1955), starring the powerfully scowling James Dean, contains images that still haunt advertising, MTV videos (and, I would argue, care-givers) to this day.

It was neat irony that the announcement in 1957 (by Macmillan's Conservative government) of the abolition of National Service should have coincided with the emergence of the seat rippers and screen shockers. What had arrived, in a reflexive relationship between the young and the rest of society, was youth (including, to be more accurate, its often older representatives and representations) as 'folk devil'. No one on the music scene fitted that image better than Jerry Lee Lewis ('Great Balls of Fire') whose 1958 UK tour collapsed when it was found out that his wife was 13 when they married! Much of the rest of this story, from Teddy boys, through Mods and Rockers, via Punk and into the raves and XTC shockers of recent times, is covered by Daren Garratt in Chapter 15. However, as a story which has run for nearly 40 years now, it is worth asking what deeper veins in the social collective unconscious it feeds from and feeds into.

One important point that needs to be noted from the start is that music became linked to clear segmentations in 'youth culture'. Within several segments, political events were beginning to be responded to by an increasingly, and diversely, 'ideological' young. Key in this – particularly for those with extended education – was CND (founded in 1958) and the first Aldermaston March. Importantly, this was a national and international movement, with the first US nuclear submarine arriving in Holy Loch in 1961 and the Polaris missile deal of 1963. Socially, liberalisation was 'in the air' and 1963 also saw the raising of the minimum age for imprisonment to 17. The following year the UK elected a Labour government under Harold Wilson, a populist who was later to court figures such as the Beatles. It was around this point that much of the UK woke up to being a 'multicultural society': the issues of 'race' and 'immigration' were an important factor in the by-election defeat of Foreign Secretary Patrick Gordon Walker in 1965. The death penalty more opposed by young people than by any other group in society was abolished the same year, which also brought the miniskirt!

Mini 'boomers'

By the height of the 'swinging sixties' London had become the world's style capital of youth, with Carnaby Street and Portobello Road places of youthful pilgrimage. The North, notably Liverpool and The Cavern (thanks to the Beatles), and its 'gritty realism' (reflected in the new wave of kitchen-sink dramas) heralded an upstart challenge (if not an end) to rigid class elitism. However, for some young people, 1966 was more notable for England winning the World Cup than for the release of the Beatles' *Revolver!* It has been widely argued that nuclear proliferation and the Cold War helped to foster in young people a sense of 'eat, drink and be merry – for tomorrow we die' and now smoking 'dope' became part of the indulgence menu easily open to young people. So, too, was the misnamed contraceptive 'pill'. With sex both technologised and (sometimes) even on the school curriculum, the decay of 'sex only within marriage' mores reached new heights (or depths, according to the Festival of Light). The Cold War angst about their vulnerability was reinforced by the early deaths of a series of pop icons (starting with Buddy Holly in 1959) and by a growing publicisation of 'juvenile' diseases such as leukaemia and 'horrors' such as the Aberfan coal-tip disaster which killed 116 children (1966). Crucial too were the assassinations of Martin Luther King and Robert Kennedy (1968) and Bloody Sunday in Londonderry (1972). Another important marker, and a contributor to the growing distrust of 'science', was the appearance in the social world of those who had been the 'Thalidomide babies' in 1959–62.

For me, the 1960s is best captured by the decade centred on 1967 (that is, 1963 to 1972). It takes us from the Beatles' 'Please Please Me' and the assassination of President Kennedy, to T. Rex's *The Slider* and the murder of four protesting Kent State students in Ohio. It brought us: Mao's *Little Red Book* and the banned *Little Red School Book; Oz* and the Osmonds; Paris 1968 and Prague 1968. For UK young people, it saw the voting age reduced to 18 (1969) and likewise the more general age of majority (1970). It also left much unchanged – for example, the male homosexual age of consent (which had to wait two and a half decades for change (to 18) and action on equal pay and sex discrimination (with laws that only came into force in 1975).

Brave new worlds?

The 1960s ended with Britain, following a referendum, entering the Common Market on 1 January 1973. If the United States was the major cultural influence upon the young in the post-war period, their major *experience* of 'other cultures' came via 'immigration' (true, I think, even for those who were in the language of the time 'immigrants' but whose families had been in the UK for generations) and from growing opportunities for 'package tours' to the Continent. Whatever the image of the 1960s, it took far more young people to the Costa Brava than ever reached Kathmandu. Yet, in its own rather insular terms, between the 1950s and the 1970s Britain became 'cosmopolitan'. To take just one index, food and drink – important because young people make major expenditures in that area – the UK had seen the emergence of coffee bars with steaming espresso machines, burger bars, 'Indian' and 'Chinese' restaurants and even a taste for wine-drinking.

The mid 1970s brought a number of new elements into youthful lives. For mainland Britain this time saw 'the troubles' (in the North of Ireland) touching home. After the Guildford bombing (1974), 'security' and 'incidents' became part of daily life, probably for the first time outside of war. Personal searches, armed police and a certain paranoia became commonplace. One woman read the *Zeitgeist* brilliantly, beating the standing candidate (former Prime Minister Heath) for the leadership of the Conservative Party. By 1979 she was Prime Minister. As I write now, I strongly suspect that it is not only the young who are 'Thatcher's children': she touched us all. From 'enterprise culture' and the rolling back of 'socialism', through the poll tax, to her role in the fall of the Soviet Empire, Margaret Thatcher made waves that still reverberate.

Both directly (and indirectly as it impinged upon parents or friends of parents), the whole generation of young people under Thatcherism experienced the impact of the threat and the reality of unemployment and also the 'dream' of yuppiedom. A more divided Britain revealed itself in disturbed and disturbing 'inner city' trouble, with governmental reaction often to 'understand less and condemn more'. Yet – and I think it is key to understanding those times – it was not the opposition parties in Parliament who gained any solid support from 'disenchanted youth'. The real beneficiaries of young people's energies often seem to have been the political extremes and forms of issue politics. Where young people did 'wave the flag' for Britain, it was often in terms of the crude nationalism of football 'hooligans' and the young soldiers and sailors heading off to the South Atlantic to the tune of 'I'm going to kill me a spic or two.' But these phenomena were not representative of most of young Britain. Thatcherism, along with other social dynamics, yielded not a 'robust individualism', nor even 'strengthened families', so much as the striving after other sites of security and sustenance.

There is, and we think our research shows it (see Chapter 3), evidence of a growing tribalism or collectivism about some of today's young people. Their worlds, multiple as ever, are increasingly constructed around 'getting a life' in which others are an essential ingredient. For this fortunate segment (mainly from the overclass of the 'two nations') it can mean strong peer bonds, a life built around not just a relationship but a supportive network for the creation of 'good times' in 'hard times'. In this sense, the 'drugs' of today are symbolic. The 'spliff' is an archetypal small group drug, as are the video and the 'soap'. Ecstasy, and the music environments associated with it, can help to foster more collective good times, senses of tribal love. For the less relatively advantaged, the menu is a little different, the search at times rather more desperate.

References

Fowles J. (1977) *The French Lieutenant's Woman*. London: Granada.

Hammond, J.L. and Hammond, B. (1947) *The Bleak Age*. Harmondsworth: Pelican.

Logan, N. (ed.) (1975) *The New Musical Express Book of Rock*. London: Star.

Pearsall R. (1971) *The Worm in the Bud*. Harmondsworth: Pelican.

Showalter, E. (1992) *Sexual Anarchy*. London: Virago.

Stainton Rogers, R., Stenner, P., Gleeson, K. and Stainton Rogers, W. (1995) *Social Psychology: a Critical Agenda*. Cambridge: Polity Press.

Wicks, B. (1988) *No Time to Wave Goodbye*. London: Bloomsbury.

Young G.M. (1960) *Victorian England: Portrait of an Age*. London: Oxford University Press.

2
Representations of the Young

Christine Griffin

> 'Youth' is . . . treated as a key indicator of the state of the nation . . .: it is expected
> to reflect the cycle of booms and troughs in the economy; shifts in cultural values
> over sexuality, morality and family life; and changes in class relations, concepts of
> nationhood, and in occupational structures. Young people are assumed to hold the
> key to the nation's future, and the treatment and management of 'youth' is
> expected to provide the solution to a nation's 'problems', from 'drug abuse', 'hooli-
> ganism' and 'teenage pregnancy' to inner city 'riots'.
>
> Christine Griffin, *Representations of Youth*

These words were published in *Representations of Youth*, a book analysing the
ways in which 'youth' as a whole, as well as specific groups of young people,
have been constructed in academic texts since World War II. In the book I paid
particular attention to British and US youth research, since these approaches have
overwhelmingly dominated academic studies on youth, and continue to do so.
Many important and interesting pieces of youth research have been produced
outside the UK/US nexus, but the ideas and arguments of Western
industrialised perspectives on 'youth' and 'adolescence' have resonances far
beyond Britain and North America. Many of the dominant representations of
youth found in academic research texts draw on a range of discourses that also
pervade more 'popular' cultural domains, such as soap operas, newspaper
coverage and feature films. Such discourses have shaped welfare policies and
practices, family life, education and training provision and policing strategies –
indeed any agency or institution involving contact with young people.

In this chapter I will examine some of the key forms through which 'youth' has
been represented within academic literature, and the impact of such
representations on social welfare policies and practices. One of the key features
of academic (and non-academic) representations of youth is the widespread
construction of youth in general, and specific groups of young people in
particular, as 'problems' (MacDonald et al., 1993). This problem status may
involve being seen as the source of a particular focus of adult concern (such as
'football hooliganism'), or as being 'at risk' of getting into difficulty of some kind
(such as 'teenage pregnancy'). Young people are frequently presented as either
actively 'deviant' or passively 'at risk', and sometimes as both simultaneously. In
general, young men are more likely to be presented as actively 'deviant',
especially in aggressive forms, and especially if they are working class and/or
black. Young women, however, are more likely to be constructed as passively 'at
risk' (Griffin, 1993).

First, however, I want to take a brief look at the origins of many contemporary concepts about youth: the 'discovery' of adolescence by G. Stanley Hall in the late nineteenth century. An early American psychologist, Hall produced an influential two-volume text in the 1900s which synthesised a range of contemporary arguments around young people and their relationships with education, family life, sexuality and employment (Hall, 1904). In pre-industrial European societies, there was no clear distinction between childhood and other pre-adult phases of life. The main age stages of childhood, youth and adulthood were defined primarily in relation to one's degree of dependence or separation from the family of origin. The concept of 'adolescence' introduced a biological foundation to notions of age stages by constructing the shift away from childhood around the onset of puberty. However vague this moment of transition might be in practice (especially for boys), Hall's text clarified the representation of adolescence as a category which was biologically determined, shaped and driven by physiological imperatives that were profoundly sexual. His work provided a point of coalescence for emerging notions about young people and society in general, reflecting economic, political and ideological changes in Western societies at that time (Gillis, 1974; Kett, 1977).

Some sociologists and historians have argued that the notion of adolescence emerged primarily as a consequence of changes in *class* relations as expanding capitalist economies demanded a cheap and youthful labour force (for example, Springhall, 1986). However, the 'discovery' of adolescence also marked a key moment for social relations around gender, sexuality, 'race' and nationality. The emerging ideology of adolescence marked out a biologically determined norm of youthful behaviour and appearance which was white/Anglo, middle class, heterosexual and male. Changes in the elite education system in the second half of the nineteenth century are one example of this process. The earlier model of schools for the sons of the upper classes was that of a monastery. Following the example of Thomas Arnold at Rugby, English public schools encouraged a new form of muscular Christian masculinity, modelling themselves on military institutions. Women, girls and the feminine were associated with weakness and fragility, and men and masculinity with virility and strength (Gillis, 1974). The emergence of the concept of adolescence coincided with this cult of heterosexual masculinity, and with the construction of 'homosexuality' as a new socio-legal category which was synonymous with deviance and sickness (Weeks, 1981).

The onset of industrialisation in Britain and the population shift from rural to urban centres brought a growing sense of concern amongst (middle class) social reformers over the conditions in which many (working class) young people were living. Such concerns amongst liberals and progressive reformers formed the basis of the various welfare and educational agencies involved in contemporary work with young people. The aspirations of these reformers cannot be greeted with unequivocal praise *or* disdain: their objectives were profoundly contradictory when viewed from the perspective of the various groups of young people they aimed to 'help'.

Social reformers in the fields of education, welfare, juvenile justice, the labour market, sexuality and moral concerns used a range of strategies in their attempts to 'protect' and 'civilise' urban working class young women and men. Religion frequently played an important role in such organisations, and from the 1900s adult-sponsored institutions for the regulation and protection of young people became increasingly professional (Jeffs and Smith, 1993). Social reformers drew on the emerging concept of adolescence to define 'normal' and 'ideal' behaviour for young people, and G. Stanley Hall's work provided a crucial meeting point for the perspectives of academics and liberal reformers. Hall associated 'normal adolescence' with unspontaneous, conformist and confident young people who hid an emotional turmoil of sexual confusion and self-doubt. Such a demeanour was particularly linked with young white middle class males, but it came to be seen as appropriate and desirable for *all* young people (Griffin, 1993).

Hall's identification of puberty as the defining moment of adolescence for young people provided a firm biological foundation for the dominant concept of adolescence which is still with us today: the 'storm and stress' model. Adolescence is seen as a potentially distressing time for *all* young people, owing to the inevitable hormonal upheavals associated with puberty that are assumed to set young people apart from the world of 'mature' adulthood. According to Hall and his contemporaries, some degree of 'freedom' was seen as necessary to enable young people to develop their full potentialities, whilst 'control' (both external and internal) would be required to maintain order and self-discipline. For Hall, *self*-control was especially necessary for the suppression of sexual impulses, notably the 'masturbatory insanity' which was assumed to plague young men at that time. Elements of these late nineteenth century arguments about the need for young people to realise their full potential and for the development of self-control form a common theme in contemporary texts on the aims of youth work and social welfare policies (Banks, 1994).

Helping troubled youth: the legacy of the storm and stress model

The relationship between young people's experiences and academic research about 'youth' and 'adolescence' is not straightforward. Youth research does not provide a simple reflection of young people's everyday lives, but nor does it merely misrepresent their experiences. No young person's life in Britain or elsewhere in the industrialised world can have remained untouched by the dominant notions underlying the storm and stress model of adolescence. Even forms of youthful resistance have been shaped by such notions. It would be a mistake, however, to see all young people as passive victims of an overwhelmingly pervasive dominant ideology. Nor would it be accurate to construct all young people as inherently resistant to dominant representations of youth. The period since the early 1980s indicates that the picture is frequently more complex than this. In addition, some young people are all but absent from contemporary academic and welfare policy approaches to youth, as I will argue later in this chapter.

The years since World War II have seen a particular boom in adult panics over youth, and an associated increase in academic youth research (Griffin, 1993). Studies about the lives of young people can be found in the fields of education, criminology, economics, cultural studies, sociology and psychology. Whilst a *biologically determinist*, individually focused approach has often characterised research on the *psychology of adolescence, sociological* research on youth has tended to emphasise the *social constructionist* approach and the activities of particular groups of young people. Although this distinction is something of an over-simplification, we can see the consequences of the uneasy relationship between 'biological' and 'social' constructions of adolescence and youth in some contemporary academic texts.

During the 1980s, for example, a series of texts appeared which expressed concern over the 'crisis' which was assumed to be facing young people, in both Britain and the USA. This 'crisis' was seen to stem not so much from rising unemployment, poverty or cuts in welfare, education and training provision, as from a growing mismatch between the 'biological' and 'social' boundaries of youth/adolescence (see Griffin, 1993). In other words, the biological foundations which were assumed to dictate the onset of puberty – and hence 'adolescence' – for girls and boys were represented as being out of synchrony with the socially determined moments through which 'youth' was defined. The latter involved entry to the full-time job market (for working class young people), and to long-term heterosexual relationships, marriage and eventually parenthood, all of which are taken as indices of 'normal' mature adulthood. Since the 'biological' and the 'social' boundary lines around the age stage of 'youth' were seen to be out of alignment, 'crisis' was represented as an inevitable if unfortunate consequence.

The approaches and assumptions I have described so far all emerged from what I have termed the *mainstream* or traditional perspective in academic literature on youth (Griffin, 1993). By this I mean an approach which would not question (at least not to any fundamental degree) the central tenets of the storm and stress model, and which is primarily engaged in constructing or reinforcing moral panics around youth in general, or specific groups of young people (for example, young African-Caribbean men, young working class women). Mainstream approaches are diverse and located in a range of academic disciplines, but they all tend to involve a process of searching for the apparent 'causes' of various constructed social problems, from youth crime and 'disaffection' to drug abuse. This is not to deny that some of these 'social problems' have very 'real', tangible and damaging effects on young people. My point is that mainstream approaches tend to operate like detective stories, searching out the causes of various 'social problems' in particular ways, and that dominant constructions of youth serve to link young people with specific 'social problems' solely or primarily as a consequence of their youth (such as 'teenage pregnancy'). In many cases, mainstream approaches tend to adopt various forms of the victim-blaming thesis, in which young people are represented as the cause of specific 'social problems' – or it is argued that such problems could be alleviated if those young people who are most affected would only change their attitudes, appearance or behaviour. So, for example, in some mainstream academic texts racism is ignored or minimised as a potential cause of differential rates of official unemployment amongst black and white youth. Some researchers have argued that young unemployed African-American men should alter their attitudes or behaviour in order to improve their employment prospects (for example, Freeman and Holzer, 1986).

Radical approaches would tend to ask quite different questions, and are far more likely to *de*construct the myriad 'social problems' that are associated with young people (for example, Hall and Jefferson, 1975). The radical perspective has been formed in part through critiques of mainstream approaches, and any one academic text may well incorporate a combination of elements from both radical and mainstream perspectives. The radical perspective is more likely to focus on the wider social systems in which young people live, economic, political and cultural, looking at relations of domination and subordination around gender, 'race', class, sexuality and (less frequently) disability as well as age (for example, Bhavnani, 1991).

Social welfare policies aimed at young people are profoundly shaped by dominant representations of 'youth' and 'adolescence', epitomised by the storm and stress model and by the different orientations of mainstream and radical approaches to youth. MacDonald et al. (1993) distinguish between the traditional 'youth as trouble' perspective, which would be associated with what I have termed a mainstream approach, and the more liberal 'youth in trouble' view. In *Representations of Youth* I discuss discourses which speak of 'controlling' young people as well as those concerned with 'protecting troubled youth' (Griffin, 1993). Policies which differentiate between young people on the basis of gender, class, 'race', disability and sexuality, do so in the context of 'common sense' representations of 'youth as trouble' and 'youth in trouble'.

In general, young men, especially if they are working class and/or black, are especially likely to be the focus of policies that operate with a 'youth as trouble' discourse. Young women, however, are more likely to be dealt with under the aegis of a 'youth in trouble' discourse. Radical analyses would tend to represent young people rather differently, in that various groups of working class youth are commonly seen as resisting oppressive conditions in school, the job market, family life and so on. Young working class people tend to be represented in relatively positive, creative and collective terms, and/or as determined survivors (for example, Willis et al., 1990). At this point it becomes increasingly difficult to speak of young people as a uniform group, and it is necessary to examine the ways in which academic youth research and social welfare policies have distinguished between different groups of young people.

Targeting and absences: diversity and representations of the young

Representations of youth operate in part to differentiate youth/adolescence as a specific age stage from childhood on the one hand, and adulthood on the other. Such representations are also differentiated by gender, 'race', class, sexuality and/or disability in specific contexts. As I have already argued, young heterosexual white and black working class men are frequently seen as 'trouble' and a source of social problems, whilst young white and black working class women are more likely to be treated as 'in trouble' or 'at risk' of 'getting into trouble'. It is no coincidence that 'getting into trouble' is a euphemism for becoming pregnant, and this is the most common event that signifies 'trouble' for young women. Getting pregnant may not be treated as such a disaster by all of the young women involved, but for some adults, this in itself can become a cause for further concern.

Britain has seen its share of moral panics over 'teenage pregnancy', to the extent that inner city disturbances and crime rates have been attributed to the growing proportion of young single mothers in the UK. In the USA, such panics are more likely to focus around the incidence of single parenthood amongst young African-American women, which was blamed for the 'riots' in Los Angeles during 1992 (Griffin, 1992). In a recent study of young women in Britain who became pregnant in their teenage years, Ann Phoenix (1991) has argued that when economic indices are held constant, many of the educational, psychological and social problems experienced by the children of 'young mothers' evaporate. That is, it is not the youth or the single status of these children's mothers that should be a cause for concern, but the poverty into which they are born, and which their mothers struggle to overcome as best they can.

Social welfare provision is also finely graded according to 'race' and ethnicity, as well as gender, from a baseline of relatively greater provision for young white males (Imam et al., 1995). Young Asian women, for example, are particularly likely to be represented as in need of 'protection' from 'restrictive' families and cultural traditions. Young African-Caribbean men are more likely to be viewed as potential threats to society, or possibly as particularly 'at risk' of getting involved in certain criminal activities. My point is that youth provision tends to be funded through a set of dominant assumptions about youth in general, and particular groups of young people, that are racialised, gender specific and class specific. Academic youth research has had relatively little to say about the lives of young black people in Britain, with some notable exceptions (for example, Mirza, 1992; Tizard and Phoenix, 1993). In addition, studies of young white people's lives have seldom examined the ways in which their experiences and identities are racialised (one exception here is Jones, 1988).

It would appear from even a fairly brief reading of the enormous academic literature on 'youth' that almost all sections of young people have been studied at some stage. There remain some notable and long-standing absences, however. The first is the group which has served as the norm against which other young people are judged: young men who are white, middle class, heterosexual and able-bodied. At a general level, this group are possibly the least visible in social welfare policies and provision aimed at young people and in academic youth studies. That is not because this particular group are unfairly discriminated against: on the contrary, they are the implicit norm against which other groups of young people are judged. They also have access to relatively better facilities in education, employment, training, career prospects and leisure. They dominate most of the spaces, but they are seldom represented as a source of 'social problems' or a cause for adult concern in the same way as their less 'fortunate' peers.

Other absences involve more marginal groups such as young lesbians, bisexuals and gay men (one exception is Trenchard and Warren, 1987). This absence is mirrored in social welfare and youth provision. Even the radical youth sub-cultures literature, which has been quick to represent young white heterosexual working class women and men as resistant in class and gender terms, has paid relatively little attention to young lesbians and gay men.

Another major absence lies in radical analyses of dis/ability as a key dimension in young people's lives. Mainstream research on young people includes a number of studies on 'handicapped young people' or 'young people with special needs' (Griffin, 1993), but such studies are usually positioned as marginal to 'general' research on the transition from school to work, family life or leisure. Such research would not attempt to deconstruct taken-for-granted distinctions between 'the disabled' and 'the able-bodied', and nor would it question the construction of certain body types as synonymous with 'normality'. Young people with disabilities are confined, in the academic literature as in the education system, to a 'separate' status, dealt with within a primarily clinical/medical domain. Again, this absence in radical analyses of youth is somewhat surprising given the importance of surveillance over the body and appearance amongst young people, especially young women, and debates about the damage caused by pressures on young women to be thin and conform to a constructed ideal of 'normal' female body shape and size (Bordo, 1993).

Summary

Dominant representations of youth are partly about setting young people apart from children and adults, as a transition point between two separate age stages. Such representations are also concerned with making distinctions between groups of young people on the basis of gender, 'race', class and sexuality in terms of discourses of deviance, disaffection and protection. From G. Stanley Hall onwards, dominant representations of youth have simultaneously treated youth as a period of inevitable turmoil and a time for 'having a fling', *and* as a time when the path to 'normal' life must be found and followed. Dominant representations of youth in mainstream academic literature operate in conjunction with social welfare policies to target specific groups of young people as in need of 'surveillance', 'protection' and/or 'care'. Radical perspectives would tend to construct particular sections of young people as in need of support and empowerment. It is this focus on *power relations* around age, 'race', class, gender and sexuality that distinguish radical approaches from the mainstream perspective. Young people are a diverse group, but these differences are not simply a matter of individual variation.

Most academic researchers or policy makers tend to view young people through the ideological veil epitomised by the storm and stress model. One of the unique aspects of age as a social relation, however, is that *all* adults were once teenagers, although their experiences will vary with time, gender, class, ethnicity, sexuality, dis/ability, region and so on. A useful exercise is to ask a group of adults to recall their memories of being 14, preferably in a session facilitated by one or two young people. This will not provide a magical insight into their 'true' experiences at 14 but it may reveal a host of traumatic memories they had long since forgotten in which a sense of powerlessness is often a common theme. Such an exercise can be one way of breaking down adults' perceptions of young people as inherently deviant or deficient. Having said this, the overwhelming force of dominant representations of youth as an age-based category remains.

References

Banks, S. (1994) 'Contemporary issues in youth work', *Youth* and *Policy* 46: 1–4.

Bhavnani, K.-K. (1991) *Talking Politics: a Psychological Framing for Views from Youth in Britain.* Cambridge: Cambridge University Press.

Bordo, S. (1993) *Unbearable Weight: Feminism, Western Culture and the Body.* Berkeley, CA: University of California Press.

Freeman, R. and Hoker, H. (eds) (1986) *The Black Youth Unemployment Crisis.* Chicago: University of Chicago Press.

Gillis, J. (1974) *Youth and History: Tradition and Change In European Age Relations, 1770–Present.* New York: Academic Press.

Griffin, C. (1992) 'Fear of a black (and working class) planet: young women and the racialisation of reproductive politics', *Feminism and Psychology,* 2 (3): 491–4.

Griffin, C. (1993) *Representations of Youth: the Study of Youth and Adolescence in Britain and America.* Cambridge: Polity Press.

Hall, G. Stanley, (1904) *Adolescence: its Psychology, and its Relation to Physiology, Anthropology, Sociology, Sex, Crime, Religion and Education*, New York: D. Appleton.

Hall, S. and Jefferson, T. (eds) (1975) *Resistance through Rituals: Youth Sub-Cultures in Post-War Britain.* London: Hutchinson.

Imam, U., Khan, T., Lashley, H. and Montgomery, A. (1995) 'Black perspectives on young people and youth work', *Youth and Policy,* 49: 1–4.

Jeffs, T. and Smith, M. (1993) 'Getting the job done: training for youth work – past, present and future', *Youth and Policy,* 40: 10–32.

Jones, S. (1988) *Black Culture, White Youth: the Reggae Tradition from JA to UK,* London: Macmillan.

Kett, J. (1977) *Rites of Passage: Adolescence In America, 1790 to the Present*, New York: Basic Books.

MacDonald, R., Banks, S. and Hollands, R. (1993) 'Youth and policy in the 1990s', *Youth and Policy*, 40: 1–9.

Mirza, H.S. (1992) *Young, Female and Black*, London: Routledge.

Phoenix, A. (1991) *Young Mothers?*, Cambridge: Polity Press.

Springhall, J. (1986) *Coming of Age: Adolescence in Britain*, Dublin: Gill and Macmillan.

Tizard, B. and Phoenix, A. (1993) *Black, White or Mixed Race? Race and Racism in the Lives of Young People of Mixed Parentage*, London: Routledge.

Trenchard, L. and Warren, H. (1987) 'Talking about school: the experiences of young lesbians and gay men', in G. Weiner and M. Arnot (eds) *Gender under Scrutiny: New Inquiries in Education*, Milton Keynes: Open University Press.

Weeks, J. (1981) *Sex, Politics and Society: the Regulation of Sexuality since 1800*, New York: Longman.

Willis, P., Jones, S., Canaan, J. and Hurd, G. (1990) *Common Culture: Symbolic Work at Play in the Everyday Cultures of the Young*, Milton Keynes: Open University Press.

3
Worlds Apart: Young People's Aspirations in a Changing Europe

Wendy Stainton Rogers, Rex Stainton Rogers,
Jozef Výrost and Ladislav Lovás

One song all four of us can remember from our youth or young adulthood is Dylan's 'The Times They Are a-Changin', and indeed they were. And, now that none of us is young any longer, we can see the profound impact of those changes on our sons and daughters. The world in which they, and we, now live is one that none of the authors could have foreseen: a world where it is possible to 'surf the Net' and instantly call up information from all over the globe; a world beset by an incurable disease which is, largely, sexually transmitted; and a world where the Iron Curtain has been pulled down, and Nelson Mandela has become President of South Africa.

We began our research with this recognition – that if we have a concern for what current life is like for today's generation of young people, or what may help them in their futures, we cannot use our own experiences of being young or the aspirations we then held as much of a guide. If we want to promote the life opportunities of young people, if we want to help them to prepare for their futures and make well-informed choices about them, then we need to find out about this 'new world' in which they are growing up. In this chapter we summarise the findings of our research so far. We have concentrated here upon the part of the work we have done together in the UK and Slovakia, although our 'Young People Project' is part of a much wider programme involving other countries (such as Spain and Hungary).

Our approach is guided by an assumption that 'young people' (as any other socially defined group) are neither all 'much the same under the skin' nor even an objectively definable segment at all. All that (largely artificially) defines them is a matter of age (we have chosen 12–25). Within this age range are those with legal statuses of 'adults' and of 'children': some, indeed, are parents themselves. Some are students, some work, some are unemployed; some are economically independent, but many are not. They vary along all manner of factors, including those of class, gender, sexual orientation and ethnicity. They also vary in their religion (or lack of it), their political affiliation (or lack of it) and the sub-cultures to which they belong. Some have travelled widely across the world, others have never left their home town. Given this massive diversity, we expect to find far more variation in their views than consensus. For this reason we have deliberately adopted research methods designed to explore diversity – which offer opportunities to identify and describe alternative viewpoints.

The conventional approach to diversity within the social disciplines (most notably psychology and sociology) is to examine the ways that differences systematically vary in relation to predetermined categories (such as class, gender, sexual orientation and ethnicity). Generally psychometric techniques are used to seek to discover, say, to what extent young men and young women respond differently from each other; how far, say, social class affects political opinions; to what extent, say, educational achievement can predict levels of aspiration.

The reason we have broken away from the conventional is this: given, as expressed at the beginning of this chapter, our conviction that young people are likely to see the world very differently from our generation, we do not think it is possible for us (an older generation) to predict and pre-define how young people's views and opinions are shaped. We wanted to avoid lumping together females against males, or 'higher classes' against 'lower' ones – and, in general, to escape from averages 'broken' by such demographic and socio-economic variables. For this reason we have adopted methods (most notably Q-methodology) which make it possible to read from the data (rather than feed into the data) what influences young people's experience (for a more detailed account of such abductive methodology, see Curt, 1994; Stainton Rogers et al., 1995).

Young people's values

In the 1960s a US psychologist, Milton Rokeach, carried out a study of young people's political thinking and action, and how these related to their values. He found that young people whose political affiliations were right-wing tended to view 'freedom' as the most important value, whereas those with left-wing political affiliations tended to see 'equality' as most important (Rokeach, 1968). The way he did this was by presenting young people with two lists of 18 values: one set he called terminal values (what is desired as an end state, such as 'equality' or 'a world of beauty'), the other instrumental values (the qualities needed to get there, such as 'logical' or 'loving'). Each value was further clarified by a short expansion. For example, 'equality' was explained as 'brotherhood [sic], equal opportunity for all', whereas 'a world of beauty' was expanded as 'beauty of nature and the arts'.

Around the 1960s and 1970s (when we were young) there was a lot of research carried out on Rokeach's values, but these days it has largely fallen into disfavour. One reason for this is obvious: the sexist language that was used. Another is that the values he chose conflated what seem to us, now, to be quite different concerns (such as aesthetic and ecological concerns about the environment). Finally, Rokeach's instrument failed to address a number of issues which have become salient these days, such as concern about health and fear of crime. As researchers we also have problems with the statistical techniques Rokeach used. Nonetheless, we decided that Rokeach's work was a good starting-point for our own research, because, in part, it would focus our minds upon how young people today – compared with yesteryear – make sense of what to do (instrumentality) and what to aspire to (terminality). By bringing Q-methodology to the study of values we also hoped to reveal something of the alternative value patterns or configurations young people evince without assuming that, say, party political affiliation was the key to unlock that diversity.

Our research involved a number of elements. Here we will report on two of them: a study paralleling Rokeach's, in which young people were asked to respond to a set of values given to them by us; and a series of 'focus groups', that is discussions between small groups of young people, each led by a young researcher. We modified the two sets of Rokeach's values, adding some extra ones (to make two sets of 22 values) and changing the language in which the explanations were expressed. The values we used are as shown in Table 3.1. We gave these lists to 60 Slovak and 60 UK university students and asked them to place them into a grid like that shown in Figure 3.1.

Q-pattern factor analysis was carried out for each list of values, first of all separately for the UK and Slovak students, and then bringing them together. Here we will look at those patterns which emerged in both sites (see Stainton Rogers et al., 1994, for a fuller treatment of these data). What this analysis does is examine the responses that each person has made, and look for general patterns of response – different ways in which a number of people have sorted the values in a particular fashion. We interpret these by looking at the pattern of values, fleshing this out with what young people said to us in the 'focus group' interviews.

Terminal values

What is noticeable here is the absence of the overtly political values which Rokeach identified as important to young people in the 1960s, such as 'equality' and 'freedom'. These simply did not figure. Instead we found three terminal (end state) value patterns that were broadly shared across the two cultures: hedonist companionship; 'street-wise' individualism; and born-again salvation.

Hedonist companionship

This set of values placed 'happiness' as most important (+4), with 'true friendship' and 'family solicitude' next (+3). Most unimportant was 'an aesthetic world' (–4), with 'salvation' and 'a world of natural beauty' next (–3). This set of values places most value upon being happy, and sees the major route to such happiness as having warm and close relationships with friends and family. The kinds of things participants in our focus groups said were:

> In the end, what matters is being happy and enjoying yourself. I'm just not prepared to do a dead-end job which would make me miserable.

> Your friends are what are most important in your life.

Table 3.1 *Terminal and instrumental values*

Terminal values

A comfortable life	An exciting life	Justice
A world at peace	A world of natural beauty	Equality
An aesthetic world	Family solicitude	Freedom
Happiness	Inner harmony	Mature love
National security	Pleasure	Salvation
Self-respect	Social recognition	True friendship
Wisdom	A safe life-space	Positive health
A sense of accomplishment		

Instrumental values

Ambitious	Capable	Clean	Forgiving	Honest
Ethical	Energetic	Logical	Obedient	Responsible
Self-controlled	Open-minded	Cheerful	Courageous	Helpful
Imaginative	Self-reliant	Intellectual	Loving	Courteous
Ideological	Realistic			

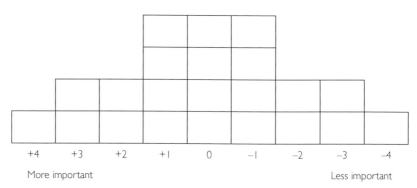

Figure 3.1

This focus on hedonism and relationships is consistent with Wilkinson and Mulgan's (1995) work on young people's values, and also the findings Brannen et al. (1994) obtained in their research into young people's health. They noted that:

> health had a lower priority than happiness, love and family relationships. Young people were asked to rank . . . 'the most important things in life to you'. Health was included along with future job security, happiness, success, peace of mind, money, friends, love and happy family relationships. Most young women and young men put happiness in their first three choices. (1994: 71)

Street-wise individualism

Here the value seen as most important was 'wisdom' (+4), followed by 'inner harmony' and 'self-respect' (+3). Again 'salvation' was the most negative (–4) with 'an aesthetic world' and 'social recognition' next (–3). This account is far more inner-directed and personal, about being 'together' and 'at one with oneself'. At first sight this looked to us very 'sixties' in its flavour, but our group discussions encouraged us to put a much harder slant on what is being portrayed here:

> You've got to be really cynical, really sussed out in the world today. Like you've got to know where you are at, and not let anybody fool you around.
>
> Wisdom – yeah, well, as they say, knowledge is power.
>
> It's about knowing what matters to you, not what matters to somebody else.

These sorts of comments offer a decidedly harsher tone, which views 'wisdom' not as a transcendental state but as a much more worldly-wise cynicism. Crucial is the ability not to be conned – either by smooth-talking politicians, or by carefully packaged advertising – but to know and trust your own judgement. Again our results here are consistent with other research. Wilkinson and Mulgan (1995) report that 96% of 18–34 year olds agree that 'everyone has to find out for themselves what sort of life they want to lead.' We picked up (as they did) a sense of alienation, especially about politics, and a strongly individualistic determination to 'be your own person' and 'do your own thing'. But it would be wrong to view this as isolationism, as 'true friendship' is also endorsed (+2). Rather the distrust is towards 'the system', towards established institutions and authority. Wilkinson and Mulgan write of a growing 'decline of deference' and of young people 'fast losing respect for, and even interest in, the people in charge'.

Born-again salvation

Here 'salvation' is accorded the strongest importance (+4) with 'wisdom' and 'family solicitude' next (+3). 'A comfortable life' (–4) and 'an aesthetic world' and 'social recognition' (–3) are viewed as most unimportant. This configuration of values was given by young people who have strong religious beliefs and affiliations. It is interesting that in this context 'wisdom' seems to have a quite different meaning from the previous account:

> It's God's love that defines what my life means, and His wisdom which guides me.
>
> I believe in Karma – what goes around comes around.
>
> Achievement in life cannot be judged by possessions.
>
> The constant pursuit of happiness can only bring unhappiness.

Instrumental values

Again there were three patterns of instrumental values which showed up in both the UK and Slovakia: being a responsible companion, a fun-loving companion and a 'mover and shaker'.

Responsible companionship

To be 'loving' was seen as the most important human quality (+4), with being 'honest' and 'responsible' (+3), 'ethical' and 'realistic' (+2) next. Being 'ambitious' (−4) was most strongly rejected, with 'ideological' and 'capable' next (−3). These qualities are very much about being a caring and warm person, but also about being dependable.

> It's about being somebody who can be trusted, who will stand by your friends no matter what.

> You have to 'be there' for somebody when they really need you.

> What matters is to be somebody that your friends can rely on.

Fun-loving companionship

Here 'cheerful' was seen as most important (+4) with 'energetic' and 'loving' (+3) next. Being 'clean' was seen as least important (−4) followed by 'ethical' and 'obedient'. This suggests a much more 'laid-back' and hedonistic kind of friendship. Our group discussions suggest that here having a good time together matters more than being caring.

> The kind of person who's great to be with, good fun.

> Going out together and having a great time.

> It's about being connected, the incredible feeling you get of being part of something bigger.

Moving and shaking

The most important value here was 'intellectual' (+4) with 'ambitious' and 'realistic' (+3) next. Being 'obedient' was seen as most unimportant (−4) with 'clean' and 'ideological' (−3) next. This seems to describe being a 'mover and shaker' – somebody who knows where they are going, and has the energy, ambition and intelligence to go far,

> I want to be a successful role model to others like me.

> You need to have a dream, to settle on what you want and go for it.

> Like, it's going to be champagne and roses, one day for sure.

Shifting values

There are parallels with the data obtained by Wilkinson and Mulgan (1995), which suggest there has been a shift away from ideological values towards far more 'personal' concerns – softer, greener and more gentle values to do with companionship and caring, at least for some young people. We were intrigued by the way that idealistic concerns with 'freedom' and 'equality' seem to have become so unimportant – generally relegated to the middle ground in young people's sorting patterns. We wondered to what extent young people had simply come to take these for granted. We tested this by asking another group of young people to sort the values again, but this time against the criterion of what would be 'worst to lose'. Sure enough, freedom (but not equality) reappeared often placed as the most distressing to lose – in most of the sorting configurations. But we also got the impression from the focus group discussions that young people have become much more cynical about idealism in general. For example, when asked directly about such values, the kinds of comments made were:

> Equality – that's a laugh! A pretty little sound-bite, to keep the punters happy.

> Like the song says – freedom's just another word for nothing left to lose!

> Politicians go on about moral values, about 'back to basics'. Sleaze-bags, the lot of them.

Aspirations

The young people we spoke to in our focus groups expressed aspirations which, in many cases, were quite traditional. A surprisingly large proportion spoke of wanting the makings of a comfortable lifestyle: a car, a home of their own, a reasonably satisfying, reasonably well-paid job. The majority saw themselves as eventually settling down and having children. However, most of them saw this as a long-term future goal, and expressed concern about whether they would ever be able to achieve it. This was for many of them a realistic appraisal – that this kind of ordinary 'settling down' would, in fact, be much more difficult for them to achieve than their parents.

There was, in both countries, tremendous uncertainty about the future. The young people in Slovakia as well as those in the UK expressed a lot of concern about unemployment. For the young Slovaks this arose from the move away from communism – a system under which their parents' generation were guaranteed a job. In the UK it arose from the limited opportunities, especially to get the kinds of jobs they felt were worth doing, and which gave them any satisfaction. As Wilkinson and Mulgan (1995) found too, we saw an enormous gap between the kinds of expectations that many young people had about the occupations they would like to follow, and the limited openings available to them: 'crap jobs for crap pay and no future'. It is hardly surprising, then, that a number of our UK groups spoke about 'opting out of the rat-race' – of giving up any real hope of a 'real job' and settling for a life of short-term, insecure 'fiddly jobs' interspersed with or augmented by welfare benefits.

This 'opting out' was by no means universal though. For instance some Slovak youngsters had already begun to speculate on the stock exchange, and were planning to set up in business on their own. One of our UK focus groups comprised four black young people all of whom were pursuing careers in entertainment and the arts. These young people were enormously ambitious: they saw themselves as determined to become both rich and famous, and expressed a willingness to work hard and make sacrifices to get where they wanted.

Conclusions

We were looking for diversity and we found it. So while we found the kinds of 'caring' values toward which Wilkinson and Mulgan (1995) have argued the young are moving, we also identified world views which, for example, are informed by strongly held religious beliefs. We also had our 'movers and shakers' and our 'street-wise individualists', who are (in different ways) far from voicing a 'warm and cuddly' perspective. Young people are no more homogeneous than any other age group studied in depth would prove to be; nor do individuals always tell the same 'story'. But equally it is clear to us that we are seeing, overall, a profound shift in values within this new generation compared with the life-stories in which we, the researchers, grew up.

To paraphrase Dylan once more, we think these data remind us that it is foolish and short-sighted to 'criticise what you don't understand'. Some politicians and social commentators seem all too ready to brand the young as 'lacking in values' because of their alienation from traditional values. They assume this means that young people have no values – they are lost, misguided, disaffected and uncaring. This is not just demeaning to the young; it demonstrates a blinkered sensibility and an unwillingness to acknowledge that young people do have value constellations – frames of means, and of ends, to which they may be strongly committed. It is just that they are very different patterns – and ones that may bring the young to castigate their elders in turn. Peter Preston (1995), writing in *The Guardian*, argued this case eloquently, describing today's young generation as follows:

> They are not ideologues; rather the reverse. They are pretty sceptical of, and pretty bored by conventional politics (because it barely acknowledges their existence in terms they recognise) . . . They have scant connection with organised religion, or indeed with any multi-disciplinary organisation. But they aren't remotely selfish – on the contrary, they throw themselves into causes where something may be accomplished. They care, but not to order. They are individuals, not party hacks. There is no easy word to describe them. But let us try: Future Pragmatists. That is because they look to the future with hope and curiosity.

References

Brannen, J., Dodd, K., Oakley, A. and Storey, P. (1994) *Young People, Health and Family Life*, Buckingham: Open University Press.

Curt, B. (pseudonym) (1994) *Textuality and Tectonics*, Buckingham: Open University Press.

Preston, P. (1995) The parties are deaf to the song of youth, *The Guardian*, 20 October 1995.

Rokeach, M. (1968) *Beliefs, Attitudes and Values*, San Francisco: Jossey-Bass.

Stainton Rogers, R., Stainton Rogers, W. and Vyrost, J. (1994) 'Ako vnímajú mladi ludia demokraciu? Metodologická tudia intra- a interkultúmych rozdielov medzi britskými a slovenskými vysokoškolský mi študentmi', *Psychológia a Patopsychológia Dietata*, 29 (3) 224–32.

Stainton Rogers, R., Stainton Rogers, W., Výrost, J. and Lovás, L. (1995) 'Future imperfect? The aspirations of Slovak and UK young people', *Studia Psychologica* 37 (3) 192–4.

Wilkinson, H. and Mulgan, G. (1995) *Freedom's Children: Work, Relationships and Politics for 18–34 Year Olds In Britain Today*, London: Demos.

4
'Pale Shadows': Racisms, Masculinity and Multiculture

Les Back

> Far from being unitary or monolithic autonomous things, cultures actually assume more 'foreign' elements, alterities, differences, than they consciously exclude. Who in India or Algeria can confidently separate out the British or French component of the past from present actualities, and who in Britain or France can draw a clear circle around British London or French Paris that would exclude the impact of India and Algeria upon those two imperial cities?
>
> Edward Said, *Culture and Imperialism*

> The Man who adores the Negro is as sick as the man who abominates him.
>
> Franz Fanon, *Black Skin, White Masks*

If we are to think again about the issue of multiculturalism it is vital to avoid any slippage into the false comfort of simple cultural archetypes which reify 'minority' and 'host' cultures respectively. Imperialism and the racist discourses that have flourished in its wake insist on what Roland Barthes (1973) called the 'simplicity of essences'. However, cultural processes themselves confound the idea that cultures exist as hermetically sealed absolute unities. Urban cultures, in particular, are highly promiscuous in their endeavour to constantly remake and invent traditions in the present. Edward Said (1993) attempts to name this process by insisting that one must view the politics of culture within 'overlapping territories' and 'intertwined histories'. The key question thus becomes how to render explicit the multiple influences that resonate within metropolitan contexts like London, Amsterdam, Paris, Hamburg and Berlin.

It is a matter not of somehow simultaneously understanding and tolerating 'foreign cultures' but of facing an imperial history that has brought different cultural groups into intense and sometimes terrible contact. In this sense the history of Europe is profoundly multicultural. Yet European racisms have equally insisted that the distinction of the European be established and maintained in the face of the barbarism and inferiority of the native, the immigrant or the ethnic minority. However, the relationship between racism and the construction of identities is not simply a matter of making non-Europeans inferior within some pseudo-biological logic. One of the cultural contradictions of racism is that the other can be seen as an object of desire, simultaneously a 'noble savage' and a 'violent avenger' (Hall, 1988). This syndrome is signalled by Franz Fanon who argued with great power that the European romance with difference was equally as devastating as the venom of racial hatred to subaltern peoples. A multiculturalism which simply celebrates the other albeit with liberal intentions – runs perilously close to this syndrome.

In this chapter I want to explore the possibility of rethinking the issue of multiculturalism with reference to the lives of young men growing up in culturally plural urban contexts in London. I want to look at the connections between white working class masculinities, multiculture and the expression of racism. Particularly focusing on the impact that black cultural forms have had on working class culture, this chapter explores the tensions between the multicultural resonances within the lives of these young men and the emergence of new and complex racialised hierarchies. The material referred to throughout is drawn from an ethnographic study of racism in young working class people's lives conducted between 1985 and 1989.

The work focused on two post-war public housing developments. The first, located next to the River Thames, is predominantly composed of white working class residents and is called Riverview. The second, in contrast, is a multi-ethnic neighbourhood which I will refer to as Southgate. Throughout the research period I lived in or at close proximity to the research area. I had a long association with this part of London and I had lived most of my life in a white working class district little more than 10 miles away. I have reflected elsewhere on the complex positionalities which emerged in the process of doing the research (Back, 1993c): for the purposes of this chapter the ethnographic work should be seen as produced through a dialogue with a white male fieldworker in his early twenties. During 1986–7 I rented a room in a tower block on Riverview estate and I used the flat as a base from which to do research in both districts. I had also worked as a youth worker for some time in this area.

'The metropolitan paradox': young men, racism and transcultural dialogue

The history of the capital is integrally connected to imperial expansion and trade. At its height during the eighteenth and nineteenth centuries London emerged as 'a kind of Emporium for the whole Earth' (Joseph Addison, quoted in Porter, 1994). Along with the flow of commodities came migrations of people from various hinterlands: Jews came to London from Poland and Germany, and French Huguenots came fleeing religious persecution. It is less well known that from the middle of the eighteenth century there were between 5,000 and 10,000 Africans living in London, of whom some were seamen but most were transported to Britain as servants and chattel (Fryer, 1984). London provided the financial centre from which Britain's slave trade was funded and it was developed economically from the fruits of slavery. The point that I want to make is that the issues I am going to talk about with regard to London are not part of a kind of 'other' England. In short, the relationship between imperial expansion and Englishness is central to the story of what it means to be part of English society in general and London in particular. Equally, the historical denial of the long-standing presence of Africans and South Asians has meant that their contribution to English society has been ignored. London has a multicultural past to be recovered but the traces of this history have been bleached from public memory (Back, 1993b).

The part of South London which formed the focus of this research had a long history of migration. From the 1920s onwards outward migration took hold as slum clearance programmes were initiated. Over the 20 years from 1930 to 1950, the local population dropped by 25%. This period was characterised by economic decline within the area's manufacturing industries. However, the decline in population was partially arrested as international migrants from several countries settled in the district. The largest single group came from Jamaica and other parts of the Caribbean. The settlement of black people in the area did not go unopposed. In 1948 agitation from the National Union of Seamen to stop black people working on British ships provoked a violent confrontation. There was also hostility to black people within the local labour movement. The result was the emergence of a far right political splinter group which commanded considerable electoral support in the area throughout the 1960s and 1970s.

During this period the black population in this part of London grew steadily. By 1981 black people constituted 25% of the 60,000 people who lived in the borough and in some of the neighbourhoods this figure rose to between 40% and 50%. This population was also youthful. The area divided into a white population that was ageing, as young white people moved out, and a disproportionately youthful black population. In 1971, 45% of people aged 15 and under were black (Hewitt, 1986). In addition, small numbers of people settled from Pakistan, India, Africa, Greece and Turkish Cyprus, and during the 1980s a large number of Vietnamese people arrived.

Paradoxically, South London is associated both with the most extreme manifestations of racism and with some of the most profound moments of inter-racial dialogue. These twin processes were most evident in youth styles. Dick Hebdige (1974a; 1974b; 1979; 1981; 1983), writing about these sub-cultures, commented that in these spectacular forms it is possible to see a 'phantom history of race relations':

> The succession of white subcultural forms can be read as a series of deep-structural forms which symbolically accommodate or expunge the black presence from the host community. It is on the plane of aesthetics: in dress, dance, music, in the whole rhetoric of style that we find the dialogue between black and white most subtly and comprehensively recorded, albeit in code. (1979: 44–5)

Here Hebdige claims we can view a dialogue of emulation and accommodation. Hebdige points out, the impact of black culture on white young people was not uniformly progressive. For example, skinhead style incorporated Jamaican forms of music (like ska and bluebeat), yet at the same time it also proclaimed white power and white pride. In this case, like a photographic negative, black culture was an emblem of white chauvinism (Mercer, 1987).

The skinhead movement attempted to construct a working class identity out of the chaos of post-war urban change (Cohen, 1972; Hebdige, 1981). Kobena Mercer has commented that within this context black cultural forms were appropriated and allied with an imperial notion of national pride in a period when Britain was in an economic sense barely hanging onto its 'First World status'. The 'skins' in this sense can be characterised as a 'Ghost dance of white ethnicity' (Mercer, 1987: 50). South London provided a key point of cultural convergence where Jamaican music in particular was made available to new audiences. The complex cultural formations which resulted show quite clearly that the integration of cultural diversity need not necessarily be connected with the rejection of racism.

The taking on of black traditions of style and language has resulted in a radical reconfiguration of white working class culture in multi-ethnic locales (Chambers, 1976; Gilroy and Lawrence, 1988). This had led Paul Gilroy to suggest that 'Black culture has become a class culture . . . as two generations of whites have appropriated it, discovered its seductive forms of meaning for their own' (1990: 273). I think it is vitally important to appreciate that folk anti-racism can be generated in the context of these encounters. The tension between dialogue and exclusion produces what I want to refer to as a *metropolitan paradox*. The point here is that working class vernacular cultures possess incommensurable (Bhabha, 1994) political impulses. It is not merely that working class young people ally themselves to a variety of racist or non-racist positions. The uneven nature of common sense produces circumstances where the rejection of racism with regard to a particular racialised group can go hand in hand with the elaboration of hostility against other groups. In order to achieve a more profound political understanding of urban multiculture it is necessary to identify the constructions of blackness that white young men find attractive. It is this issue that I now concentrate on.

Black icons? The doubling of fear and desire

Young white people in the districts of South London had an intimate relationship with black cultural forms of speech and style. In both districts the dialogues occurring within multi-racial peer groups had opened up black cultural practices to white appropriations. While this process was most profound on the estate I referred to as Southgate it was also found to lesser degree of intensity within adolescent communities in Riverview. The identification with black culture and people incorporated a whole range of social practices from the blazonry of black musical cultures and styles to the adoption of creole usage and black London argot. Amongst young whites there existed a continuum of identifications with black culture which started with the most rudimentary usage of creole and extended to some cases where young whites talked about a stage in mid-adolescence where they expressed a desire to be black (Back, 1991b). These identifications occurred equally between white young men and women. Roger Hewitt and others have commented on the potential of these identifications to yield non-racist positions for whites. In no way do I want to deny that such a potential exists but I want to look at the ways racially divisive processes are also in operation within such multi-ethnic settings.

Black young men could be viewed by whites – both male and female as prestigious figures in particular adolescent communities. Their status often relates to their position as cultural innovators and through their association with prestigious youth styles. Yet at the same time black young men could be characterised by whites as undesirable, violent, dangerous and aggressive. Many of the black young men refer to instances in South London where white (adult) people with whom they come into contact 'hold on to their bags tightly' or 'put their heads down and walk away'. As Tim points out here:

> White people fear black people. Lotta people out there don't know black people. It's only what they hear and read in the newspapers – that is how they know black people, that is how they see black people. Walking down the road you see white ladies holding onto their bags tight as you pass them, as if you are gonna rob dem.

These do not merely result from a stereotype of blackness, but relate more specifically to a gendered construction of black masculinity. This notion is loaded with a whole range of connotations, from fantasies about black male heterosexuality and sexual potency to aggressiveness and violence.

From black locations these notions of fear and desire are both restricting and unrepresentative. Indeed, 'uniform whiteness' is closely correlated with a fear of racial attack and violence in the minds of some black young men. Writing on her experience of growing up in the American South, bell hooks comments: 'whiteness in the black imagination is often a representation of terror' (1992: 342). In a similar fashion 'white areas' in South London were viewed by black men as dangerous places to be avoided. While the stereotypes of black masculinity were embraced by some, many of these young men felt constrained and alienated by the mythology of 'black macho'. Wilson, a young man of 17, comments here:

> Yeah, there is this expectation to be this big black macho thing. Some people play to that, that's OK if they want to do that. But I think that's like making black people to be like, you know, closer to the beast. It's pure wickedness. There's a lot of stuff about how black men treat women and that. It is true that some black men are pure idiots but to make it like saying all black men are this, or all black men are that is just rubbish.

Others spoke of the way in which particular archetypes of black men were sometimes 'played to' while in other circumstances the same images would be rejected.

The existence of an interlocked dualism of 'fear and desire' in white constructions of black masculinity is an essential feature of my argument. This syndrome was acted out in the starkest terms during a visit by the Southgate basketball club to an area outside London. I played on the team with the young men and I was the only white player. The events that I want to briefly give an account of took place during a tournament that was held in a provincial area of coastal England in a region known as East Anglia.

When we arrived it was immediately apparent that we were entering a completely different social and political landscape. On the Saturday we played two games, the second of which we lost by the smallest of margins. The young men contested the result and the team was disqualified from the tournament. I have no doubt that the decision was influenced by the racist images the presence of these young men evoked in the minds of the white organisers. Wayne, the team captain, saw this clearly: 'I don't say this often, Les, but these people are racist. It is because we are a black team that they are being so hard on us.' It was clear that the panic which the officials showed towards the team was not simply a result of the protests which we made. Pauline, the team coach, commented that exactly the same sequence of events had happened the previous year when a women's team from a neighbouring part of South London had participated in the tournament. She said, 'The people here will do that if we don't behave properly. You see we make it easy for them to say, "What do you expect from them ghetto boys?"' Yet these young men were hardly 'children of the ghetto': they were all employed, some in 'white collar' jobs, or studying. It seemed clear to me that the fear which was so apparent in the behaviour of the white officials and organisers was the most important factor shaping the outcome of these events.

On the Saturday evening a dance was held to celebrate the tournament. The team attended with mixed feelings. We sat in a corner of the function room where the event was being held. I kept thinking of the extent to which basketball is predominantly a white game in Britain. Black players were perfectly fine as long as they remained just a few charismatic figures. It was a very different matter when black teams participated, as this experience had shown. The irony of the situation was that during the course of the evening the organisers ran a 'best-looking player' competition, and it was won by one of our players. Just a few hours earlier the team had been characterised as a riotous group of black youngsters. Suddenly black became beautiful! There was a suggestion that Derek should not accept the prize as a protest against the earlier behaviour of the organisers. However, this did not happen and the team celebrated a strange victory. Paradoxically it seemed as if our white hosts characterised young people as being individually glamorous and attractive while at the same time were fearful of them collectively. This comes close to what Stuart Hall, inspired by the suggestive comments made by Franz Fanon (1967), calls the 'doubling of fear and desire' (1988: 28) where contradictory feelings towards black subjects can be felt simultaneously. The contradiction is at the core of the white construction of black otherness. The white organisers of the competition used the fact that a black person won the 'beauty contest' as a way of denying that their prior actions had been informed by racism.

With this in mind I want to explore how the *fear and desire couplet* manages white identifications with black people in South London. The aim is to demonstrate how the partial suppression of particular racisms can go hand in hand with the elaboration of other racist discourses and actions.

White working class masculinities and establishing a racialised hierarchy

While accepting and adhering to the idea that non-racist sensibilities are communicated to white people through the process of cultural dialogues (Hewitt, 1986; Jones, 1988), it must also be understood that the *fear and desire couplet* is present both alongside and sometimes inside these processes. For white young men the perceptions of black masculinity in heterosexual codes of 'hardness' and 'hyper-sexuality' are some of the core elements which attract them to their image of black masculine style. This is located around racialised definitions of masculinity. The image of black masculinity as invulnerable, 'hard' and 'bad' is alarmingly similar to racist notions of dangerous/violent 'black muggers'. At the moment when racist ideas are most vulnerable, in situations where there is intimate contact between black and white men, stereotypical ideas can be reproduced 'dressed up' as positive characteristics to be emulated. This kind of identification can find itself locked within the discourse of absolute difference which renders blackness exotic and reaffirms black men as a 'race apart'.

Whites create a racialised image of black masculinity, assembled from fragments of their own experience and a range of other discourses, which they then identify with as the 'qualities' possessed by the other. The paradox here is that this image of blackness is a white artefact. The end result is that a particular version of black heterosexual masculinity is adopted in the styles and rituals of white men without any radical transformation of their use of racist discourses. This may have specific payoffs with regard to white attitudes towards black men (albeit confined to fear and desire and a specific construction of blackness), but this kind of iconography is of little relevance to a wider refutation of racism. I am arguing that these processes are going on simultaneously with more profound and politicised dialogues. The situation is not monolithic; rather, very complex exchanges occur which are, to a greater or lesser extent, constituted by the racialised social constructions mentioned above.

Previously I have shown that the notions of race and racism adopted by the young men in this district are contradictory and ambiguous (Back, 1991a; Back, 1993a). In the predominantly white working class district of Riverview this process was starkly apparent. While there existed a widely held view that racism and prejudice were wrong, young whites repeatedly used racist discourse to characterise black people outside the area. Equally, racist name-calling was prevalent amongst the young men. In the name-calling context racist names were operated in 'wind-ups' and other forms of play mentioned earlier. In this sense there was a clear relationship between the ritual expression of masculine identities and popular racism: the former provided the platform for the latter.

While black young people were subject to such forms of abuse, the use of racism in these strategic settings violated the widely held view that it was 'out of order' to use racism or bring colour into multi-racial peer interactions. The contradictory nature of these ideas allowed for contingent forms of racial inclusion to be attained by black young people in the area. This also has to be seen alongside the resistance to racism which black young people operated within these peer settings. However, the situation was very different for the newly settled children of Vietnamese refugees who were housed in these areas during the 1980s. In many ways Vietnamese youth operate outside of the linguistic and cultural exchanges that take place in multi-racial groups and constitute a subordinate youth group, or what Roger Hewitt (1990: 141) has termed a *sociolinguistic underclass.*

White young men justified the absence of the Vietnamese young people by asserting that they 'liked to keep themselves to themselves' and that they 'won't mix'. Their lack of participation in friendship groups was the result of the kinds of constructions that were mobilised against them by whites. In the course of fieldwork I noticed that a Vietnamese boy – Tanyi – started to come into the club with two white boys, Cliff and Jack. Cliff and Jack were from established 'estate families'. Cliff's father, in particular, was reputed to have been a supporter of the National Front in the 1970s and vehemently opposed the settlement of the Vietnamese on the estate. The three boys were said to 'hang around together' which usually meant that they spent time together on the estate and in the youth club.

The three boys would come into the club and spend their time playing football and pool. Occasionally, Tanyi's Chinese/Vietnamese origins were mentioned in masculinist forms of play called 'wind-ups' (which are the process of getting another person angry then ridiculing their anger by exposing its illegitimacy: 'I was only joking . . . only winding you up'). The most recurrent reference point was the association of Tanyi's background with a stereotype of 'Orientals' who are proficient in martial arts. On one occasion the three boys were playing pool and Cliff rolled the pool cue over his shoulder and adopted a fight stance in front of Tanyi. He then withdrew, saying, 'I'd better watch it. Tanyi would make Bruce Lee [a famous martial arts hero] take up pool'. All three boys laughed at this. While Tanyi was accepted as part of the peer group, his 'difference' was often referred to in these exchanges, making it apparent that his presence was always contingent on Cliff's and Jack's approval. It was clear that the three boys used their masculinity as a common register around which to build friendship. In this sense these masculine forms of play that they were involved in were expressions of this process at work (Back, 1990). However, these friendships did not last long.

After two months I started to feel some tension between Tanyi, Cliff and Jack. On one occasion at the entrance of the club a new worker asked Tanyi to spell his name. Cliff, who was standing behind him, said, 'just put Tony.' This process of Anglicisation of names is common amongst British Asian young people who move in white peer groups. In this area the Vietnamese young men would justify this by claiming that the whites could not pronounce their names properly. On this occasion I think that Cliff's 'naming claim' was of greater significance. It signalled an increasing resentment towards Tanyi's 'difference'. This change also manifested itself in their interactions within the club. Cliff challenged Tanyi in 'wind-ups' more often and subsequently the boys spent less time together. Three weeks later Tanyi stopped coming to the club.

When I asked Cliff and Jack about this they told me that Tanyi had decided to 'go back to his own kind'. A few days after this discussion I saw Tanyi on the estate and asked him why he had stopped coming to the club. He said:

> I was jus[t] sick of the way they treat me. You know, yellow this, yellow that, 'Chink' this, 'Chink' that. Then I decided that I was not going to come to the club any more. I decided that I didn't want them to use me as something to play with. See they say we don't come to the club because we don't want to but would you want to be treated like that? I go to the club when they have Vietnamese disco and the club on Sundays but no more in the week.

Clearly, the manifestation of racist practices was the most important factor in the breakdown of this friendship group. So, rather than a matter of voluntary absence, the lack of a Vietnamese presence in the club was the result of an informal exclusion.

While Vietnamese youth were excluded from the youth club they were also subject to racial harassment and attacks. There were several instances reported by the Vietnamese refugees of harassment on their way to local shopping facilities. There were also stories of young men urinating into the letter-boxes of Vietnamese residents and burning torches being placed outside their homes.

In the face of this kind of harassment it is hardly surprising that the Vietnamese young people were reluctant to use the youth club or to enter into close relationships with other young people in the area. The question which emerges here is: why can young black people gain access to a contingent insider position while the Vietnamese cannot? The answer I suspect lay in the way that racism and gender interact in the construction of black and Vietnamese 'otherness'.

The internal configurations and contradictions found in white working class masculinities police the determinants of racial exclusion. Here the Vietnamese young men are constructed as generally weak and feeble. Although there were on a few occasions references to an imagined relationship between 'Orientals' and prowess in martial arts, the Vietnamese young men were viewed as vulnerable, soft and effeminate. Thus within these white constructions black men are viewed in terms of the *fear and desire couplet,* while the Vietnamese young men are labelled as soft and effeminate and vilified.

When I met Chas in 1987 he was 14 years old. He lived in Riverview and he is white but intimately involved with the musical cultures of black London. He had taken on the full blazonry of black style forms. One of his front teeth is gold capped, he had 'tramlines' shaved into the sides of his blond hair, and he wore a medallion with the symbol of Africa coloured in red, gold and green. We would talk about the relative worth of black British musicians like Soul II Soul compared with the American rap aces Public Enemy. He was unequivocal about the issue of colour. 'It's pure wickedness to cuss people's colour – you know what I mean? Like my black friends have as much right to be here as I have.' For a short time Chas 'went out' with a black young woman from the area. However, the politics of this posturing was not extended beyond his identifications with his particular image of blackness.

On one occasion we were walking through South London sharing discourse on the state of dance music when his model of racial hierarchies became clear. We passed a Vietnamese refugee and her son walking back from a shopping excursion. Chas turned, 'there is one thing though – I can't stand the Chinks. Their cooking stinks and they keep themselves to themselves like. They don't want to mix.' I asked, 'But isn't that just as bad as saying that all black people are muggers?' He replied, 'Na! That's not the same at all! My black mates wouldn't let people walk over them the way the Vietnamese do – do you know what I mean? Black people have nuff respect for who they are. If you said things to dem you'd get nuff licks [physical retribution].'

In this short extract we see the articulation between gender and racism rising to the surface of consciousness. Here a dualism develops which connects racialised boundaries with gendered characteristics. In the framework of white working class masculinities black and 'Oriental' youth are characterised in terms of a set of dualistic oppositions. The terms of inter-racial dialogue are set by this process of *race/gender othering*. An image of blackness is defined in the context of white common sense which is in turn viewed positively. This results in the definition of black young men as contingent insiders. In contrast, the Vietnamese young men are castigated within a kind of Orientalist discourse and are attacked and excluded. What follows from this discourse is that particular minorities are designated as being 'hard' and assertive, while others are designated as being 'soft' and vulnerable.

The configurations of 'white masculinity' are inextricably linked with the processes of constructing various 'others'. Franz Fanon (1967) showed that in colonial and neo-colonial societies the division between self and other is often a crude simplification of the complex psychological legacy of racism. His aim was to deconstruct the 'white masks' which racism imposed on black people, or as Homi Bhabha puts it, 'the white man's artifice inscribed on the black man's body' (1990: 188). Bhabha himself suggests that the divisions between self and other are always partial, with the result that neither is sufficient unto itself (1990: 193). Appropriating Fanon's metaphor one might pose the question of how white young men are adopting 'black masks'. What I am suggesting here is that white masculinity does not involve the assertion of a monolithic racialised self. Rather it embraces and rejects differently positioned images of masculine otherness. On the one hand, white young men identify with particular constructions of blackness, and in doing so they appropriate these images as part of *their* selfhood.

On the other hand, they reject any form of identification with images of the 'Oriental' as being anti-self. Complex configurations of identity emerge in a situation where 'The Shadow of the Other falls upon the Self' (Bhabha, 1990: 203).

The racialised identities which are rejected, or from which individuals distance themselves, are as important as the ones which are embraced. In the process of saying 'I am not like him/her' the subject is saying something about who they are and how they conceive themselves. I have referred to this elsewhere as a process of vacating particular socially available notions of identity (Back, 1991b). In view of the issues discussed here this manifests itself in a process whereby particular combinations of masculine identity are embraced while others are rejected. My point is that all of these forms of masculinity are racialised.

Conclusion

> The white Negro accepts the real Negro not as a human being in his totality, but as the bringer of a highly specified and restricted 'cultural dowry'. In doing so he creates an inverted form of keeping the nigger in his place. (Ned Polsky, 1961: 313)

This quotation refers to Norman Mailer's famous essay 'The white negro'. In it Mailer claims to show how white hipsters in 1950s America took on black language and style. Or, as Mailer put it, they were 'a new breed of [white] adventurers, urban adventurers who drifted out at night looking for action with a black man's code to fit their facts' (1961: 285). Polsky's key point is that the hipsters' appropriation of blackness was restricted to a particular stereotype of what being black meant. Echoing Fanon's (1967) famous pronouncement on this process, he holds that these stereotypes of blackness are really the property of white folks: a black image but a white artefact. Polsky suggests the hipsters did not want black men to be 'Uncle Toms' but they still wanted them to be 'spooks' (1961: 313), a damning commentary on the radical potential of such mimesis. The issues raised here are resonant throughout all instances where white people have appropriated black cultural forms.

The taking on of black cultural forms by white young men may have transformed the sight and sound of South London neighbourhoods but this clearly has not banished racism from their lives. I do not want to deny that there is a progressive cultural politics of racial dialogue in these locations, yet the contemporary urgencies of the growth of racial harassment in South London prohibit any slippage into banal optimism. I have argued in this chapter that in order to understand the contingencies of folk rejections of racism we have to cross our analysis of racism with the politics of various masculinities. It is only here that we can begin to decipher why it is that Vietnamese young people – male and female – in this part of South London are so viciously harassed.

It is here that I want to return to the vexed question of multiculturalism. I have argued that racist cultures incorporate difference. As a result there is no necessary opposition between complex and plural forms of racism on the one hand and multiculture on the other. Contemporary fascist cultures themselves are increasingly becoming syncretic, transnational and globalised. The incorporation of the swastika and the Nazi salute by British and other European far right groups provides evidence of this symbolic traffic. New information technologies are accelerating these processes, providing fascists throughout the world with the means to develop a multicultural and virtual fascism (Solomos and Back, 1995). In these circumstances extreme forms of localism in the guise of racial chauvinism can go hand in hand with a white supremacist multicultural globalism. The liberal impulse to promote tolerance through 'valuing cultural difference' is redundant in the context of the multifaceted nature of racist cultures. Rather the crucial issue is how to understand complex articulations between culture and power and the manner in which these feature in everyday experience.

If multiculturalism is to have any meaning in the context of the twenty-first century, the idea of the existence of homogeneous cultures and identities must be undermined irrevocably. Edward Said concludes that identity labels provide little more than a departure:

> Muslim, or American are not more than starting-points, which if followed into actual experience for only a moment are quickly left behind. Imperialism consolidated the mixture of cultures and identities on a global scale. But its worst and most paradoxical gift was to allow people to believe that they were only, mainly, exclusively, white, or Black, or Western or Oriental. (1993: 408)

Here he points clearly to the connection between racism and the reification of cultural difference. Historically, in Britain at least, multiculturalism has operated within such absolutist models of 'minority culture' (Gilroy, 1987). But such cultural hermetics ignore the intense contact which is also a part of the largess of imperialism. If multiculturalism is to be politically reconfigured, the strange comforts of cultural absolutism must be abandoned. It is only then that we can fully embrace and reckon with the intense relationship between modernity and multiculture.

Cultural hybridity and the emergences of decentred subjectivities (Hall, 1992), while providing important sites for cultural contest, do not necessarily produce progressive outcomes. I have argued that the range of identifications elaborated by young white men in South London point to the complex intersection between plural forms of racism, masculinity and multiculture. Any attempt to intervene politically within such urban contexts needs to develop a grounded understanding of these relationships. It is only then that young whites, and for that matter their multicultural educators, can engender inclusive ways of life which move beyond the assimilation of shadows.

Note

This chapter was given as the Henry Luce Memorial Lecture at Clarke University, Massachusetts, on 17 February 1993. I would like to thank Parminder Bhachu and Michael Keith for their incisive comments on earlier drafts. I would also like to thank Barbara Tizard, Ann Phoenix, John Solomos and Roger Hewitt. The research is drawn from New Ethnicities and Urban Culture: Racisms and Multiculture in Young Lives by Les Back, published in London by University College Press in 1996.

References

Back, L. (1990) 'Racist name calling and developing anti-racist strategies in youth work', Research Papers no. 14, Centre for Research in Ethnic Relations, University of Warwick.

Back, L. (1991a) 'Social context and racist name calling: an ethnographic perspective on racist talk within a South London adolescent community', *European Journal of Intercultural Studies*, 1 (3): 19–39.

Back, L. (1991b) 'Youth, racism and ethnicity in South London: an ethnographic study of adolescent inter-ethnic relations', unpublished PhD thesis, Goldsmiths' College, University of London.

Back, L. (1993a) 'Youth, race and nation in a predominantly white working-class neighbourhood in South London', New Community, 19 (2): 217–33.

Back, L. (1993b) 'The African heritage of white Europeans', in L. Back and A. Nayak (eds), Invisible Europeans: Black People in the 'New Europe', Birmingham: AFFOR.

Back, L. (1993c) 'Gendered participation: masculinity and fieldwork in a South London adolescent community', in D. Beli, P. Caplan and W. Jahan Karim (eds), *Gendered Fields: Women Men and Ethnography*, London: Routledge.

Barthes, R. (1973) *Mythologies* London: Granada.

Bhabha, H.K. (1990) 'Interrogating identity: the postcolonial prerogative', in D.T. Goldberg (ed.), *Anatomy of Racism* Minneapolis: University of Minnesota.

Bhabha, H.K. (1994) *The Location of Culture* London: Routledge.

Chambers, I. (1976) 'A strategy for living: black music and white subcultures', in S. Hall and T. Jefferson (eds), *Resistance through Rituals* London: Hutchinson.

Cohen, P. (1972) 'Subcultural conflict and working-class community', Working Papers in Cultural Studies, no. 2, University of Birmingham.

Fanon, F. (1967) *Black Skin White Masks*, London: Grove Press.

Fryer, P. (1984) *Staying Power: the History of Black People In Britain* London: Pluto Press.

Gilroy, P. (1987) *There Ain't No Black In the Union Jack*, London: Hutchinson.

Gilroy, P. (1990) One nation under a groove: the cultural politics of 'race' and racism in Britain', in D.T. Goldberg (ed.), *Anatomy of Racism*, Minneapolis: University of Minnesota.

Gilroy, P. and Lawrence, E. (1988) 'Two tone Britain: white and black youth and the politics of anti-racism', in P. Cohen and H. Bains (eds), *Multi-Racist Britain* London: Macmillan.

Hall, S. (1988) 'New ethnicities', in *Black Film/British Cinema*, Institute of Contemporary Arts Documents 7, London: ICA/BFI.

Hall, S. (1992) 'The question of cultural identity', in S. Hall, D. Held and T. McGrew (eds), *Modernity and its Futures*, Cambridge: Polity Press and Open University Press.

Hebdige, D. (1974a) 'Aspects of style in the deviant subcultures of the 1960s', MA thesis, Centre for Contemporary Cultural Studies, University of Birmingham.

Hebdige, D. (1974b) 'Reggae, rastas and rudies: style and the subversion of form', Stencilled Papers 24, Centre for Contemporary Cultural Studies, University of Birmingham.

Hebdige, D. (1979) *Subculture: the Meaning of Style*, London: Methuen.

Hebdige, D. (1981) 'Skinheads and the search for a white working-class identity', *New Socialist*, September: 38.

Hebdige, D. (1983) 'Ska tissue: the rise and fall of two tone', in S. Davis and P. Simon (eds), *Reggae International*, London: Thames & Hudson.

Hewitt, R. (1990) 'A sociolinguistic view of urban adolescent relations', in F. Roegilds (ed.), *Every Cloud Has a Silver Lining*, Studies in Cultural Sociology, 28, Hostebro: Akademisk Foriag.

Hewitt, R. (1986) *White Talk, Black Talk: Inter-Racial Friendship and Communication amongst Adolescents*, London: Cambridge University Press.

hooks, b. (1992) 'Representing whiteness in the Black imagination', in L. Grossberg, C. Nelson and P. Triecher (eds), *Cultural* Studies, London: Routledge.

Jones, S. (1988) *Black Culture, White Youth: the Reggae Tradition from JA to UK*, Basingstoke: Macmillan.

Mailer, N. (1961) 'The white negro: superficial reflections on the hipster', in N. Mailer (ed.), *Advertisements for Myself*, London: Andre Deutsch.

Mercer, K. (1987) 'Black hair/style politics', *New Formations 3*, Winter: 33–56.

Polsky, E. (1961) 'On hipsters', in N. Mailer (ed.), *Advertisements for Myself*, London: Andre Deutsch.

Porter, R. (1994) *London: a Social History*, London: Hamish Hamilton.

Said, E. (1993) *Culture and Imperialism*, London: Chatto & Windus.

Solomos, J. and Back, L. (1995) *Racism and Society*, London: Macmillan.

5
Children's Rights: Participation and Dialogue

Jeremy Roche

Few areas have been so riddled by political hypocrisy as children's rights and welfare.

T. Hammarberg, in B. Franklin, *The Handbook of Children's Rights*

In this chapter I consider recent changes in the law relating to children and young people contained in the Children Act 1989, emphasising the significance of the child's 'new' right to be an independent legal actor. Next I look at the United Nations Convention on the Rights of the Child (UNCRC) and explore some points of continuity and discontinuity between the Children Act 1989 and the UNCRC. I argue that two sets of tensions are common to both the domestic legislation and the UNCRC, namely protection versus autonomy and universalism versus social difference. The rest of the chapter explores these two tensions and argues that it is only through a commitment to enhanced participation on the part of children and young people that these tensions can, in part, be resolved; the idea of rights as a form of 'public conversation' is central to this commitment.

Arguments around children's rights are rarely straightforward. Often the supposed interests of children and young people are used by adults with their own separate agendas. We can see this in recent debates around single parents, divorce law reform and the operation of the Child Support Act 1991. At the same time it is important to recognise that, given that children are rarely in a position to fight for themselves, it is very often adults who are the most determined campaigners and fighters for children's rights, be it over their education, health or welfare rights. Some argue that the increasing focus on the language of rights and use of the law to resolve disputes involving children and young people is harmful to both their own interests and those of society. This line of argument suggests that such 'juridification' of issues relating to children and young people denies the complexity of their relations with adult society, diverts resources away from more constructive and effective ways of responding to their interests and, at a rhetorical level, simply operates to make adult society feel better (King and Trowell, 1992). However, for others, the increasing emphasis placed on children's rights is a sign of progress, even if somewhat overdue. Flekkoy argues that children 'constitute a unique group in a democracy in three respects': they have 'no influence in the choice of persons . . . that are responsible for decisions influencing the conditions' under which they must live and grow: that is they do not have the vote; they do not have access to other means of swaying public opinion; and what rights they do enjoy are often either indirect, that is exercisable by adults on their behalf, or conditional (1995: 180–1). From this perspective mechanisms of empowerment, including an emphasis on rights, are seen as integral to any project concerned with improving the position of children and young people.

Young people, rights and the Children Act 1989

In the 1990s there has been a proliferation of rights charters including the Citizen's Charter. While it is doubtful that children have been socially empowered as a result of such developments (for example the Education Charter, revealingly subtitled 'You and Your Child's Education', is a parents' rather than a children's charter), it is also the case that the 1990s witnessed radical reform of the law relating to children throughout the United Kingdom. The Children Act 1989 was heralded as the most far-reaching reform of the law relating to children this century and is concerned, amongst other things, to enhance their rights.

However, the Children Act 1989 had a history including the Department of Health and Social Services Review of Child Care Law and the Law Commission Report on Guardianship and Custody. In 1986 the House of Lords in *Gillick v. West Norfolk and Wisbech AHA* [1986] AC 112 had decided that the 'mature minor' possessed certain rights, in this case the right to a confidential relationship with a doctor for the purposes of receiving contraceptive advice and treatment. In one sense all that the House of Lords had done was to say that as long as the young person concerned understood fully all the issues involved there was no reason why they should be discriminated against: adult patients are entitled to such a confidential relationship.

In addition a series of scandals regarding the physical and sexual abuse of children both at home and whilst in 'care' had an impact on the Children Act. Out of the many enquiries and reports triggered by these scandals a number of themes emerged. First, the professionals entrusted with the task of caring for and protecting children all too often lost sight of who the client was and at times were unclear as to what their powers and duties were. Second, the child was cast as a victim to be rescued or protected and on this basis a range of interventions were justified, for example the number of intimate medical examinations that children caught up in the Cleveland scandal were subject to, and in the Orkney case the interception of letters written by parents to their children who had been taken to the mainland. Third, the solution to such events was to be sought in part through increased legal accountability and a redrawing of the rights and responsibilities of parents and the local authority. The Children Act 1989 (and parallel legislation throughout the UK) thus represented Parliament's response to a range of concerns.

The Children Act 1989 (including the new Rules of Court and Regulations and

Guidance) introduced radical changes to law and procedure. It redefined the basis on which a care or supervision order could be made, it clarified local authority responsibilities towards children they are looking after, it gave the courts increased and more flexible powers to control their proceedings and to make appropriate orders, and it repositioned children in the eyes of the law. For example it gave children of sufficient understanding the right to refuse to submit to a medical examination even when it had been ordered by the court (but now see *South Glamorgan CC v. W and B* [1993] 1 FLR 574) and new Rules of Court gave children the right to instruct a solicitor. The public concern over the misnamed 'children divorcing their parents' cases illustrates the radicalism of the latter development.

The Children Act 1989 contains a 'welfare checklist' which makes court decision-making more child-centred. The first item on this checklist is the 'ascertainable wishes and feelings of the child' and, increasingly, the more mature the child concerned the more the court, and professionals, will take account of what their feelings are on the matter in dispute. It is now almost axiomatic to state that any decision which is made on the basis of the welfare principle, that is out of a concern for that person's well-being, will, or ought to, pay serious regard to what they have to say about the matter. However the Children Act, for the first time, allows children to instruct a solicitor to start family proceedings on a matter which concerns them – to be independent legal actors. They do not need the permission of any adult; the solicitor need only be satisfied that the child has the requisite understanding to initiate the action. However before the child is able to make an application to the court for a Section 8 order they will require the court's permission and any such application will now be heard by the High Court (see Practice Direction [1993] 1 FLR 668). So the Children Act 1989 can be seen as encompassing a traditional concern with the welfare of children as well as the more radical aim of allowing children direct access to the law. While it is not hard to justify such a development on a child protection basis the child autonomy argument has less purchase in society and the legal system (O'Donovan, 1993). There is a sense in which the law is entering unchartered waters here: adult society does not know the kinds of issues that will be brought before the courts.

The United Nations Convention on the Rights of the Child

The UNCRC has been described in a number of ways. It has been referred to as providing a benchmark whereby decisions about and for children can be measured, while others see it as a piece of political rhetoric. The UNCRC can be described as being concerned with 'the three ps': provision (of services), protection and participation. The Convention indicates on a human rights basis what rights children ought to enjoy and what are the obligations of signatory states. The rights contained in the UNCRC are not rights in a strict legal sense (because if breached you cannot go to court for a remedy): rather they are standards to be met by the signatory states.

Three principles underpin the UNCRC: (1) all the rights in the Convention must be available to all children without discrimination of any kind; (2) the child's best interests must be a primary consideration in all actions concerning them; and (3) the child's views must be considered and taken into account in all matters affecting them. This last principle, the principle of representation and participation, is seen as the key to the UNCRC.

In many ways the Convention goes beyond the principles contained in the Children Act 1989. Two examples will suffice. First, the Children Act established that courts have to regard the child's welfare as the paramount consideration, that is as outweighing all other considerations. Under Article 3 of the UNCRC the child's welfare is a primary consideration, but the range of settings in which those making decisions must treat the child's welfare as a primary consideration is much wider. It could be argued that Article 3 would include decisions taken by a school to exclude a pupil or by a tribunal hearing an immigration appeal. So for the UK to meet its obligations in full under this article would involve a transformation in the way in which decisions concerning children are made throughout society.

Second, Article 19 seeks to protect children from all forms of maltreatment and neglect. It is arguable that current legislation in the UK falls short of this standard: corporal punishment of children is still permitted in private schools which do not receive any public funding, and child-minders are allowed to 'smack' those they are caring for as long as the parent consents. Such reliance on notions of parental consent reinforces the idea that children are the property of parents and echoes Franklin's (1986) observation that 'children because of their age are denied human rights which as adults we consider to be basic human rights'. We still sanction the hitting of children (of course we like to 'name' it as something else), albeit for their own good or as reasonable punishment. No one else in our society can be lawfully assaulted, but children can (Gulbenkian Foundation, 1993).

However similar tensions are to be found within the UNCRC as are present in the Children Act 1989. The desire to protect the child (Article 19) can clash with the UNCRC's concern for family privacy (Articles 5 and 16) and the autonomy rights of the child (Articles 12–15). The idea that all the rights contained in the UNCRC are to be enjoyed without discrimination (Article 2) might conflict with Article 30 which refers to the right of children from minority communities to enjoy their own culture, to practise their own religion and to speak their own language. Further, Article 12, with its emphasis on representation and participation rights, might result in children challenging the rights and responsibilities which attach to adults in their communities – adults who have their own vision of children's best interests.

Before looking at these two tensions in more detail it is important to note that there are three features of the wider socio-legal context to the debates surrounding children's rights that require comment. First, notions of family privacy and parental responsibility render problematic the idea of children's rights. For some the question of children's rights, and the concern for their welfare, resemble a 'Trojan horse' whereby the integrity and sanctity of family life are undermined. According to this argument, talk about the rights and welfare of children is simply used to justify further state interference in family life. This was the position adopted by Victoria Gillick. She argued that the Department of Health and Social Security circular regarding the giving of contraceptive advice to children under the age of 16 was an infringement of her parental rights which the state ought to be upholding not undermining. The recent controversy over 'children divorcing their parents' (see generally Houghton-James, 1994) can also be read in this way – that the law has gone so far in advancing rights for children that family life itself is under threat. The UNCRC has been similarly criticised.

Second, there is the need to consider the economic position of children. In this context a celebration of the language of rights might appear irrelevant to some. What real meaning does such language have when so many, and increasing numbers of, children are being brought up in conditions of poverty (Department of Social Security, 1994; Kumar, 1993)? Furthermore, for many young people the future after their education is marked either by the fear, or by the direct experience, of unemployment. Article 4 of the UNCRC provides that in order to meet the economic, social and cultural rights contained in the Convention, signatory states must undertake legislative and administrative measures 'to the maximum extent of their available resources'.

Third, there are different groups of children alongside an almost kaleidoscopic range of images of children in society. Children who are differently situated on the basis of race, ethnicity, gender, class and religion encounter the law and its institutions in different ways. At the same time they are seen by some as primarily citizens (or citizens-in-waiting) and by others as primarily victims or threats to the well-being of society. Thus a critique of the condition of children is intimately linked with a broader critique of society and its institutions and attitudes.

Common standard versus social difference

The law applies throughout the legal community without formal discrimination: we are all equally bound by the law's prescriptions and prohibitions. However, children live in differently constituted households: rich and poor, black and white, girls and boys, at home or in institutional care. These variations create different needs and agendas for action, resulting in different claims being made of adult society for change. Some claims will have more legitimacy than others by virtue of the prevailing social and political climate, of what is being demanded or of who is doing the demanding. Further, some of these demands will impact directly on the beliefs and conventions of upbringing of some sections of this society.

The case of *Re B* [1993] 1 FLR 386 provides an illustration of how the courts have responded to this challenge. Here the parents of a boy aged 15 years and 9 months refused to give their consent to a blood transfusion to treat his leukaemia. His parents were devout Jehovah's Witnesses and such a transfusion was against their beliefs: their 15 year old son also objected to the transfusion. The High Court, overriding the parents' refusal to give consent and ordering that the transfusion take place, observed that the parents were free to make martyrs of themselves but not of their child and that 'this court . . . should be slow to allow an infant to martyr himself'.

As noted earlier such judicial caution is understandable; the courts will act to protect children from themselves if necessary and to impose some minimal protective standard: otherwise children would always be vulnerable to the claims of culture. The deployment of the language of rights thus carries different meanings for different groups within society. For some it is clear that such language represents progress; for others it might be a sign of the wider society's indifference, if not outright hostility, to their religious beliefs and traditions of family life (Roche, 1996).

The argument around universalism and relativism is linked with the other critical tension in the law relating to children, protection versus autonomy. However the contexts in which the courts consider and act on what they see as being best for the child are varied.

Protection versus autonomy

Disputes over contact ('custody' under the old law) provide another illustration of the way which the courts have attempted to reconcile the conflict between their sense of what is best for the child and the child's clearly stated preferences. For example in *Re B* [1992] 1 FLR 140 the children did not want to have contact with their father, whose behaviour the court acknowledged to be bizarre, but the court nevertheless ordered that there should be contact. The court asserted that in the long term they would benefit from having their relationship with their father preserved; a continuing relationship with both parents is now seen as integral to the welfare of the child. This tension between what the child wants and what adults want for the child runs throughout most discussions on children's rights. Some proponents of children's rights qualify their commitment to the idea of an autonomy right with the proposition that while children should have the most precious right of all, that is to make their own mistakes, this does not mean that they should be allowed to expose themselves to a life threatening or permanent injury sustaining situation (Eekelaar, 1986). Freeman tackles the issue in a slightly different way by arguing that there is nothing necessarily wrong with paternalistic restrictions: they merely require justification (1992: 68). Many would agree. Of course parents spend much time and energy on trying to make the world safe for their children and they would expect little else from those in positions of public power (such as judges) who make decisions for children. Yet as children get older their definitions of their welfare and interests will become more important.

The participating child

The UNCRC's emphasis on the right to participate (Article 12) moves beyond a limited shopping-list vision of rights towards a more open and uncertain agenda in which children and young people can shape their future and make new demands of adult society. It is for this reason that Articles 12 and 2, and their relationship to other provisions of the Convention, are so important. Article 2 states that all the rights in the UNCRC must apply without discrimination (based on either 'race, colour, sex, language, religion, political or other opinion, national, ethnic or social origin, property, disability, birth or other status') to all children. As the article itself makes clear, this provision is of general application throughout the UNCRC: none of the rights laid down in the UNCRC can be treated as having been secured if some children by virtue of some form of discrimination are excluded from the enjoyment of these rights.

Of course the ability to discriminate against children is increased if you do not have to take their well-being seriously and if you do not have to listen to them. In this sense a commitment to an anti-discriminatory practice is fundamental to a commitment to the principle of participation. If you are concerned to treat young people as people rather than on the basis of their colour, sex, disability etc., then it follows that this must carry with it a commitment to dialogue with that young person. This is why the combination of the prohibition of a wide range of discriminations with Article 12 is so important. Yet the Children's Rights Development Unit argue that in the UK there is not a 'culture of listening to children' and that they feel as if they have almost no control over their lives (Lansdown, 1995).

To comply with the letter and spirit of Article 12 does not require that young people be given the right to make decisions. What Article 12 requires is that they should be able to participate in the decision-making process either directly or via a representative and that their views should be taken into account. In other words their participation should be an integral part of any such process. This requires adults in positions of power and authority over children and young people to work with, and relate to, them differently.

Conclusion

The 'politics of children's rights' generates strong feelings within society. For some the agenda is about the expansion of notions of citizenship wherever possible to include children and young people; for others the concern is to ensure that they are brought up with a proper respect for social institutions and authority; and for yet others their primary concern is with protecting children from themselves as much as from others. Often there are ambiguous agendas and motivations at work. Central to the different approaches to the position of children in society today are very different views of family life, state power and the abilities of children. The UNCRC's focus on participation opens up a new way of thinking about rights – rights as conversation – which can be seen to offer a way forward (Minow, 1987).

By way of conclusion I want to explore two linked questions. How should adults who work with children and young people alter their practice in order to act in accordance with the participation principle? What kinds of conversations between adult and child might then result?

Three broad developments are needed in order to enhance the participation of children and young people. First, they will need to have access to appropriate information about matters which concern them. This in itself would require significant changes. This will include doctors, teachers, social workers and other professionals working with children being much more forthcoming about the options facing the child, what the likely consequences of a particular course of action might be, and who or where to go to for further advice and support. It will also include improved access to lawyers and others with legal skills and knowledge and those professionals acquiring new skills and developing new ways of working (King and Young, 1992).

Second, it will require the presence of appropriately trained adult professionals to act as enablers for children in certain settings, such as advocacy projects. Allied to this there is an argument in favour of the setting up of a Children's Ombudsman (Rosenbaum and Newell, 1991). Third, it will require that professionals and institutions alter their practices so that children themselves can act and speak for themselves, that is self-advocacy. This will include not only encouragement and support in speaking out, without fear of retribution, but also an acceptance of the changing nature of adult-child relationships. New spaces for children and young people will have to be created both formally and informally whereby they can be actors in their own causes.

But what kind of 'conversations' or dialogue can realistically take place between adult professionals and children? The idea of a conversation is quite cosy and non-threatening, yet it involves substantial change on the part of many who work with children: they need to be open and not closed, inclusive not exclusive. By this I mean that participation is not limited to those of a particular class or ethnic group and that the agenda for discussion is not so shaped as to exclude certain ideas or values. The participants, in particular the more powerful ones, must have genuinely open minds as to what might best be done. It should not be a case of 'consulting' the child or young person in order to persuade him or her of the rightness or inevitability of a certain outcome. Rather it should be open to the future: the mind should not be bureaucratised. Children have much to say and contribute to conversations in which they are, in theory, the central concern. Participation is about making sure that they do not simply become exhibits in a show of concern or fear.

While an imbalance of power is inescapable in all conversations, especially when they are taking place in a decision-making context (Cahn, 1993), if they are conducted in accordance with the spirit underlying Articles 2 and 12 of the UNCRC the imbalance will be at least acknowledged and minimised. To be committed to a practice with children and young people in which they are provided with proper information, in which they are able to express their thoughts and feelings on the matter in question at an appropriate time and place, in which the various possible courses of action are fully explored with them, and in which their views, whatever their social origins or location, are listened to and treated seriously, will be to transform the experience of child and professional: it will also be more rewarding and valuable for both. Children, whatever the circumstances, should be able to expect respect and openness in their dealings with others, just as we desire such for ourselves in our dealings with the world. In this sense the children's rights project, of which the UNCRC and reformed child care legislation are simply signposts, is one which is about the extension of notions of participation and a redrawing of what it is to be an adult and a child.

References

Cahn, N. (1993) 'Inconsistent stories', *The Georgetown Law Journal*, 81: 2475–531.

Department of Social Security (1994) *Households Below Average Income: a Statistical Analysis 1979–1991/92*, London: HMSO.

Eekelaar, J. (1986) 'The emergence of children's rights', *Oxford Journal of Legal Studies*, 6: 161.

Flekkoy, M. (1995) 'The Scandinavian experience of children's rights', in B. Franklin (ed.), *The Handbook of Children's Rights: Comparative Policy and Practice*, London: Routledge.

Franklin, B. (1986) *The Rights of Children*, Oxford: Blackwell.

Freeman, M.D.A. (1992) 'Taking children's rights more seriously', in P. Alston, S. Parker and J. Seymour (eds), *Children, Rights and the Law*, Oxford: Clarendon.

Gulbenkian Foundation (1993) *One Scandal Too Many . . . the Case for Comprehensive Protection for Children in All Settings*, London: Calouste Gulbenkian Foundation.

Hammarberg, T. (1995) 'Preface', in B. Franklin (ed.), *The Handbook of Children's Rights: Comparative Policy and* Practice, London: Routledge.

Houghton-James, H. (1994) 'Children divorcing their parents', *Journal of Social Welfare and Family Law*, 16: 185–99.

King, M. and Trowell, J. (1992) *Children's Welfare and the Law: the Limits of Legal Intervention*, London: Sage.

King, P. and Young, I. (1992) *The Child Client*, Bristol: Jordans/Family Law.

Kumar, V. (1993) *Poverty and Inequality in the UK: the Effects on Children*, London: National Children's Bureau.

Lansdown, G. (1995) 'The Children's Rights Development Unit', in B. Franklin (ed.), *The Handbook of Children's Rights: Comparative Policy and Practice*, London: Routledge.

Minow, M. (1987) 'Interpreting rights: an essay for Robert Cover', *Yale Law Journal*, 96 (8): 1860.

O'Donovan, K. (1993) *Family Law Matters*, London: Pluto.

Roche, J. (1996) 'The politics of children's rights', in J. Brannen and M. O'Brien (eds), *Children in Families: Research and Policy*, London: Falmer.

Rosenbaum, M. and Newell, P. (1991) *Taking Children Seriously: a Proposal for a Children's Rights Commissioner*, London: Calouste Gulbenkian Foundation.

6
Citizens or What?

Tom Storrie

People are like cats,' I told my son, 'you can't teach them anything.' He looked suitably grave, but held his tongue.

Salman Rushdie, *Midnight's Children*

What processes can offer young people a grasp on *what* forms of collective decision-making rich enough to engage them as creative participants in the politics of their societies? The answer proposed here is contained in an outline for a craft apprenticeship in democratic citizenship. The ground for this proposal is first prepared by a general exploration of the related concepts of democracy and citizenship in historical, social and political terms.

Democracy in crisis

The democratic crisis is widely ignored, a fact which compounds the crisis itself. If democracy is supposed to discover the 'general interest', there is often little general interest in democracy itself: people are interested in successfully using political power to achieve their specific objectives but not in reflecting more generally on the means used. This fits only too well with a certain ill-founded Western satisfaction which presumes that our democracies are already decently matured, allowing us unreflectively to assume that any outcomes obtained are justified because duly sanctioned by procedures which are correct because democratic.

Secularisation, urbanisation, the recognition of moral, ethnic and cultural diversity, galloping consumerism set against deepening and widening structural unemployment, withdrawal from welfare state interventionism, the assertion of the moral superiority of private liberty, the sheer size of nation-states where Kafkaesque governing bureaucracies and elective aristocracies cannot adequately engage with 'the erratic and runaway character of modernity' (Giddens, 1991: 30) – all such phenomena contribute to a retreat from a presumed consensus into an uneasy pluralism characterised by a negative and implicit citizenship where each person defensively observes the rights of others to pursue their own ends within the rules of the game. At the same time the unprecedented hegemonic penetration of the modem nation-state into patterns of individual identity, perspectives and value systems remains in place. As Stephen Howe has remarked, 'it is not the state that has withered away but civil society' (1991: 133).

It is very difficult for the ordinary citizen, beyond the cocoon of local space where the potential for participative decision-making arrangements can at least seem possible, to feel anything other than powerless in the face of the wider world of stranger, more threatening and uncontrollable events. And the notion of local communal space is itself fast becoming a nostalgic utopia: '"Community walls" now zigzag wildly around the urban mass. Immediate next door neighbours may know nothing about each other's work, workplaces or wider kinships. Often they share only their postcodes. Organic communities and organic communications are slowly disappearing' (Willis, 1990a: 141).

Globally capitalist democracy is said to be in the ascendant, boosted recently by the liberalisation of the ex-communist territories, but it is often hard to deny the charge that it functions as little more than a gloss on processes of consumerist expansionism which tend to repeat the exploitative negativities of old-fashioned colonialism. Fellowship, in an ideal consumerist market economy, is reduced to a minimum: 'All are out to maximise their own advantages... Any relationship of exchange endures for only so long as it suits all the parties to it' (Dennis and Halsey, 1988: 6).

Even supposedly powerful politicians, local or global, are caught systemically in processes of chronic disempowerment: 'the outlines of an alternative society are no longer seen in the debates in parliament or the decisions of the executive but rather in the application of microelectronics, reactor technology and human genetics ... the political system is being threatened with *disempowerment* ... decisions in science and business are charged with an effectively political content for which the agents possess no legitimation' (Ulrich Beck, 1992: 186).

At the same time, perhaps with a raw intuition, there is a marked tendency amongst the young to disengage from formal 'old politics', and indeed from established institutions of many kinds. 'Much of the cultural creativity we have identified would evaporate when transferred to institutions. Many of the real symbolic energies of young people are essentially informal in their logic, meaning and motivation' (Willis, 1990b: 55). Willis further notes that the young form 'proto-communities': 'social groupings not connected through direct communication but through shared styles, fashions, interests, empathies, positions and passions – sometimes shared simultaneously "off-air" through the communication media'. These communities are often 'serial', a spaced-out queue of people rather than a talking circle, though they can 'sometimes make or be made a living circle of communication . . . Proto-communities, or aspects of them, have lain behind or helped in the development of much of the "new politics" – feminism, anti-racism and especially grass-roots "greenism"' (1990a: 141–2).

Citizenship

Britain did for a time embrace policies of a moral and interventionist nature with justification attempted in terms of citizenship. Towards the end of the nineteenth century T.H. Green and Arnold Toynbee were central figures in an influential group of philosophers and social reformers, known as the Idealists, who provided a moral and philosophical framework for the emerging social democratic and welfare capitalist state as it developed during the first half of this century. Breaking with the previous *laissez-faire* liberalism by attributing to the state the moral obligation to intervene radically in matters of social policy on behalf of its citizenry, they grounded their philosophies and policies in a consensus of Christian values already established, albeit implicitly and unconceptualised, in the everyday lives of the population (Plant and Vincent, 1984).

Powerful arguments can be ranged against this ideology: no recognition of class as a political factor; religion-based consensus would no longer suffice today; the view of the local community in harmony with the state can be reversed so that community action can more easily be understood as a necessary bulwark against state intrusion and coercion. However they did hold an optimistic view of individuals' capacities, and thought that they could and should participate in the political life of the society of which they were by formal right members. They posed the question, and suggested one answer, as to how people may be integrated into socio-political life in a manner which recognised them as citizens and depended on their co-operation in matters relating to the common good, thereby transcending the basic compulsory nature of the bond tying citizens to the state. They recognised that the possible futures of a society are already immanent within the codes of everyday life with the consequent requirement to work with communities to discover and develop the best of these futures.

In recent decades 'citizenship' as a word was virtually absent even from informed political debate in Britain but towards the end of the 1980s this changed radically. The Conservative government claimed the word by strongly encouraging 'active citizenship', thereby putting heavy emphasis on volunteering as a civic virtue to be recognised, developed and rewarded. A Commission on Citizenship, set up in 1988 by the government, produced its report in 1990 (Morrell, 1990) which recommended that all programmes of education and training at all levels, not only in schools but also including youth work, community work, adult education and continuing professional education and training, should incorporate considerations of citizenship. Higher education institutions were exhorted to give credit to applicants who demonstrated active citizenship by participation in worthy acts of volunteering, and an extension of the civic honours list was proposed in order to highlight and reward such activities.

The Labour Party in 1992 set up a Commission on Social Justice whose report (Borrie, 1994) recommended its own variation on this theme: a Citizen's Service, a national voluntary community service scheme primarily for people aged between 16 and 25 where volunteers should receive financial support and credits for further learning. The Left here also runs true to form in proposing an expensive state social service. This consensus across the political spectrum to promote volunteering can be read as an implicit recognition, despite political rhetoric to the contrary, that unemployment – and youth unemployment in particular – remains a seriously structural phenomenon. A *Guardian* report (7 June 1995) wryly comments that while volunteering has recently increased, neither the unemployed nor the retired are much attracted to it.

J.M. Barbalet (1988), in his critique of T.H. Marshall's (1950) seminal work on citizenship, asserts that there is as yet no adequate theory of citizenship. Similarly Raymond Plant (1989) states

> that the history of the concept of citizenship is far from simple and reveals contending features and characteristics . . . the complexities cannot be resolved or some kind of core, impartial, politically neutral definition arrived at. Any definition of citizenship is going to rule out as irrelevant or unimportant some features which have been central to its history . . . Citizenship is an example of what philosophers have come to call an essentially contested concept . . . characterised by an array of different, sometimes incompatible criteria . . . This is not surprising as citizenship raises questions about the nature of the state, the role of the market, obligation to one another, the idea of the common good or common interests, and ideas about rights and entitlements.

Definitions of citizenship are themselves therefore politically committed and in varying degrees internally contradictory (for example, individual civil rights versus collective industrial rights) or in competition with each other. Plant identifies the 'classical/liberal' and the 'liberal/social-democratic' approaches as the two most influential models affecting citizenship in Britain. Both uphold a commitment to the market and to a high degree of personal freedom, but disagree on the legitimacy of state welfare provision to mitigate market approaches. The one tends towards a minimal state, with a 'procedural framework' to regulate civil society where it is claimed individuals can less easily escape personal responsibility and where 'active citizenship' will therefore have more scope. The other advocates a more interventionist state where the socio-economic dimensions of citizenship are supported and developed, thereby controlling the market in the cause of social justice.

Marshall recognised the developmental quality of citizenship: civil rights emerging in the eighteenth century, political rights in the nineteenth and social rights in the twentieth. The incorporation particularly of social rights into citizenship attempts directly to mitigate patterns of inequality and therefore to extend empowerment but their delivery is mediated through an extensive bureaucracy with the tendency, as Marshall noted, to relate 'to individuals as consumers, not as actors'. He saw that entitlement to citizenship rights is necessarily mediated through appropriate institutions which are themselves the product of a particular history or histories. As the Morrell Report has it, citizenship is 'a cultural achievement, a gift of history, which can be lost or destroyed' (Morrell, 1990: xv). The dialectical tension between such particularist achievements and universalist concepts of human rights is therefore usefully exposed.

This development has continued in Britain with the establishment of the Equal Opportunities Commission (Sex Discrimination Act 1975) and the Commission for Racial Equality (Race Relations Act 1976). And there is now surely an urgent case to include an ecological category of rights and duties, effectively an extension of the concept of equal opportunities, in order to protect and enhance the quality of opportunities for present and future generations. In coping with environmental issues, fraught with grave uncertainties and irreversibilities, where the 'environment' itself is subject to many different interpretations and society is as stubbornly unruly as the weather is uncontrollable democratic citizenship offers perhaps the only operational reference framework, weak though it may be, for the necessary interactive social learning and decision-making.

The pull from Europe with radical requirements to adapt to an emergent socio-economic and political European Union is a major influence on the development of citizenship. While the future form of the Union remains deeply uncertain, this process is already profoundly modifying the pattern and functions of nation-states, with inevitable effects on the nature and institutions of citizenship. It is also important to look beyond Europe to understand the more global imperatives which have affected the development of citizenship. The Universal Declaration of Human Rights, promulgated by the United Nations in 1948 in reaction to the atrocities of World War II, asserted that these rights be granted to all individuals regardless of national citizen status, thereby both recognising that all individuals have a status in international law and also setting limits of acceptability regarding the conduct of any nation-state towards those individuals, citizens or otherwise, within its jurisdiction.

> These rights, which the Universal Declaration identifies, and which have been concretised by the UN Covenants on Civil and Political Rights and on Economic Social and Cultural Rights, as well as by the European Convention on Human Rights and the Social Charter, are rights enjoyed by everyone. They are human rights because they must be granted to all, without distinction on nationality or any other ground . . . these rights particularly address the position of the disadvantaged, women, the disabled and those subject to discrimination . . . [these rights] may be described as constituting new citizenship. (Gardner, 1990: 65–6)

Incorporation of such new citizenship rights into British law is at best partial and uneven. Apart from Britain and the Scandinavian countries, all other parties to the Convention have either incorporated it or have a domestic bill of rights. In a number of cases, the human rights institutions in Strasbourg have had to consider arguments about these rights in the United Kingdom for the first time, which the UK courts have not been able to consider. Rights in Britain are residual: individuals are free to do what is left over after laws have imposed piecemeal restrictions when Parliament thought them necessary. British law accumulates to itself a wilfully opaque complexity, a form which is itself an obstacle to the proper enjoyment of rights, further exacerbated by anxiety about 'the extent to which authorities encroach on rights which the individual thought he had' (Gardner, 1990: 71–2). This anxiety doubtless fuels current demands in Britain for a written bill of rights.

The tendency to confuse citizenship merely with a given number of rights can distract from the idea that citizenship is primarily a specific cultural achievement which can indeed be lost or destroyed. Citizenship invokes bonds uniting citizens amongst themselves and to their society. This suggests that the primary task of the citizen, collective in nature, is with fellow-citizens to maintain and enhance this cultural achievement: working in the present on a specific inheritance in search of better futures. This task, essentially one of interpersonal and intercultural negotiation, exchange and learning, should generate an existential appreciation of the relativity of one's own perceptions, practices and values with a corresponding increase in understanding and control over one's own everyday life. At the most general level, guidance for this task lies not at the level of procedures but at that of values.

The hypothesis is maintained here that the complex of values at the heart of democracy is liberty, equality and fellowship (Storrie, 1994). It is of interest to note that the Treaty of Rome cites liberty, equality and social justice. The fellowship version is however preferred here because social justice, as an end to be achieved, does not function as adequately as fellowship within the dynamics of the democratic *process:* democracy, into which fellowship introduces the essential human ingredient where otherwise there would remain a trilogy of entirely abstract values, is one means to attempt to achieve such desirable ends as social justice. The procedural majority-minority conflict is mirrored at a deeper level by the tension between the values of equality and liberty, a tension which can never be permanently resolved but at best only held within acceptable bounds by the tough elastic bonds of fellowship. In reality of course each person will operate within their own value system, interpreting its different terms according to personal understanding, preference, disposition or ideology, themselves in turn profoundly influenced by the particular cultural, ethnic and indeed ethnocentric context in which they are embedded. The practice of democracy therefore regularly demands very difficult compromises, given not only the differences but also the misunderstandings at play. The values of democracy can serve as an ethical sextant to negotiate the cross-currents of social transaction. As Edgar Morin (1987) says, democracy is a solution which gives us problems.

Towards a craft apprenticeship in democratic citizenship

Any adequate answers to the double question posed at the start of this chapter must be framed in terms of appropriate learning strategies taking account of citizenship as it can be subjectively experienced, perceived and adopted. Citizenship, participative membership of a body politic, is objective in that it can be formally possessed or granted and subjective in that it depends upon personal competence to know how to enjoy the rights and discharge the responsibilities. In developing political competence, the analogy with language learning is exact: learning will be effective if the contexts, and the interactions within them, are suitably rich and varied and if contributions from the learner are sought and valued.

Citizenship is best learnt through an engagement in relevant contexts where the everyday codes of social, cultural and political behaviour can be observed, rehearsed, experimentally used and developed. Apprentice citizens are in effect invited, in the best traditions of action research, to use intervention into social processes as a tool to gain knowledge about those same social processes. These codes are often inscribed in what Anthony Giddens calls 'practical consciousness':

> Human beings can in some degree . . . give accounts of the circumstances of their actions. But this by no means exhausts what they know about why they act as they do. Many most subtle and dazzlingly intricate forms of knowledge are embedded in, and constitutive of, the actions we carry out. They are done knowledgeably, but without necessarily being available to the discursive awareness of the actor. (1987: 63)

The problem is: if citizenship is such a contested, even theoretically undeveloped concept, how may one grasp it sufficiently to use it in the construction of learning strategies? Can one get beyond prescriptive or partisan descriptions of good democratic behaviour to a more existential position where an actual democratic moment is reflectively caught in the attempt to assess its quality? Such democratic moments of course belong not to any one individual but to the collectivity of people who have together created them. This renders the problem more complex – how can the individuals concerned manage this together? – but it also points to a framework for an appropriate apprenticeship. Two categories of citizen, of democratic actor, now emerge: the individual citizen and the collective citizen. In other words, a craft apprenticeship in citizenship ideally requires contextualisation over time in the social and sociable rhythms, rich in democratic moments, of a collective citizen. This satisfies the precondition that for any political activity, democratic or otherwise, some recognised institutional structure must already exist. It is the 'rationalist illusion . . . that social or political order can be the product of agreement. We are on far safer ground if we affirm, with Hume, that social life is primordial, and agreement . . . a possibility only within the framework of a common life' (Gray, 1989: 254).

Some recognised institutional structures can take many forms: youth clubs, school councils, local voluntary associations, pressure groups (such as Greenpeace), single issue campaigns (anti-motorway protesters) or simply informal friendship groups. But are they rich, or potentially rich, in democratic moments? How open is membership? How transparent are procedures? Is conflict intelligently accepted and explored for opportunities for participative and peaceable resolution? Is decision-making linked to social learning? Is power shared? Does it circulate? The collective citizen is here conceived as becoming in a sense concerned in its own endogenous learning: members are invited to reinvent and enhance their democratic inheritance. How the more powerful share their power inventively and experimentally is a key factor in the promotion of this process: 'Only power can fight power. The greater threat of abuse comes not from allowing the actor to take initiatives, but rather from suppressing his freedom to do so in order to restrict all initiatives to a monopoly of certain actors or higher authorities' (Crozier and Friedberg, 1980).

One way of assessing the strengths and weaknesses of the democracy in one's group could be to invite a few trusted outsiders to attempt an audit of its internal democracy. The questioning in the previous paragraph could for instance be expanded into a checklist as one flexible tool for such an audit. More ambitiously, the group could twin with another similar group over an agreed period of time (three months?) in an exchange where each would simultaneously have the privilege of studying at close quarters the democratic rhetoric and practice of the other while being a similar object of study for the other. Using each other mutually as resources in this way, the groups would find their risks fairly equally distributed, in happy contrast to much formal teaching. This strategy provides a learning structure within which an agreed agenda is held steadily in focus over a certain limited period of time in order that relevant arguments, attitudes and structures may be usefully examined, becoming in the process more susceptible to considered change. The participation of valued outsiders can obviously serve a useful purpose, able on occasions to offer pertinent comments and questions which an outsider can more easily articulate. In this latter model the groups can most clearly be seen as collective citizens, voluntarily face to face in reciprocal learning exchanges.

Conclusion

Widespread indifference or alienation, whether generated by material complacency or by powerlessness, leads directly to the ironic classification of democracy as a strictly minority interest, itself in interminable competition with other supposedly more efficient and powerful decision-making processes, either market or messianic in nature, and predisposed to exploitation or even violence. The democratic game is an incessant and often frustrating search against the odds for multiple working compromises where nothing is ever finally removed from the agenda.

Sociable inventiveness is the spark which one must always be looking for. Positive contextualised invitations need to be extended to young people to become *actors* implicated, with their own agendas, in the invention of democratic citizenship. This perspective gains reflexive strength from the insight that democracy exists as much in the doing of it as in general prescriptions of it. This echoes the duality of Giddens's structuration theory where 'Structure is both the medium and the outcome of the human activities which it recursively organises' (1987: 61).

Questions of citizenship have assumed an urgency today because of intensifying pressures and uncertainties linking local and global dimensions. They bear with especial keenness upon young people who 'face each other with fewer and more fragile masks' (Willis, 1990a: 22), who are both our future and suffer more than others the negative effects of modernity's socio-economic, political and cultural crisis.

References

Barbalet, J.M. (1988) *Citizenship: Rights, Struggle and Class Equality*, Buckingham: Open University Press.

Beck, U. (1992) *Risk Society: Towards a New Modernity*, London: Sage.

Borrie, G. (1994) *Social Justice: Strategies for National Renewal*, London: Vintage Press.

Crozier, M. and Friedberg, E. (1980) *Actors and Systems: the Politics of Collective Action*, Chicago: University of Chicago Press.

Dennis, N. and Halsey, A.H. (1988) *English Ethical Socialism*, Oxford: Oxford University Press.

Gardner, J. (1990) 'What lawyers mean by citizenship', Appendix D in F. Morrell, *Encouraging Citizenship*, London: HMSO.

Giddens, A. (1987) *Social Theory and Modern Sociology*, Cambridge: Polity Press.

Giddens, A. (1991) *Modernity and Self-Identity*, Cambridge: Polity Press.

Gray, J. (1989) *Liberalisms*, London: Routledge.

Howe, S. (1991) 'Citizenship in the new Europe: a last chance for the Enlightenment', in G. Andrews (ed.), *Citizenship*, London: Lawrence & Wishart.

Marshall, T.H. (1950) *Citizenship and Social Class*, Cambridge: Cambridge University Press.

Morin, E. (1987) *Penser l'Europe*, Paris: Gallimard.

Morrell, F. (1990) *Encouraging Citizenship*, London: HMSO.

Plant, R. (1989) 'Citizenship: problems of definition', paper presented at the Speaker's Commission on Citizenship seminar (leading to the Morrell Report).

Plant, R. and Vincent, A. (1984) *Philosophy, Politics and Citizenship*, Oxford: Blackwell.

Rushdie, S. (1981) *Midnight's Children*, London: Picador.

Storrie, T. (1994) 'la citoyenneté, un auto-apprentissage institutionnel', in M. Blanc, T. Storrie, M. Mormont and J. Remy (eds), *Vie quotidienne et Démocratic*, Paris, L'Harmattan.

Willis, P. (1990a) *Common Culture: Symbolic Work at Play in the Everyday Cultures of the Young*, Buckingham: Open University Press.

Willis, P. (1990b) *Moving Culture*, London: Gulbenkian Foundation.

7

Racial Formations of Youth in Late Twentieth-Century England

Gargi Bhattacharyya and John Gabriel

Late twentieth century England has witnessed immigration from Eastern Europe, Britain's former colonies (for example, Ireland) and the New Commonwealth, notably from the Indian subcontinent, the Caribbean and Africa. The most recent period of immigration, in the aftermath of World War II, and the racialisation of immigrant groups and their descendants (which drew on racist ideologies dating back several centuries), coincided with other political and cultural developments, for example: the growth of the leisure, fashion and entertainment industries; the emergence of distinctive classes of consumers both of public services and of privately produced goods; the growth of a service sector; a population growth prompted by the post-war baby boom; and the formation of distinctive youth sub-cultures. The focus of this chapter is situated against this historical background. Its aim is to examine racial formations amongst young people in England in the latter half of the twentieth century.

Under such circumstances as those sketched above, notably the coincidence of immigration and youth sub-cultures, it was no surprise that 'whiteness' became a key cultural symbol of one of the first youth formations to emerge in the post-war period. In fact, Teddy boys made their name terrorising immigrants in Notting Hill and Nottingham in the late 1950s. Equally predictable was the way in which the mainstream media at the time dubbed the events 'race riots' rather than the perpetrators 'racists'. It was not until the 1970s that young people were specifically identified in racial terms and unsurprisingly it was black and not white youths who were marked as such. Mugging became synonymous with black street crime and the police used any law at their disposal, in this case the Vagrancy Act 1824, to arrest young blacks merely on suspicion that they might commit a crime (Hall et al., 1978). Community protest led to the repeal of this law, only for it to be replaced by stop and search powers introduced in the Police and Criminal Evidence Act 1984 (PACE).

Racism refers generally to ideas and practices of inferiority and subordination and to the structuring of social relations between groups defined in racial terms (Anthias and Yuval-Davis, 1992). Racialisation has been used to stand for the processes whereby groups have come to be marked or signified in racial terms (Miles, 1989; Small, 1994). Historically such processes entail a complex interplay of political, economic and cultural factors, the particular significance of each varying according to circumstance. Alleged biological factors, including superficial markings like skin, have served to underpin claims to racial differences. The experience of the Holocaust and UNESCO's denial of biologically defined races in the late 1940s merely encouraged the recoding of racist forms, although biological arguments continue to retain their appeal. Moreover, cultural difference and religion in particular have a long history of marking racial difference. For example, Edward Said's (1979) concept of Orientalism (which stood for the discourse of Western hegemony) embraced a virulent strain of Islamophobia, the origins of which he traced from the twelfth century to the Gulf War in the late twentieth century. Anti-Irish racism and anti-Semitism, too, have both built on the racialisation of religious differences (Allen, 1994; Cohen, 1988).

In overviews of contemporary racist culture, the significance of sexuality, which has been a site of excessive racist anxiety, is often ignored or at least underplayed. Moreover, such discussions are often restricted to sexualised racisms in the past – and clearly there are well-documented historical precedents for what we are describing. Angela Davis (1981) explores this issue in a piece called 'The myth of the black rapist'. Here she argues that African-American men were constructed as a violent sexual threat to white women and that this mythology allowed white men to terrorise the post-slavery African-American community. Davis argues that this terrorisation in response to a mythical sexual threat is still used against black people today. In his book *White Hero, Black Beast* (1979), Paul Hoch suggests that similar myths have been used to justify violence against Indian men in the aftermath of the Indian Uprising in 1857 and Jewish men in Nazi Germany. In all cases, the anxious fantasies of dominant men lead to violence.

This mythology of an engulfing and dangerously unpredictable black sexuality exists even today, and can still be used as a justification for repressive violence against black communities. The criminalisation of young black men referred to above, and again below, feeds on this myth of depravity. Even more frighteningly, in cases of obvious abuse violators have explained their actions as responses to black sexual threat, for example the police accounts of the Rodney King beating in Los Angeles (Fiske, 1994).

Although black women are not immune to this damaging mythology, the sexual myths around black women tend to concentrate less on violence and more on titillation. Historical accounts link this to the experience of colonialism and slavery, where Asian and African women were sexually available to the white men who dominated them (Collins, 1990). Contemporary mythologies typically cast black women as more hyper-sexual than white women – whether this be in terms of their ability to serve or their rampant and domineering sex drive. This contemporary exoticism can be seen in a range of pornographic representations and sexual services.

Racial markings: who's defining whom?

Even within the limited time span of the last 40 years or so, young people have been the object of widely divergent and shifting racist cultures. The latter have been supported by legislation, policies and routine procedures. For example, the Prevention of Terrorism Act has been used on a routine basis to discriminate against young people of Irish descent (Hillyard, 1993). Likewise anti-Semitism has remained a recurring experience for young Jewish people throughout this period. Since the early 1970s the revival of extreme right-wing organisations like the National Front, the British National Party (BNP) and Combat 18 in Britain and the growing links between neo-fascist groups across Europe have led to an escalation of anti-Semitic racial violence (Runnymede Commission on Anti-Semitism, 1994: 52ff).

Elsewhere, amongst academics and policy makers, the old biological arguments about race gave way to ideas of cultural difference. A growing social science literature sought to characterise race relations as sequence or cycle, the end result of which was assimilation. The latter referred to the point at which immigrant cultures became indistinguishable from English culture. These new racist cultures of subordination and denial were met with stiff resistance from first generation immigrants and inevitably encouraged the reassertion of relatively rigid and static ethnic identities and formations. Groups were defined and sought to define themselves in terms of cultural baggages (religion, language, nationality) which appeared non-negotiable on both sides. A black consciousness, inspired by political developments in the United States in the 1960s, expressed itself most notably but not exclusively amongst young people of African-Caribbean background.

Official discourses on race shifted largely in response to pressure from minority organisations and pressure groups: assimilation was displaced and instead terms like 'integration', 'diversity' and 'multiculturalism' were incorporated into policy documents and political speeches. Such thinking remained rooted in the idea of ethnicity as something you carried round in a suitcase: understanding difference meant explaining differences between Sikhism and Islam, bhangra and calypso, akki and dhal. As far as policy makers were concerned the paramount problem for young people of diverse ethnic backgrounds was the conflict between traditional values of their home background and the modern freedoms that white English Western culture had to offer. Hence, assumptions of backwardness and superiority remained rooted in these allegedly liberal agendas.

For many young people growing up in the 1970s and 1980s, media and 'official' characterisations of their situations bore little resemblance to their lives and their sense of themselves. They were not just Sikh, Cypriot, Jewish. Nor were they just English either (and not just because Conservative politicians told them that trying to be black and English was a lost cause). Many did not see themselves just as exclusively black either, especially when town hall bureaucracies and academics were the ones telling them that this was what they were and that racism was their only experience.

New understandings emerged from the writings of novelists and playwrights like Hanif Kureishi, black intellectuals (such as Stuart Hall and Paul Gilroy) and film-makers like Isaac Julien and Gurinder Chaddha, all of whom spoke a new language of hybridity and Diaspora, neither torn between two cultures nor simply one or the other but complex, dynamic fusions – new ethnicities which could not be described in terms of set characteristics or passively received experiences but were born of conscious self-definitions. For example, working in the arena of cultural production some artists have challenged myths of exoticism. These productions can be characterised by their ambiguous relation to myths of black sexuality. Although there has been a recognition that certain myths are used to justify repression and that the objectification of black sexuality may be disempowering, some work has also tried to reclaim dominant ideas of black sexuality. This work uses the mythology of exoticism to create a sense of black sexual pride. This has been most apparent in the work of women and gay cultural producers.

Sexuality, gender and class are thus important facets of these new articulations and youth cultures, marked by dress, music, language, and humour. Whiteness, however, would just not go away. It continued to shape the experiences and destinies of young people, however hard they sought to subvert and resist it.

Family

The racialisation of families has been a recurrent feature of post-war British social policy. The Moynihan Report, published in the United States in the mid 1960s, blamed youth delinquency, educational failure and unemployment in the inner city on the black family and in particular on the absence of a strong male breadwinner role model. Its influence has been felt on both sides of the Atlantic (Dominelli, 1988: 95). In England racial assumptions have been more coded in official statements on parenting and families but the implied message of black dysfunctionality remains.

At the Conservative Party Conference in 1993 lone parents were held responsible for excessive levels of welfare expenditure. A report by Kensington and Chelsea Council in 1993 blamed single mothers who had several children by different fathers for the rise in delinquency in London schools (*Runnymede Trust Bulletin*, no. 271: 1, December 1993/January 1994). What makes such statements racialised is not their explicit content but the common sense assumptions regarding black families and the criminalisation of black youth which underpin them (Phoenix, 1988). If Conservative delegates played down the statistics on black lone parents, the BNP and the tabloid press certainly did not. Linking the Cabinet report on single parents to the figures in the 1991 census which revealed that 42% of African-Caribbean families were headed by a lone parent, the *Daily*

Mail ran a series of articles in mid December 1993, making explicit racial gendered connections that work on ideas of sexuality discussed above: that black men were prone to sex and violence and black women to passivity, welfare dependency and promiscuity (8 December 1993). One of many ironies in Conservative government rhetoric on lone parent families and its implied attack on 'problem' black families is its immigration policy which has successfully managed to keep children, husbands, wives and grandparents from being reunited with their families (Divided Families Campaign, 1990).

Ideas of dysfunctionality alongside a policy of assimilation, which prevailed in the 1960s, added weight to policy makers' arguments both to place a disproportionate number of black children in institutional care (see Barn, 1990) and then to place the disproportionately few *black* children who were found foster and adoptive homes with *white* parent families. Against this background, black groups, community organisations and black social workers began campaigning for what became known as racial matching in the 1970s: the policy of allocating black children to black foster and adoptive parents. Projects like the New Black Families Unit sought to recruit more black foster and adoptive parents and succeeded in doing so. Moreover, many local authorities incorporated race matching policies into their equal opportunity and/or anti-racist policies from the late 1970s onwards.

From the point of view of a strategy of getting more black foster and adoptive parents and fewer black children in care, the principle of racial matching made much sense. Moreover, numerous cases of young black people who had been brought up by black and white parents respectively confirmed the importance of a black family network for support against racism and for identity and self-esteem (Lewis, 1985; see also Yvon Guest's account in *The Guardian*, 28 August 1989).

However, a number of concerns regarding racial matching were expressed by researchers, politicians and policy makers from the late 1980s onwards. Several cases were exploited by the national press to highlight these concerns, including one in Croydon in 1989 (Gabriel, 1994: 62ff) and one in Norfolk, where Jim and Roma Lawrence, an 'inter-racial' couple, were refused the right to adopt a mixed race child because of their lack of racial understanding. The press had a field day, accusing social workers of political correctness, left-wing dogma and what was by then a well-worn slur against anti-racist and equal opportunity policy makers – acting like thought police (*Runnymede Trust Bulletin*, no. 268, September 1993). Academics, too, expressed concerns that decisions regarding fostering and adoption could not be reduced to skin alone. According to Phoenix and Tizard (1995) such policies assume that racially defined groups are homogeneous whereas in fact they are divided in terms of religion, social class and national/cultural allegiance. How would you place a white Bosnian Muslim child: according to skin or religious criteria? And where do you place a mixed race child? Moreover, in their research; Tizard and Phoenix (1993) encountered a political understanding of racism (which was one important argument for same race placements) amongst some white parents and a corresponding absence of such an awareness amongst some black parents.

So, in a political climate in which anti-racist policies and initiatives are under attack; in the wake of guidance which advises against the placement of children with parents on racial grounds alone; and, to cap it all, amid disagreement amongst academics and professionals regarding the political and cultural benefits of such a policy, councils are increasingly operating more flexible policies. Some race placement policies, with hindsight, undoubtedly mobilised black groups, encouraged local authorities to employ more black social workers, discouraged the institutionalisation of black children in care facilities and increased the numbers of black foster and adoptive parents. The shift away from such policies accommodates a more complex understanding of identity and social relations within a family. Nevertheless, the invisibility of race may, once again, encourage local authorities to: channel resources towards white families; ignore the complex reasons for the disproportionate numbers of black children in care; and overlook routine racial stereotyping by social workers when processing such cases (Barn, 1993).

Education

The area of schooling and education has been a key arena of debate about racism in society – particularly in relation to youth. There are two main foci for these debates. Firstly, schooling is seen to be an important arena in terms of determining people's wider life chances. Schools have been charged with the responsibility for addressing the continuing disadvantage faced by young African, African-Caribbean and Asian people. Both the lack of employment opportunities and the over-representation of young black people in the criminal justice system have been linked to failures of education. Secondly, anti-racist thinking has identified the school as a key institution in the formation of white consciousness. This means that racism can be challenged most effectively at this formative stage in white youth's lives.

The earliest references to the particular needs of black children concentrated on their status as immigrants. This period, which begins with the White Paper *The Education of Immigrants* (DES, 1965) and continues in some ways throughout the seventies, can be characterised by policies which encourage the assimilation of migrant populations. These policies assumed that the problem was immigrants themselves: newcomers antagonised the natives by being unfamiliar with local customs. The role of schools was to smooth over this friction by teaching immigrants the ways of the British – in terms of language and culture more generally. White racism was seen to stem from too great a concentration of newcomers in certain areas – reasoning which gave rise to policies such as the dispersal of black pupils across several schools, which meant bussing black children out of their home area (Saggar, 1991).

Black writers argued against this sort of policy, saying that it blamed the victims instead of examining white racism. Particularly, the assimilation model of education was criticised for failing to address the needs of black children. Writers like Bernard Coard (1971) argued that institutional racism caused black children to underachieve in school. This problem required an attack on racist practice, not a policy which tried to minimise differences between black cultural heritages and the monoculture of the white population.

In the 1980s there were at last some institutional responses to racism in education. Many initiatives originated in local authorities, but central government also adopted recommendations about schooling for diverse populations. The continuing scandal of poor achievement among black children, and African-Caribbean children in particular, led to the commissioning of a report unfortunately entitled *West Indian Children in our Schools* in 1979. This report eventually became the Swann Report, *Education for All* (DES, 1985). It advocated an education based on pluralism and argued that schools should develop a respect for cultural diversity. However, this 'multiculturalism' too often took the form of token gestures – saris, samosas and steelbands at open days with no impact on mainstream schooling. Some anti-racists argued that this version of multiculturalism encouraged the idea that black people were exotic and 'other'. Instead, they demanded that education address the issue of white racism as the real cause of unrest and underachievement.

In the aftermath of multiculturalism and anti-racism, black people in Britain remain dissatisfied with the education the state offers them. This dissatisfaction can be registered in a number of developments. Many minority groups run community 'schools' which function alongside compulsory schooling. These may be religious or language schools teaching children about their home culture after the school day or at weekends – or they may seek to supplement the work of state schools such as Saturday schools which build on mainstream schoolwork and offer help with homework and core subjects. These institutions operate largely outside the state education system: for example, full-time Muslim schools do not receive state funding. They perform two roles: to teach the cultural values of language, faith and history which are not registered by mainstream schooling, and to counteract the 'underachievement' of black children by investing community resources in extra schoolwork. Both roles could be seen as interventions against racism. Elsewhere in mainstream education, black teachers have worked in the classroom as well as in autonomous black teacher organisations to: challenge the white Anglocentrism in the curriculum; promote respect for cultural differences; and acknowledge the ever changing pattern of ethnic allegiances on the part of young people.

Policing and protesting

Policing has been a key area of dispute around black youth for many years in Britain. Black people are hugely over-represented in the criminal justice system (see, for example, Reiner, 1989; Chigwada, 1991; Keith, 1993; *Runnymede Trust Bulletin*, no. 262, February 1993; no. 278, September 1994; no. 283, March 1995) and this has been put down to a racist police force and legal system.

We can link these statistics to the myths of black criminality which we discussed earlier. Many of the racist mythologies which we have outlined reveal racism to be an indication of white fear. This links with a number of themes: the myth that black people are beyond reason and are less than human; the myth that black people are driven by ravenous and dangerous sexual hunger which must be contained; the myth that black people cannot succeed educationally or hold down paid employment. All these mythologies contribute to the criminalisation of black people, and particularly of young black men.

The criminalisation of black people also takes place through immigration law and its implementation. Since the Immigration Act 1971 black communities have been harassed by the accusation that they are 'illegal immigrants' – both in popular mythology and in state practice. In recent years this harassment has also taken the form of forced deportations and refusal of rights of abode to black families. Many people fall foul of British immigration law – and many more are terrorised by their fear of its powers. The death of Joy Gardner at the hands of immigration officials in 1993 has come to symbolise the violence of contemporary practices around immigration. Proposed extensions of immigration law which render a range of service providers liable to check the immigration status of their clients increase the sense that immigration law is designed to make all black people seem illegal and illegitimate (*JCWI Bulletin*, vol. 5, no. 10, Autumn 1995).

There are many accounts of racist practice by the police – developments in community policing have been an attempt to address some of these accusations. The infamous 'sus' laws of the 1970s and PACE, both referred to above, allowed police to stop and search people at will according to their own suspicions. Predictably, suspicion was informed by racism, whether consciously or unconsciously, and young black men were made vulnerable to harassment by police officers. The Criminal Justice and Public Order Act 1994 again makes black communities particularly vulnerable to police harassment by increasing police powers to search vehicles and people at will, without specific reason or justification.

This ongoing and everyday antagonism between black people and the police is sporadically fuelled by cases of deaths in custody or during arrest of black people. Brian Douglas, a young black man from South London, was killed in police custody in 1995 – shortly after police began to carry US-style side batons. In December 1995 another young black man, Wayne Douglas (no relation), died in police custody in the same area of London. Angry response to this killing was reported as a lawless riot sparked off by professional agitators. At no point has the police force acknowledged that the black community has a legitimate grievance: between April 1994 and March 1995 Scotland Yard acknowledges 15 deaths in custody, yet police claim no responsibility for any of these deaths (at time of writing 9 cases still had not had proper inquests).

In response to police harassment and violence, black communities have formed monitoring projects to organise resistance and advise complainants. Groups such as Newham Monitoring Project (NMP), Southall Monitoring Group and Birmingham Racial Attacks Monitoring Unit, along with many similar projects nation-wide, work to monitor police behaviour and other racist violence and to provide an avenue of support for those suffering harassment. In June 1995 NMP launched a campaign under the slogan 'Policing the Police', working with local black and white communities suffering from violent policing. The tactic of offering immediate support and information to individuals while campaigning about the wider issues has been an important thread of anti-racist activity in Britain. This kind of campaign has been a key forum for the politicisation of young black people.

Street protest has also played a key role in responses to police brutality, racist violence and disenfranchisement. Public displays of dissent are of prime importance for communities who are excluded from sites of authority in society. They offer an alternative forum for those disaffected with mainstream politics, often seen to have no relevance to the realities of black life. However, public protest is too often an occasion for further harassment – and these histories have become part of popular mythologies of black criminality in Britain.

Youth, too, often appears in policy as a problem – as a cause for concern. This increases when you add the dangers of 'race' to the equation. Youth is seen as unruly and in need of direction and management. Racist culture makes black youth appear doubly dangerous. The added turbulence of racism increases the threat of white youth. The response of a range of key institutions, schools, police, employment schemes, has been to regard young people as a danger to be contained and appeased (Solomos, 1988; 1993).

Recent work has highlighted the extent to which we conceptualise 'race' as taking place in the city (see, for example, Cross and Keith, 1993). The problems of 'race' and racism become part of how we conceive of late urban living in the West – linked to a sense of degeneration both in the economy and in our immediate surroundings. In this mythology black people are at once a sign that cities, and by implication Britain, are in decline and are principal victims of this process. Discussions of 'race' in Britain must take account of both this damaging mythology and the consequences of the concentration of black British communities in some areas and the isolation of black people in others.

The histories of uprisings have become an important part of the disputed stories of 'race' in this country. Dominant representations refer to these events as 'riots' – stressing the dangerous lawlessness of youth, particularly black youth, and erasing the grievances which give rise to these uprisings (Gilroy, 1987). In response, black cultural productions, both in local oral histories and in more public forms, have retold uprisings as central events of black (and white) resistance in Britain. Perhaps even more significantly, the organisational lessons learned from uprisings and their aftermaths continue to shape anti-racist politics in this country.

Work

The transformation of inner cities referred to above relates to a wider restructuring of the economy which has entailed: the shift from manufacturing to service industries; the deunionisation of workforces; the privatisation of public service employment; the increase in part-time short-term contract work; and the increase in youth unemployment. These changes have been examined in terms of a dual labour market characterised by a core of relatively secure white collar work and a periphery of part-time, unsafe low paid insecure jobs; by the growth of post-Fordism (a term which seeks to capture the collapse of mass production in Western economies, the growth of high technology industries and flexible production, where production lines are quickly adapted to changes in market conditions); and by the reconfiguration of an underclass made up of young people, women and refugees who invariably end up in part-time employment characterised by a lack of rights, little or no job security and low pay, and unprotected by the now abolished wages councils (Sivanandan, 1989).

Successive Conservative governments have blamed this economic decline on the lack of skilled labour produced by the education system: hence the emergence over the past 15 years of a plethora of training programmes for young people aimed at equipping them with the skills appropriate to changing market conditions. The creation of training and enterprise councils in 1990 heralded yet another false dawn and the 'special needs' focus prevalent under the Manpower Services Commission was again revived. In other words English language provision took priority over issues of discrimination and equality of outcome (Wrench, 1991).

Research on youth training programmes has confirmed the failure of such schemes for young working class people as a whole but particularly for ethnic minority trainees. In the first place, black school leavers are less likely to have a place on such schemes (despite the latter's supposed universal availability) than their white counterparts. For example, in one London careers' office 75% of those waiting for a place are black, yet black people account for only 40% of the local 16–18 population). Moreover, only 27% of black trainees left training schemes with any qualification compared with 32% of all school leavers (*Runnymede Trust Bulletin*, no. 278: 11, September 1994). In another survey, two-thirds of black people left training schemes early compared with 49% of all early leavers (*Runnymede Trust Bulletin*, no. 272: 9, February 1994).

The Race Relations Act 1976 outlaws both direct and indirect discrimination and encourages employers to commit themselves to equal opportunity policies. In 1994 a survey of 100 companies revealed that only 34 or one-third complied with legal requirements to provide adequate information on equal opportunities in their annual accounts (*Runnymede Trust Bulletin*, no. 274, April 1994). Surveys elsewhere confirm disproportionately high rates of unemployment amongst black workers, for example 28% for Bangladeshis and Pakistanis, 27% amongst workers of African-Caribbean background and 10% for whites (*Runnymede Trust Bulletin*, no. 282, February 1995).

In 1995, statistics revealed that inequalities have grown wider in Britain than any other industrialised country apart from New Zealand, and that in terms *of* income black and ethnic minorities are more likely to be in the poorest fifth and less likely to be in the richest fifth than their white counterparts. Meanwhile, local studies confirm an increase in racial harassment at work *(Runnymede Trust Bulletin*, no. 277: 9, July/August 1994).

Middle class graduates from ethnic minorities are also at a disadvantage, along with women and mature students. In one case, cited in a report published by the Association of Graduate Recruiters, a black woman was recalled for a medical examination and asked about diseases in the Indian subcontinent before being offered the job *(Runnymede Trust Bulletin*, no. 265: 11, May 1993). Elsewhere evidence of racial discrimination has been confirmed within the government's own ranks in the civil service *(Runnymede Trust Bulletin*, no. 268: 7, September 1993).

Different class locations have entailed different forms of resistance. Within the peripheral or secondary labour market young workers have sometimes foregrounded their black identities in their alliances with workers struggling for better working conditions, equal pay and union recognition. Their support has come through their participation in trade unions and community organisations. Members of youth-dominated organisations like the Anti Nazi League participated in trade union sponsored marches and events. Organisations like the Action Group on Irish Youth, based in London, provide advice and training for young people of Irish background ('Meeting the needs of young Irish people', *Newscheck*, vol. 4, no. 5, March 1994). As trade unionists, young black workers have spoken out against the proposed introduction of internal immigration checks by public sector and social services providers referred to above *(Runnymede Trust Bulletin*, no. 288: 10, September 1995). Meanwhile autonomy groups of black professionals, such as teachers, lawyers and journalists, have used their institutional base to campaign for improved employment conditions and a more equitable service.

Conclusions

This chapter has only scratched the surface, both of the experiences of young people and of related research and policies. We have alluded to, though not developed in detail, an understanding of constructions of youth and race which always beg a discussion in historical and historically specific terms. For example sexuality has been a prime motivator in racial violence, which took particular forms in the United States (rapes, beatings, lynchings), but nowadays plays an important role in underpinning policy and common sense ideas about the family, policing and the inner city. Such ideas have played a crucial role in the constructions of white consciousness.

Equal opportunities policies have always been tainted by their own limitations, by a widespread view that anything more than tokenism puts whites at a disadvantage, and by their capacity to become incorporated into policy-speak and provision removed from the everyday life of young people. The potential impact of equal opportunity policies and anti-racist initiatives was systematically undermined by cultural agendas of the new right, ably supported by sections of the tabloid press. Perhaps of greater concern were their liberal-minded agendas which were invariably built on an assumption of, and the need to maintain, white supremacy.

Significant cultural practices have emerged out of such conditions around which young people of diverse ethnic backgrounds have mobilised, from inner city uprisings, through campaign groups against deportations and police violence and homophobia, to autonomous organisations of young professionals (autonomy varyingly defined according to race, ethnicity, gender or a combination). In the meantime, cultural producers attempt to capture the diversity of young people's experiences in art, cinema, television, music, theatre and literature in ways which defy old ethnic boundaries and institutionally prescribed definitions as well as challenging racist notions and practices.

References

Allen, T. (1994) *The Invention of the White Race*, London: Verso.

Anthias, F. and Yuval-Davis, M. (1992) *Racialized Boundaries: Race, Gender, Colour, and Class and the Anti-Racist Struggle*, London: Routledge.

Barn, R. (1990) 'Black children in local authority care', *New Community*, 16 (2): 229–46.

Barn, R. (1993) *Black Children in the Public Care System*, London: Batsford and British Agencies for Fostering and Adoption.

Chigwada, R. (1991) 'The policing of black women', in E. Cashmore and E. McLaughlin (eds), *Out of Order*, London: Routledge.

Coard, B. (1971) *How the West Indian Child is Made ESN in the British School System*, London: New Beacon.

Cohen, P. (1988) 'The perversions of inheritance: studies in the making of multi-racist Britain', in P. Cohen and H. Bains (eds); *Multi-Racist Britain*, Basingstoke: Macmillan.

Collins, P. Hill (1990) *Black Feminist Thought*, London: Harper Collins.

Cross, M. and Keith, M. (1993) *Racism, the City and the State*, London: Routledge.

Davis, A. (1981) *Women Race and Class*, London: Women's Press.

DES (1965) *The Education of Immigrants*, Department of Education and Science, Circular 7/65, London: HMSO.

DES (1985) *Education for All*, Department of Education and Science, London: HMSO, Cmnd 9453.

Divided Families Campaign (1990) *Give Us a Happy Ending: How Families Are Kept Apart by British Immigration Law*, London.

Dominelli, L. (1988) *Anti-Racist Social Work: a Challenge for White Practitioners and Educators*, Basingstoke: Macmillan.

Fiske, J. (1994) *Media Matters*, London: University of Minnesota Press.

Gabriel, J. (1994) *Racism, Culture, Markets*, London: Routledge.

Gilroy, P. (1987) *There Ain't No Black in the Union Jack*, London: Hutchinson.

Hali, S., Critcher, C., Jefferson, T., Clarke, J. and Roberts, B. (1978) *Policing the Crisis: Mugging, the State and Law and Order*, London: Macmillan.

Hillyard, P. (1993) *Suspect Community*, London: Pluto and NCCL.

Hoch, P. (1979) *White Hero, Black Beast: Racism, Sexism and the Mask of Masculinity*, London: Pluto Press.

Keith, M. (1993) *Race Riots and Policing: Lore and Disorder in a Multi-Racist Society*, London: UCL Press.

Lewis, G. (1985) 'From deepest Kilburn', in L. Heron (ed.), *Truth, Dare or Promise? Girls Growing up in the Fifties*, London: Virago.

Miles, R. (1989) *Racism*, London: Routledge.

Phoenix, A. (1988) 'The Afro-Caribbean myth', *New Society*, 83: 10–13.

Phoenix, A. and Tizard, B. (1995) *Race, Ethnicity, Gender and Social Class: Social Identities In Adolescence*, London: Routledge.

Reiner, R. (1989) 'Race and criminal justice', *New Community*, 16 (1): 5–21.

Runnymede Commission on Anti-Semitism (1994) *A Very Light Sleeper*, London.

Saggar, S. (1991) *Race and Public Policy*, Aldershot: Avebury.

Said, E. (1979) *Orientalism*, New York: Random House.

Sivanandan, A. (1989) 'The new racism', *New Statesman and Society*, 4 November: 8–9.

Small, S. (1994) *Racialized Barriers*, London: Routledge.

Solomos, J. (1988) *Black Youth, Racism and the State*, Cambridge: Cambridge University Press.

Solomos, J. (1993) *Race and Racism in Britain*, London: Macmillan.

Tizard, B. and Phoenix, A. (1993) *Black, White and Mixed Race?: Race and Racism in the Lives of Young People of Mixed Parentage*, London: Routledge.

Wrench, J. (1991) 'Employment and the Labour market', *New Community*, 17 (2).

8
Young People and Political Participation

Claire Hackett

In the public debate about young people today, assumptions about the apathy and indifference of young people abound. This chapter discusses some of the arguments surrounding young people's apparent lack of participation in constitutional politics in the context of the changes that social policy has made to the lives of young people today. The chapter focuses on the participation of young people in the community and voluntary sector – a sector, it is argued, which is increasingly relevant to the lives of young people. I will argue that participation is a learned activity in whatever context it takes place. I will examine the dynamics of young people's participation and explore the contribution they make, drawing on examples from my own working context.

Problems or participants?

Much of the public discourse about young people in our society is formulated as the social problem young people present to society: juvenile offending, youth unemployment, teenage pregnancy, drug misuse. A much more benign viewpoint casts young people as alienated from society. Even this more sympathetic stance implies however a problematised and passive position. A common assumption is the necessity to solve the problem young people present and bring young people back into society. This doctrine informs our media and the policy making of our political and public establishments. It is time for a new standpoint, one which sees young people as active participants in our society with contributions to make if opportunities are afforded to them.

Commentators who contend that young people are politically apathetic cite as evidence the fact that relatively few numbers of young people (those under 25) vote in elections. Evidence from the British Youth Council survey in 1993 found that a fifth of 16–25 year olds were not registered to vote, four times as many as in any other age group. Is this apathy or is it a rational response to the negative impact of party and constitutional politics on the lives of young people? If the latter, it is a response shared by other groups of people. It is perhaps no coincidence that non-voting is also high in the poorest sections of our population who have also been marginalised by social policy. For example, although it is not quantifiable, there is no doubt that the poll tax left a legacy of non-registration for young people as well as other groups of people. Explaining non-participation as apathetic behaviour is a superficial argument. We must instead ask if there are barriers to political participation.

Containment and control

One approach to the issue of young people's distance from party and constitutional politics is to see it as related to the development of political consciousness. In his interpretation of data collected in the Young People's Social Attitudes survey, David Walker (1996) discusses the proposition that there is a minimum base of knowledge necessary for effective participation in the political process. The survey data reveal a low consumption of newspapers which Walker posits as a possible problem because of the under-informed political consciousness it implies. While I feel unsure about the equation of newspaper and media consumption with political knowledge, I agree with the concept of a developing consciousness as an entry into political action. Learning to participate, acquiring the means of participation is necessary when one is moving from a position of exclusion and powerlessness. In that sense it certainly may be the case that participation in constitutional politics is more difficult for this generation of young people because there are fewer opportunities.

The wave of social policies in the 1980s and 1990s directed at young people has constrained young people's lives and deprived them of independence. An increasingly market-oriented education system, the removal of social security and a punitive response to juvenile offending have all contributed to reducing choices for young people. There has been a recognition that this generation of young people occupy a different political space than the one before. Bessant (1995) uses the concept of delayed adulthood to describe the situation of young people today who no longer have access to economic independence through employment. This, she argues, has led to an extension of adolescent dependency. Government policy has exacerbated this situation by interventions such as youth training schemes. She argues instead for policies which will provide the means for young people to acquire full citizenship.

> Rather than prolonging the institutionalisation and childish dependence of young people as a means of containment we should be considering how to provide experience that presents opportunities of full citizenship to young people in the context of a diminishing labour market. (1995: 29)

If one looks at two of the traditional arenas for development of political consciousness, work and further and higher education, we can see that these have radically changed for today's young people. Their attendance at further and higher education has increased. Now, however, it usually entails taking on part-time work and/or the accumulation of debt. This is a situation which fosters only the concentration on an individual future and leaves little room for collective political action. The world of employment, which offers an avenue for political participation through independence and trade union involvement, is one which is denied to the majority of our young people in increasing numbers. Young people today have fewer choices and fewer routes to financial independence. The social spaces they occupy offer dwindling opportunities for exploring and fostering a traditional political identity within what is in any case an increasingly narrow party political landscape.

In considering the non-participation of young people in constitutional politics it is therefore perhaps more appropriate to interrogate the exclusionary and containment policies of political elites. The issues of public policy which have such a huge impact on young people's lives are not arrived at through any agency or input from young people themselves. If the spotlight is turned instead on most policies and public statements of political parties it is clear that, by formulating policies which are aimed at solving the problem presented by young people, they overwhelmingly address an adult middle class constituency. A more positive and inclusive approach would take a critical look at how public policy has problematised young people and redress this by a direct engagement with young people themselves. Until government and political parties do this, there will be no rise in young people's membership of political parties and no increase in party political participation.

New arenas

While the opportunities and incentives for participation in party politics are becoming more limited there is another area which is becoming increasingly pertinent to young people and where participation is being explored by many young people. This is the community and voluntary sectors whose growth represents a changing arena of political participation for adults as well. Increasingly political participation is taking place through community groups, self-help groups, and single issue pressure groups. The diversity of these groups reflects the actual diversity amongst young people. Young people are not a homogeneous group and any analysis of the exclusion and oppression of young people must take account of the differences of class, gender, race, sexuality and disability amongst young people. The multiplicity of community and voluntary groups organising around their own issues offer routes for young people's participation through the politics of identity and diversity. Because these groups do not view people as an undifferentiated mass they offer real possibilities for participation and representation of young people's interests.

Some of this voluntary sector addresses the welfare of children and young people. There are many community and voluntary groups which are concerned about young people, which provide services to young people and which speak on behalf of young people. To some extent the growth of this sector reflects the shift in state regulation referred to earlier. Increasingly service provision for young people is made in partnership between statutory and voluntary sectors, and voluntary sector representations on young people's issues are addressed to statutory intervention issues such as education, social care and criminal justice. There is therefore an onus on these voluntary organisations to involve young people and to encourage their active participation. If this is not done the risk is surely that they will end up colluding in the exclusion and problematising of young people.

Professionalisation has accompanied the growth of the voluntary sector and this means that the participation of young people will not happen automatically or without active support from the organisations. There are however many examples of young people's willingness to engage with the issues which affect them when opportunities are created to do so by organisations claiming to speak and act for them. My own experience convinces me that it is to the mutual advantage of each when this is done. If these groups are to be truly representative of young people's issues and concerns, they must engage with young people, listen to them and be prepared to involve young people in a meaningful way.

Participation

One of the most important things for adults to learn from young people's participation is the unique contribution young people make. I worked with a group of young people who set out to publish a guide to the United Nations Convention on the Rights of the Child. The group aimed to interpret the Convention in a way that would make sense to young people. Their resulting work, a booklet called *A Guide To Rights* (Rights For Us Group, 1994), is I believe powerful because the young people interpreted the Convention in their own words with reference to their own lives. Their work graphically illustrates the centrality of these rights and offers a rebuff to those who become alarmed at the idea of young people's rights. Rights to protection, to health care, to education and to be with your family do not pose a threat to our society. The authors identify the right to have your opinion heard and taken into account as one of those which underpins many other rights. Their own work has been a practical exercise of this right.

The *Guide to Rights* as written by the young people gives a concrete reality to the UN Convention on the Rights of the Child. Another group of young people, the Youth Rights group, chose to take one of the articles in the Convention, the right to participation, as their theme for action and, to this end, organised a conference aimed at young people, practitioners and policy makers in the statutory services and intervention aimed at young people. The conference, held in April 1995, discussed young people's experience of the care system, the juvenile justice system and the youth service. The workshops were led by young people who used a variety of techniques to engage the conference attenders, both youth and adult. For example, the workshop led by young people in care began by role-playing a case conference of social workers, parents and young person. This raised many issues which were then hotly debated by everyone in the workshop. The plenary session took the form of a panel of policy makers chaired by young people who directed the ensuing question, answer and discussion session.

As a conference attender one of the striking things for me was the way in which the young people who had been working together in a supportive environment were thus enabled to take charge of a situation involving adult experts and professionals. A very similar opportunity arose more recently in my own work with a group of young people in West Belfast who are carrying out a piece of research on drugs issues in the area. The young women in the group participated in the annual conference of a voluntary organisation promoting alternatives to care and custody systems for young people. The theme of the conference was responses to the adolescent drug culture. The young women ran an activity-based workshop with exercises encouraging the adult participants to look up and interpret statistics, to discuss their own attitudes to drugs use and to examine the connections between drug use and other issues such as fashion, economics etc. These were exercises which had been designed and used for our own group work and were now being reclaimed by the young women to assert their authority in the workshop context. In this situation the young women were not just participating as equal partners, but were directing and facilitating adult participation on their terms. In their research on the drugs culture and economy the young people have highlighted the many different aspects of this issue: health, information, criminalisation and the social and economic consequences. Moreover, they repositioned young people as active participants in the public debate about drugs, and not simply objects of anxiety.

Confidence building

The cornerstone of this kind of participation is confidence building in the group. In my experience the group must have confidence not just in themselves but also in the process they are engaged in. Self-confidence is built in personal development work within the group. Confidence in the project comes with testing their ability to make decisions *vis-à-vis* the adults and adult organisations they are working with.

The process of enabling young people to tap their own power and abilities is essential to facilitating their participation. In an article describing her work with a group of young mothers, my colleague Lorna McDonald (1994) outlines her initial impressions:

> What became clear almost immediately was that I was working with a group of young women who had lived most of their lives without anyone else having positive expectations for them as individuals.

Lorna goes on to describe the impact of the group work on the young women:

> The most significant learning for me is how valuable personal development work is in enabling young women to learn to trust, to value themselves, to support each other and to understand their rights to bring up their own children with a sense of physical, mental, spiritual and emotional security and pride.

One of the key elements of participation is the decision-making process. In my experience of group work with young people this is something that increases as the life of the group goes on and each step forward is successfully negotiated by the young people. Vivian McConvey (1994–5), who worked with the Youth Rights group, has written about the shift in young people's consciousness as the group continued. She quotes one young person's realisation of his power to make decisions:

> Then it came to me. It was the direction of the group. Before the group started, the idea of self-direction was simply theoretical, it wasn't until the group put this into practice that we realised that the destiny of this group lay in our hands, not the worker's, not Save The Children's, not the Children's Rights Alliance's, but ours. And for me that was an awe inspiring feeling. At the tender age of seventeen I was making decisions with minimal adult influence. I felt in charge and how good it felt!

For adults in the process this can be a challenging experience, consciously surrendering control and trusting the outcome of the process which has been started. What we need to realise as adults is the rewards that come from the active participation of young people. Sometimes it is uncomfortable, sometimes there is conflict; but if, as adults working with young people, we believe in an inclusive and representative society, it is something we must stand behind and support.

Common interests

Sometimes the input of young people can point up the common interests and experiences of adults and young people rather than divergence. Work with young women over a number of years led to the identification of women's centres as a ideal location for provision for some young women. A group of young women called Taking A Stand, aged between 18 and 21, were looking for an organisation to host and support their meetings and were attracted to the ethos of the local women's centre. Their idea was furthered by another group of young women calling themselves Dreamscape who set out to explore the lives and needs of young women by collecting information from a wide variety of groups and individuals. They used a range of methods: interviews, group discussions, diaries, visits to women's centres. They discovered that for young women over 16 and particularly those who had children, the provision already offered by women's centres for older women was very relevant. The desire for child care, a return to education, counselling and the breaking of isolation was similar to that experienced by older women using the network of community-based women's centres in Belfast. Contacts with the women's centres themselves established that there was a great willingness to engage with and provide for young women. There was a recognition that resources of staff and funding would be needed to further the work. The whole project was written up by an independent consultant, Marie Quiery (1996), in collaboration with Dreamscape, and this document is currently being used by women's centres to try and secure funding.

Conclusion

One of the features of young people's participation is the mushrooming effect once the process has begun. In the West Belfast drugs research project, for example, the young people have attended and represented their project at several conferences. These experiences encouraged some members of the group to attend and speak out at a major international human rights conference discussing the impact of armed conflict on children. As the only young people at the conference their input was invaluable. In turn this led to production of a written submission to the United Nations facilitated by the Committee on the Administration of Justice, a human rights organisation in Northern Ireland. Once begun, participation takes on a momentum. Invitations come from other organisations eager to involve young people and the young people themselves grasp other opportunities.

What emerges for me is a picture of young people eager to participate in a world which impacts upon them. What is involved for young people is commitment, the courage and confidence to take decisions, to act on them and accept the consequences of them. The culture of young people's participation in our society is not well developed. Certainly the lack of structures for participation create major barriers for young people. There are however many young people striving to make our society more representative of them.

References

Bessant, Judith (1995) 'Delayed adulthood', *Young People Now*, 76, August.
British Youth Council (1993) 'Young people: changing the face of British politics', Briefing Paper, London: British Youth Council.
McConvey, Vivian (1994–95) 'The impact of the worker in self-directed practice', Social Action, 2 (3), London: Whiting & Birch.
McDonald, Lorna (1994), 'Personal development work with young single mothers', *Child Care in Practice*, 1 (2), Belfast: Minprint.
Quiery, Marie (1996) *Unfilled Needs, Unlimited Potential*, Belfast: Save The Children.
Rights For Us Group (1994) *A Guide To Rights*, London: Save The Children.
Walker, David (1996) 'Young people, politics and the media', in H. Roberts and D. Sachdev (eds), *Young People's Social Attitudes*, Essex: Barnardo's and Social Community Planning Research.

9
Youth Working: Professional Identities Given, Received or Contested?

Stanley Tucker

Playing 'the game'

Those who work with young people witness, almost on a daily basis, a myriad of criticisms concerning the lifestyles, attitudes and ambitions of the young. Those criticisms come in different guises: criticisms about school achievements, public behaviour, willingness to work, or acceptance of social responsibility. The sources of criticism are also varied: the media, government, religious organisations, parents, and so on. Indeed, criticisms of the young are not new, for through time they have been variously urged, persuaded and coerced into 'playing the game' (Baden-Powell, 1909). So what is this 'game', and where do those who work with young people fit into it?

This chapter seeks to answer that question by exploring the ways in which youth working is defined through complex social and political relations. Here, the term 'youth working' is used as a shorthand definition for the occupational activities involved in the fields of health, welfare, and education. Accordingly, consideration is given to how those who undertake this kind of work, particularly in the public sector, construct their professional identities. Crucially, it is argued that such identities are developed in response to 'the game', that ideas about the nature of 'the game' are contested at every level, and that policies and practices are generated through the filters of social policy, training, work priorities and visions, as well as the conditions of existence that impact on the lives of young people, such as unemployment and homelessness.

'The game', then, varies according to the demands being made on young people and those who work with them. Those demands can be potentially empowering: to promote rights and responsibilities; to engage young people in decision-making; or to assist them to voice their opinions. However, they can also be constraining: concerned with control, regulation and conformity. They can manifest themselves in the form of social customs and practices, legal regulations, or sanctions. Thus, although the arena of 'the game' may vary, be it education, social work, or youth justice, such arenas often serve to advance congruent, and sometimes very different, representations of youth working.

So, what are we likely to find out by considering the issue of professional identity construction? First, it is argued that a whole range of groups lay claim to possessing a unique ability to understand the needs and aspirations of their client groups (see Esland, 1980). In turn, assertions of skill and knowledge capability are made, and codes of practice and work methods developed, in an attempt to stake out particular positions in 'the game'. Second, public support for that expression of uniqueness does not come cheap. For public sector professions, in particular, are expected to directly respond to state expressed 'concerns' (Wilding, 1982) about 'problematic' youth behaviour. Here then, the pitch for 'the game' is marked out. Third, there is debate about 'the game' plan. How should we intervene in the lives of young people? What kind of interventions are necessary? What values and visions should underpin different forms of professional work? Finally, there is the issue of equality of treatment. There exist various divisions or leagues of young people, principally constituted around notions of 'race', gender, disability or social class. In turn, groups of professionals are assigned the task of controlling, gatekeeping, guiding and educating these particular groups.

Developing professional identities in a changing world

The world of youth working appears to be changing at a rapid rate. How to most effectively facilitate the management of change is an issue facing many professional groups operating in the public sector. Teacher control of curriculum matters; opting-out processes within the NHS and education systems; and the purchaser and provider separation as it relates to the provision of social welfare, are all examples of contemporary developments, which serve to alter established service delivery patterns, methods of working, and roles and relationships. The influence of external pressure for change is becoming increasingly apparent, particularly in relation to the actions and activities of political parties and government departments. Indeed, it appears that those groups who want to hold on to their professional status must acknowledge, and at least in part embrace, the constraints and controls applied by such bodies (see Abbott and Wallace, 1990).

Now, perhaps this has always been the case, in that no occupational group is ever completely free to 'do its own thing'. Yet, the socio-political climate for public sector professionals working with young people has changed so fundamentally, that there is a need to understand not only the nature of that change, but also how it impacts on professional work and the identities adopted by particular individuals and groups. The roots of that change are grounded in the significantly altered structure and functioning of the welfare state. There is a need to draw a distinction between the role of the professional in 'traditional' welfare systems such as that which existed prior to the election of a Conservative government in 1979, and those activities carried out within the contemporary 'liberal' state (Bertilsson, 1990). In the former, some emphasis is placed on the 'redistributive', 'guarantor' and 'restitutive' aspects of maintaining the 'positive' rights and participation of young people; whereas with the latter, ideas about professional work stress the need to focus on the anti-collective aspect of human experience, the effective treatment (or at the very least control) of the troubled and troublesome, 'negative rights' that limit state intervention, and the development of services which 'cheer to the echo' notions of economic efficiency and choice based on ability to pay.

Youth working has had to encounter such changes head on. Choices have had to be made, new ideas either accepted, modified or resisted. For the world of the public sector professional in the new 'liberal' state cannot be sheltered from the icy blasts of welfare reform. In essence, a very different kind of discursive agenda is created to construct the boundaries of professional work. Crucially, a whole range of 'ideological effects' are used to constitute, and separate off, different groups of young people. For example, what is the hoped for 'ideological effect' of a discursive intervention that urges us to 'condemn a little more and understand a little less'? Or another that argues for the special treatment of black young people to counter their presumed social, personal and educational inadequacies? Or one that narrowly defines the actions of single pregnant young women as being irresponsible and self-centred? Essentially, in all this, an attempt is made to create a very different kind of terrain for working with young people: a terrain that divides and declares different groups and individuals as being 'suitable for treatment'; a terrain that extends the boundaries of those considered to be 'at risk' to include anyone who might have 'delinquent potential' (see Edelman, 1974); a terrain where 'ideological effects' are utilised to create symbols for youthful behaviour that 'other' those who are active in political demonstrations, grass-roots community politics, or protests about the environment.

How, then, do such processes shape matters of identity construction and development? To answer that question we need to understand what purposes such 'ideological effects' serve in terms of shaping professional roles and relationships, social policies, and work practices. In essence, there is a need to consider carefully the influence of particular forms of discourse constituted through various forms of 'knowledge, talk and texts' (Wetherell and Potter, 1992). For how we speak about young people, research into their needs, develop services for them, etc. is essentially underpinned by the views that are expressed by policy makers, those who hold sway in powerful institutions, the enforcers of legislation, professional groupings, academic writers and researchers – those able to influence and shape 'social meanings' and assist in their wider dissemination. One intention of using discourse in this way is to influence the boundaries of professional activities. Various representations of the period of youth compete for our attention. Youth can be seen as a period for fostering and developing ambitions; as a time of transition; as a period where the 'problematic' behaviour of some must be regulated and controlled. Different discourses create different ideologically inspired professional tasks. Thus, as Hall (1981) maintains:

> Ideologies . . . work by the transformation of discourses (the disarticulation and rearticulation of ideological elements) and the transformation (the fracturing and recomposition) of subjects for action.

The quote from Hall is cited not least of all because it captures the fluidity of the process concerned with ideological construction. Different ideas about the young are present in a society at different points in time. However, the currency of those ideas is largely dictated by the ability of individuals and groups to project them, and pronounce on their appropriateness, in the key institutional arenas of society – education, legal system, government, etc. And yet, the power to influence discourse does not simply lie with one group (even if they are considered to be the most powerful). For as Foucault (1991) argues, power is accorded to differing 'strategic positions' that are adopted, and it can be 'resisted' and 'struggled against'. So, although 'liberal' ideological forces have been used to mark out particular forms of professional work, they are not merely transmitted, received and acted on. Social policies have intentions, workplace practices have intentions: sometimes these are congruent, and sometimes they are in opposition. It is the interface between the two, namely policy and practice, that creates the dynamic forces of professional identity construction.

A framework for considering identity

Any framework which attempts to assist reflection on matters of professional identity construction must be able to:

1 explore the impact of 'ideological effects' on the socio-political terrain and the conditions of existence for those working with young people;
2 assist analysis of those forms of discourse that are used to define particular forms of work;
3 show how ideas are struggled over and contested at various levels of experience;
4 demonstrate how such matters directly impact upon the professional identities which individuals and groups adopt in their everyday work.

The socio-political terrain upon which society encounters its young people in the 1990s is one that has consistently been characterised by a series of visible 'moral panics' (Cohen, 1973). These 'panics', perhaps not surprisingly, have tended to focus on the behaviour of working class young people (often young men), located in socially and economically deprived inner city communities. In addition, media scrutiny has been applied to specific aspects of youth activity. For example, forms of collective recreation such as 'rave parties' are consistently depicted as offering opportunities for presumed 'illegal' activities, that is drug taking and sexual experimentation; incidents of 'joy-riding' are reported so as to create a representation of working class youth as being collectively corrupted by limited opportunities for 'meaningful' (middle class adult approved) forms of activity; and work with young offenders is frequently couched in the terminology of 'soft options' and 'treats for bad boys'. Professional intervention in community life, expenditure on education, health and welfare programmes for young people, and the tackling of deprivation by means other than Victorian-style 'self-help', are disputed by a government which values self-reliance and choice based on individual wealth.

In creating this kind of terrain, 'ideological effects' are used to classify those forms of behaviour that are not considered to be entrepreneurial or worthy as 'problematic', deviant, hedonistic or just plain mad or bad. The failure of young people to conform is placed at the door of particular groups of public sector professional workers – teachers, social workers, youth workers, etc. They are also castigated for their 'trendy' ideas and practices, inability to impose discipline, and do-gooder intentions. The discourse of the 'problematic' is thus extended to include both young people and those who work with them. Both groups, it is maintained, need to be controlled, regulated and changed.

Accordingly, a different official discourse, one that largely manifests itself through social policies, enquiries and reports, emerges that portrays a very different kind of knowledge about the needs of young people. Crucially, to impose that knowledge a form of ideologically generated power is used, that proclaims the rightness of particular approaches and solutions. For, as Foucault (1991) points out, the exercise of power itself is influential in the production of specific forms of knowledge; there is no 'disinterested knowledge' – there are those who know the answers and those who do not! The discourse of the official, then, is used to reinforce liberal ideological values. Self-improvement can be promoted through testing at 5, 7, 11 and 14 years; the three Rs and a return 'to basics' are linked to a 'golden age' of Victorian endeavour and voluntary activity; the power of the teacher is openly challenged through the creation of a 'mums' army' of on-the-job trained teachers and unqualified classroom assistants.

Yet, at the same time, forms of discourse are developed concerning work with young people that effectively 'fly in the face' of liberal official discourse. For example, during the mid 1980s (at the height of the welfare state transformation) and into the 1990s we witnessed the development of an increasingly active lobby who fought for an improvement in youth work services for women and girls. Essentially, a critical dialogue was pursued which attempted to openly question the historical thrust of youth work – its male-dominated senior management structure, as well as its preoccupation with providing activities to meet the needs and 'interests' of young men (see Smith, 1983). Women youth workers, encouraged by the arguments of writers like Smith, who maintain the need for the creation of 'single sex work', set about developing a whole range of innovatory projects designed to encourage young women and girls to question patriarchal arrangements and their treatment by the institutions of society.

In reality, some women youth workers chose to challenge one of the main assumptions that has influenced the provision of social welfare within UK society. For it is through the use of the representations (discursive messages and images) contained within 'family ideology' that social policies and educational and welfare arrangements are constructed and maintained:

> Family ideology has been a vital means – the vital means – of holding together and legitimising the existing social, economic, political and gender systems. Challenging the ideology thus means challenging the system. (Gittins, 1985)

This kind of ideological 'challenge' can have a profound impact on the professional identities of those who embrace it. For, far from accepting the discourses of the official, such ideas are used to challenge and resist it. A deliberate attempt is made to deproblematise the young; emphasis is placed on facilitation and enabling; and a political dimension is added to practice in order to contest existing power relations.

Thus, a further important element of the process of professional identity construction is revealed. For it can be argued that the process of identity development does not occur in a uniform fashion. The formation of identities takes place within different arenas, at different points in time, and in different ways. As we have seen, attempts are made to determine the shape of professional work through social policies. Yet, we do not always find a degree of congruence between policies pursued at national and local levels. Indeed, during the early years of the 1980s, Labour-controlled councils actively encouraged their employees to promote policies and practices that would counter the efforts of the Conservative government to 'dismantle' parts of the infrastructure of public welfare. Similarly, alternative practice lobbies use trade unions, grass-roots pressure groups and political alliances to press their different claims. Crucially, those with official, political, charismatic or collective forms of power utilise such arenas as the conduits for the development of particular forms of discourse about professional work and the knowledge base that should underpin it.

To advance this point a stage further, consider the influence that training has on the values, attitudes and performance of public sector professionals working with young people. Almost all groups who undertake work of this nature undergo some form of training. Yet, there exist widely divergent views about what should be taught; the skills that are necessary to perform particular types of work; how training should be organised and delivered; as well as the criteria that should be adopted around issues of assessment. Take, for example, the value positions that are pursued with regard to the development of competency-based training, such as that inspired by S/NVQs. Some commentators have proclaimed the importance of these approaches, declaring that they offer the opportunity to develop work related skills and abilities, will improve performance, and are employer-led (see Jessup, 1990). On the other hand, competency-based learning has been criticised for its attempts to 'parcellize' the workforce, limit opportunities to explore the social, economic and structural inequalities of society, as well as 'narrow the initiative' of individual workers and groups of workers (Field, 1993).

The important point to grasp is that those who are in the position to determine the organisation of training potentially have the power to shape its knowledge base. For different approaches to knowledge acquisition contain different discursive positions that are concerned to turn out different kinds of professional workers. Thus, it becomes all the more important to locate such changes within the context of the significant power shifts that have occurred around the welfare state. The control of training is seen as a way of constructing different kinds of professional identities. For example, if the focus of social work training can be moved from its present academic institutional network, central government will be able to become far more instrumental in determining not only the process of accreditation, but also the actual forms of knowledge and skills to be assessed and legitimised.

And yet, as with other areas of professional work, groups and individuals, operating at ground level, also assert a degree of autonomy and relative power to contest macro-based assertions concerning the direction of training. There exist various layers of interaction between the macro and the micro. Trainers, students in training, and those who support workplace learning, all play a role in interpreting, defining and assessing competence, educational achievement and practice. The curriculum of professional training itself should be viewed as a 'site of struggle', for as Apple (1993) argues there is a need to question:

> the comforting illusion that there can (and must) be one grand narrative to which all relations of domination can be subsumed, the focus on the 'microlevel' as a site of the political . . . the idea of the decentered subject where identity is both non-fixed and a site of political struggle . . . all of this [is important.

Apple creates a powerful picture of the dynamic of human relations that are revealed in just one arena of professional activity: training. The knowledge base of particular kinds of professional work is contested; there is at the same time resistance by some, and acceptance by others, of the problematising discourses of youth; competency-based work is acclaimed by employers for specifically meeting their needs, and yet is rejected by some academic educators and trainers as being anti-intellectual, narrow and lacking a value base in its orientation.

So, we can see from the above that in considering how professional identities are established, developed and maintained, there is a need to examine a whole range of socio-politically inspired discursive interventions. We also have to consider the impact of power and knowledge in shaping the priorities, practices and activities of different forms of work. The nature, skills and priorities of professional work are contested in many different arenas – at both macro and micro levels of experience. Accordingly, a framework for analysis can be utilised to capture the crucial elements and factors entailed in the process of professional identity construction, as shown in Figure 9.1. The framework offers a very

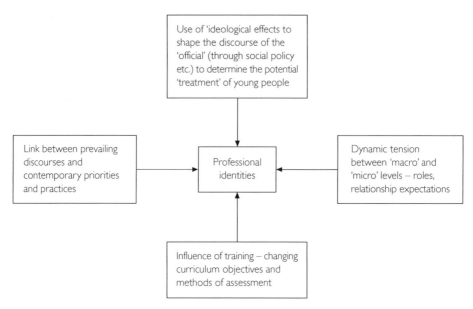

Figure 9.1

different way of looking at the issue of professional identity construction. For example, it challenges the altruistic illusions of trait theory – those qualities that set the professional apart from others in the workforce – as well as notions that professional groups merely operate on behalf of the state (see Wilding, 1982). Instead, we begin to concern ourselves with understanding the socio-political background, dynamic tensions and struggles that occur to influence matters of identity development. Even the process of training assumes a different purpose – one where power struggles are acted out for the control of the knowledge base of professional work.

Returning to 'the game'

To understand the nature of 'the game' that those who work with young people find themselves in, there is a need to consider carefully the totality of the arena that effectively delineates the field of play. For it is on that field of play that professional identities are constructed. Shirts are worn containing the 'colours' of different ideological positions – conveying discourses that represent sometimes complementary and sometimes conflicting approaches and underlying values. Some players in the game are more powerful than others, and can, therefore, increase their opportunities for defining the features of professional work. However, there are those who frequently resist the game plan, whilst in turn promoting their own visions and aspirations.

In essence, it is argued that at any moment competing definitions of professional work are advanced. There is no one simple 'version' that everyone adopts, merely because they have been schooled in the profession. Professional identities are created and developed within particular institutional settings; via the 'ideological effects' of social policy; through discursive interactions; and at the level of macro and micro social and political relations. On the field of play there are particular key social actors. Individually and collectively they 'shout at' the onlooking crowd of politicians, academics, managers, students in training, parents, young people and workers. They say this is how the world is, and this is how those who work with young people should behave and act; they strive to create the rules of 'the game' and orchestrate its tactics.

References

Abbott, P. and Wallace, C. (1990) *The Sociology of the Caring Professions*, London: Falmer.

Apple, M. (1993) 'What post-modernists forget: cultural capital and official knowledge', *Curriculum Studies*, 1 (3).

Baden-Powell, R. (1909) *Scouting for Boys*, London: Scout Association.

Bertilsson, M. (1990) 'The welfare state, the professions and citizens', in R. Torstendahl and M. Burrage (eds), *The Formation of the Professions*, London: Sage.

Cohen, S. (1973) *Folk Devils and Moral Panics*, London: Paladin.

Edelman, M. (1974) 'The political language of the helping professions', *Politics and Society*, 4 (3).

Esland, G. (1980) 'Professions and professionalisation', in G. Esland and G. Salmon (eds), *The Politics of Work and Occupations*, Milton Keynes: Open University Press.

Field, J. (1993) 'Competency and the pedagogy of labour', in M. Thorpe, R. Edwards and A. Hanson (eds), *Culture and Processes of Adult Learning*, London: Routledge.

Foucault, M. (1991) *Discipline and Punish: the Birth of the Prison*, Harmondsworth: Penguin.

Gittins, D. (1985) *The Family in Question*, London: Macmillan.

Hall, S. (1981) 'The white of their eyes: racist ideology and the media', in G. Bridges and R. Brund (eds), *Silverlinings*, London: Lawrence Wishart.

Jessup, G. (1990) 'National Vocational Qualifications: implications for further education', in M. Bees and M. Swords (eds), *National Vocational Qualifications and Further Education*, London: Kogan Page and National Council for Vocational Qualifications.

Smith, N. (1983) *Youth Service Provision for Girls and Young Women*, Leicester: National Association of Youth Clubs.

Wetherell, M. and Potter, J. (1992) *Mapping the Language of Racism: Discourse and the Legitimation of Exploitation*, Brighton: Harvester Wheatsheaf.

Wilding, P. (1982) *Professional Power and Social Welfare*, London: Routledge and Kegan Paul.

10
Welfare Services for Young People: Better Connections?

Bob Coles

This chapter charts recent developments in the provision of 'welfare' services for young people in the UK*. Welfare is defined as the means through which a person's well-being is provided for, encompassing health, shelter, nutrition, social support, education, training and personal development. It also covers protection from exploitation or abuse, and the development of skills and opportunities for participation in the economy and the community. As we will see, the recognition of these needs and the development of the means through which the state can be assured that they are met have changed significantly in recent years. This chapter focuses on changes in youth policy since the election of the Labour Government in 1997 mainly on the grounds that, only since then has anything that could be reasonably called a coherent 'youth policy' been developed (Coles, 2000; Jones and Bell, 2000). The chapter also explores some conceptual issues such as, what do we mean by 'youth' and 'young people' and how has our understanding of these changed over time?

Perspectives on 'youth' and 'youth transitions'

Different disciplines within the social sciences have different conceptualisations of 'youth', although these have come together more closely in recent years (Coleman and Hendry, 1999). 'Youth' is often defined as a phase in the life course between childhood and adulthood and 'young people' as that group of people going through that phase (Coles, 1995; Jones and Wallace, 1992). Some disciplines use alternative terms. 'Adolescence' is often used within psychology to describe the common biological, psychological, emotional and sexual maturation phases associated with the onset of puberty and the teenage years. Psychologists do recognise issues of difference, especially gender differences and how issues as diverse as diet, culture or family relationships can impact upon the developmental process (Shaffer, 2002). Sociological writings illustrate the ways in which socially constructed boundaries between childhood, youth and adulthood are determined by social institutions; for instance, schools, the labour market, families and housing. Also associated with the different statuses within the life course are legal rights and responsibilities that are often granted at specific chronological ages. These vary from, for instance, the age of criminal responsibility (the age of 10 in England and Wales), the end of compulsory edu-cation (the age of 16 across the UK), the age at which young people can vote and marry without parental consent (the age of 18 in England and Wales), to the age at which a person can claim benefits at a full adult rate (the age of 25 across the UK). Political scientists and others have focused on rights and responsibilities, examining the ways in which the 'protection rights' according to children become gradually supplemented by participation and entitlement rights associ-ated with citizenship (Coles, 1995). These have become more important in recent years with the development of youth charters and an increasing emphasis on the involvement of young people in the design, delivery and governance of services (Cutler, 2002).

The 'youth transition model' is used to help understand the way in which 'youth' was transformed in the last quarter of the twentieth century. Sociologists describe this as involving three main transitions: completing full-time education and gaining employment (the school-to-work transition); attaining (relative) independence of families of origin and embarking on partnering and parenting careers (the domestic transition); and leaving home and living away from par-ents (the housing transition). The use of the words 'transitions' or 'careers' suggests that these are often not simple 'one step moves'. Sociologists emphasise the ways in which these have become ever more complex, extended and beset with risk and uncertainty (Furlong and Cartmel, 1997). So-called 'traditional transitions', widespread until the mid 1970s in the UK, involved young people first leaving school at minimum school leaving age and immediately, and with few difficulties, getting a job – the school-to-work transition accomplished in a matter of days. As young people developed their employment career, they con-tinued to live at home, but were able to save, form partnerships, get engaged, then married, and upon marriage leave home to live with their spouse. This was followed by the married couple having children in their late teens or early twen-ties. The order was almost invariable, with early employment enabling a degree of financial independence that could fund a domestic transition (culmination in marriage), followed by a housing transition (living away from the parental home and starting a family of their own).

Some young people still embark on one or more of these transitions in their early to mid teens. Some become parents. Others leave home. Around one in ten nationally still manages to leave school and get a job at the age of 16. But these transitions are now undertaken by only a very small minority. Teenage parents, leaving home 'prematurely', youth homelessness, and even employment with-out training are regarded as 'problems' to be addressed (Jones, 1995). Early transitions are often associated with so-called 'failed' transitions, although such terminology is obviously judgemental and, as such, contentious (Coles, 2000). Such transitions involve young people: leaving school but not obtaining secure employment or promising careers; leaving (or running away from) home or care placement only to experience various forms of homelessness; leaving the support of family or carer without other forms of support. Early transitions are also associated with other factors such as underachievement at school, problems at home, drug misuse, mental health problems, self-harming and criminality – in short, threats to young people's 'welfare'. Much of the policy agenda in the late 1990s was focused on how 'vulnerable groups' experienced 'failed' transitions and various forms of 'social exclusion'.

The majority of young people have not replaced traditional with 'failed' transitions but with 'extended transitions'. In most parts of the UK four out of five young people stay on in education at the age of 16 and more than a third go on into full-time higher education at the age of 18. Whilst many may leave home in their late teens, this is not to live with a partner and start a family, but to go to college or university or embark on other forms of training. Those not going to college are highly likely to continue to live at home during their early twenties. More than half of men and around a third of young women aged 20–24 in the UK live at home with their parents, a much higher proportion than much of the rest of Europe (Coleman and Schofield, 2003). The average age of motherhood also rose steadily during the last quarter of the twentieth century, with the average age of those giving birth within marriage reaching 30.4 years (Matheson and Summerfield, 2000). Some of the key milestones for completing youth transitions have thus been extended until a young person's mid-to-late twenties or early thirties. There is also recognition in some research that factors such as ethnicity, impairment, and poverty impact upon identity and upon the expectations and experiences of 'independence' and living away from home (Bignall and Butt, 2000). Meanwhile, the costs of these extended transitions have to be borne by young people and their families. Most undergraduate students now have to pay substantial fees and by the time they graduate the average amount of debt they have accumulated is estimated in tens of thousands of pounds. Young people in their twenties either live at home or now follow extended housing careers through various forms of intermediate, (largely rented), multi-occupied housing. If they wish to gain a foothold in the owner-occupied sector of the housing market, they have to do so in a climate in which the average deposit required by first time buyers has quadrupled in the last six years to around £24,000 and is set to reach £35,000 by 2011 (Howard, 2002).

Extended youth transitions require a great deal of family support, both financial and emotional. Yet, given the rise in lone parenthood and divorce and separation during the last quarter of the twentieth century, far fewer families are in a position to give this. Moreover, fewer than half of 16 year olds now live with both their married biological parents and with divorce and separation comes the cost of maintaining two households. Many young people's extended transitions therefore rely upon extensive financial support from parents, which they are unable to afford. But it was not this issue that forced youth policy development to the front of the political stage. It was the huge cost of policy failure amongst the most vulnerable.

The social exclusion agenda and the development of youth policy in the UK

A case can be made that the push towards developing more coherence and strategy in youth policy pre-dated the 1997 election. The year before saw the publication of a highly influential report that detailed the cost of youth crime, and the ineffective and inefficient response of the youth justice system to it (Audit Commission, 1996). Of the seven million offences committed by young people each year (estimated to cost around £7 billion a year), only 3% resulted in an arrest. Yet the youth justice system was reported to cost a further £1 billion pounds and was laboriously slow. Furthermore, as the report revealed, many of the known causes of youth crime lay beyond the police or the criminal justice system, in poor performance and disaffection at school, especially through truancy and school exclusion. The latter had increased by a staggering 450% in the first half of the 1990s. To be tough on the causes of crime, therefore, required better co-ordination of policy across government departments.

The Social Exclusion Unit (SEU) was set up shortly after the 1997 election to address the complex and multi-faceted syndromes of disadvantage – the so-called 'joined-up' problems (Coles, 2000). Within two years it had produced five major reports on:

- Truancy and School Exclusion (SEU, 1998a);
- Rough Sleeping (SEU 1998b);
- Poor Neighbourhoods (SEU 1998c);
- Teenage Pregnancy (SEU, 1999a); and
- 16–18 year olds not in Education, Employment or Training (NEET) (SEU, 1999b).

As well as charting the rise in permanent exclusions from school, the first report pointed to the relationship between school exclusion and the lack of school-based qualifications, later unemployment, and involvement in crime and drug use. Exclusions were also spatially clustered, with a quarter of all secondary schools producing two-thirds of all exclusions. Some groups were heavily over-represented: four out of five of them boys. African-Caribbean boys were five times more likely to be excluded than their white peers; those with special educational needs were seven times more likely to be excluded; and those children 'looked after' (in foster or residential care) were ten times more likely to be excluded than their peers. Truancy was also shown to be widespread, with around 5–10% of hard-core non-attenders many of whom rarely went to school for months or years at a time. Truancy was also as much a female as a male issue. This first SEU report provided a recipe to be followed by subsequent ones: hard hitting indictment of the lack of policy co-ordination; brave new targets on the reduction of the problem; new planning and co-ordination mechanisms; and re-assignment of the responsibilities of key stakeholders for doing things differently in the future. In terms of targets, truancy and school exclusions were to be reduced by a third by 2003 (with exclusions but not truancy rates now well on course to meet these targets). New guidelines were given to schools and LEAs, first, to ensure that schools stopped excluding pupils for trivial reasons and, secondly, to ensure that LEAs made adequate provision so that those who were excluded were re-integrated into full-time education within 15 days.

The second report on *Rough Sleepers* was about a much wider problem than 'youth' homelessness. This report claimed that relatively few of the street-homeless were under the age of eighteen years old but a quarter of them were between the ages of 18 and 25. The initiatives it suggested included targeting particular groups, including 'looked after' children and care leavers, policy and practice for which will be described in more detail below. The third report was not specifically focused on youth policy issues but on the spatial concentrations of poverty and disadvantage. This inquiry gave rise to 18 separate Policy Action Teams (PATs), one of which was given the task of examining policy and provision for 'young people' and how government could do better in co-ordinating services for them. This report from PAT 12 proved to be highly influential in providing recommendations for the wholesale transformation of youth policy making and the co-ordination of policy within Whitehall. It pointed out that the UK was alone in Europe in having no minister for youth, no ministry, nor any cross-ministerial group for the co-ordination of policy. It produced a map of different responsibilities that covered eight government departments, six units, and at least ten other agencies all potentially pulling in different directions. There was no one with the job of ensuring coherence; no single point of contact; no one to speak; no one to listen; no one to take a lead. The recommendations from PAT 12, now largely implemented, were for the development of a cross-ministerial group (chaired by the Chancellor) and a new Children and Young People's Unit in Whitehall to develop an overarching strategy and co-ordinate intelligence gathering and policy. This unit has proved highly influential in consulting with interest groups, including children and young people themselves, and setting a range of principles, outcomes and delivery plans for the enhancement of their welfare, including the reduction of child poverty by a half by 2010 (CYPU, 2002).

The fourth report on *Teenage Pregnancy* drew attention to the size of the problem. In 1997 there were 90,000 conceptions to teenagers, nearly 8,000 to girls under the age of 16 and over 2,000 to those under 14; conception rates which were twice that of Germany, three times that of France and six times that of Holland. Those who became pregnant were again shown to be spatially clustered in areas of social housing, deprivation and poverty, and high levels of parental unemployment. Teenage mothers were also more likely to have had mothers who had been parents themselves in their teenage years and were also linked to truancy and school exclusion before the age of 16 and disengagement from education, employment and training after that age. Also over-represented were other 'vulnerable groups', such as those 'looked after' in public care, with one estimate that half those young women looked after were mothers of at least one child by the age of 18 (Biehal et al., 1995). The policy initiatives on teenage pregnancy followed a similar pattern to those in previous reports, including a 28 point action plan and a Teenage Pregnancy Strategy launched in 1999. This was to be co-ordinated in each local authority area by Teenage Pregnancy Co-ordinators. Targets for reducing teenage pregnancy rates were given a longer period than truancy and school exclusions, with the aim to reduce conceptions to young women under the age of 18 by half by 2010. Sure Start (announced before the report in 1998) and Sure Start Plus (pilot schemes announced in March 2000 for 20 'hot-spot' areas) aim to provide information, guidance and support. Sure Start plus offers young people personal advisers to help them make informed choices about the future of their pregnancy, packages of support to help them access health care, parenting skills, education, child care and housing, as well as advice on contraception. These initiatives are largely based upon a US programme which claims that, for each $1 invested, there is a net saving of $7 in later welfare payments. This is, therefore, part of the commitment to investing in early interventions because they are less expensive than meeting the costs of disadvantage later in the life course. Indeed, it is clear that the strategy is not only about reducing conceptions but ensuring that teenage motherhood, should it occur, is not a well worn path into educationally unqualified, economic (and social) marginality, unemployment and welfare dependency.

The fifth report, *Bridging the Gap*, was on a topic few commentators had even noticed at the beginning of the 1990s. This was young people aged 16 or 17 who had left school but took no part in any form of education, employment or training, now commonly called 'the NEET group'. The SEU report suggested that this group numbered around 160,000 young people, around 8% of the age group, although this is likely to be an underestimate (Britton et al., 2002). Perhaps unsurprisingly, the report said that disengagement between the ages of 16 and 18 was closely linked to experiencing unemployment subsequently and that, prior to 16, the NEET group were highly likely to have either truanted, been excluded from school or under-performed in terms of school qualifications. There was also evidence of spatial concentrations and associations with other forms of disadvantage, such as membership of minority ethnic groups (especially African-Caribbean boys and members of Pakistani or Bangladeshi communities), having special educational needs or a mental health problem, being a young carer, or being 'looked after' in care. Three quarters of young men in the age group charged with a criminal offence also had no involvement in education, employment or training. Whilst some of the NEET group were virtually permanently disengaged, the majority had tried some form of employment, education or training after reaching the minimum school leaving age and before dropping out. A third dropped out of further education, with a further 40% dropping out of either employment or training suggesting poor levels of guidance and support. A report by the 'left of centre' think-tank DEMOS had looked at the problem in 1999 and suggested the need for a generic youth support service as a single point of contact for young people between the ages of 13 to 19 (Bentley and Gurumurthy, 1999). This, it was argued, would see young people through the difficult years of transition, prevent drop out and facilitate the 'brokering in' of more specialist support. The SEU report came to similar conclusions and was published alongside a White Paper announcing the development of the Connexions Strategy and the Connexions Service. This was to be linked with a re-organisation of all post-16 education and training through Learning and Skills Councils (LSCs). The identified 47 sub-regions across England now have co-terminous LSCs and Connexions Partnerships. Interestingly, Scotland and Wales have not followed suit, although similar sorts of 'joined-up' solutions are being developed under unitary local authorities. But before looking at the Connexions Strategy in more detail, we turn to other significant developments taking place outside of the policy arena influenced by the SEU.

Meanwhile . . .

Independently of inquiries instigated by the SEU, other radical and far reaching policy reviews and developments were taking place. Nowhere was this more apparent than in support and services for children and young people who are 'looked after', a term introduced by the Children Act 1989 for those previously described as being 'in care'. Shortly before the 1997 election, the Conservative government commissioned a wide ranging review of the measures taken to protect children living away from home and published as *People Like Us* (Utting, 1997). Throughout the 1990s, there was continued evidence of physical and sexual abuse of those in care and the Secretary of State, in responding to the Utting Report, also accepted that it 'painted a woeful tale of failure' and that 'the whole system failed' (DoH, 1998). Utting documented the sorry plight of the most vulnerable young people who often came to be 'looked after' because of being brought up in some of the worst social and economic conditions, only to find that when the state took over responsibility, it did little better and produced alarmingly poor welfare outcomes. A startling majority of those 'looked after' were also known to have mental health problems yet received little coherent treatment or support (Koprowska and Stein, 2000). Three quarters of care leavers had no academic qualifications and more than a half became unemployed. Nearly a third of the young single homeless had been in care, and 38% of young prisoners had been in care at some time. Part of this was due to the fact that, whilst most young people were experiencing extended transitions, many of those who were 'looked after' were being asked to find work and live independently shortly after their 16th birthday, despite their disadvantaged and damaged pasts.

The Government's response to the Utting Report resulted in a series of important reforms. A 'Quality Protects' programme was introduced in an attempt to raise standards in foster and residential care, set new targets relating to the average number of placements a young person was likely to experience and enhance their educational attainments. It has also drawn particular attention to the identification of the needs of young people from minority ethnic groups and disabled children and young people (Robbins, 2001). The Children (Leaving Care) Act 2000 introduced a new duty on local authorities to assess and meet the needs of care leavers until the age of 21 or when the young person completed their education, whichever was the later. Prior to the 2000 Act, local authorities had a power (but not a duty) to assist and befriend young people leaving care after the age of 16. Under the new Act needs assessments were to be incorporated into a 'pathway plan', detailing expected progress and giving care leavers a named Personal Adviser to co-ordinate support and ensure that needs were met. Pathway plans are expected to cover education, training and employment, accommodation and personal support (such as mentoring or befriending), health care, life skills and financial support. Young people are also expected to play a key role in drawing up such a plan, together with other professional workers.

Similar developments have taken place in the areas of youth justice and special educational needs. In the case of the latter, individual education plans (reviewed annually) are supplemented by 'transition plans' after the age of 13. Young offenders also have their case reviewed by a multi-agency youth offending team (YOT), through whom their Personal Adviser will be allocated (in conjunction with Connexions). As we have seen with teenage parents, the aim with all these groups is to make a more holistic assessment of their welfare needs and provide personal adviser support in ensuring that all their needs are met.

The Connexions strategy and the 'welfare' of young people

Announced in February 2000, the proposal for a Connexions Strategy was signed by the Prime Minister and seven Cabinet Ministers, a symbol that Connexions is intended to be a single and coherent strategy across government to give 'the best start in life for every young person' (DfEE, 2000). The 'strategy' is intended to co-ordinate policy across a number of partner agencies. This includes schools, colleges, employers and training providers, youth justice services, drug action teams, housing, social services and leaving care teams, teenage pregnancy co-ordinators, the youth service and the voluntary sector, particularly those working with 'hard to reach' groups. The aim of the strategy is to provide a support service for all 13–19 year olds through a network of personal advisers delivered through multi-agency teams. The development of the new Connexions Service, at the heart of the strategy, is intended to provide a universal service for all young people, but with resources targeted at those most in need. Three levels of need have been identified. Around 10% of young people are thought to be facing severe, and often multi-faceted, problems and to require the intervention of a Personal Adviser to broker in specialist support. This can be from professionals working in health, drugs or social services, for instance. A further 30–40%

of young people are thought to be 'at risk' of under-achieving or disengaging and are anticipated to require in-depth intensive support with Personal Advisers. The remainder (around 60%) will benefit only from the universal service. Even this basic service is intended to be enhanced by the development of one-stop-shops, where a number of youth support agencies have a presence, and on-line support via telephone contacts and 'chat-rooms' through Connexions Direct on the web and open 24 hours a day, 7 days a week. A further feature of both the service and the strategy is the involvement of young people in their design and delivery, with many already involved in the appointment of Connexions staff (including chief executives) and the drawing up of young person's charters detailing rights, entitlements, principles and standards of service expected.

The 47 Connexions Partnerships across England are responsible for the strategic development of coherence and co-operation with other services within the sub-region. Membership of the Partnership Boards that govern each local service include chief officers from local authority services, Health Authorities, the Police and employers as well as representatives from the voluntary sector. Between them they have a budget of around double that allocated to the old careers services. Whether Connexions has re-badged, replaced or eclipsed careers services is a contentious issue. Some of the partnerships have followed a 'transmuted model', developing partnerships by building the new service on amalgamated careers companies. Here welfare services are largely built as 'careers service plus'. The other dominant model of partnership development involves a 'sub-contracting model', whereby the Partnership Boards make a contract for the delivery of services with a range of different partners, including previously existing careers companies. During the 1990s and before the arrival of Connexions, careers companies had been 're-focused' by their contracts with government to pay increasing attention to the needs of the 'hard to reach' groups. From 1997 onwards, these were also those groups who,were being scrutinized nationally by the Social Exclusion Unit. Under the sub-contracting model, some careers companies are being forced into mainly providing only the universal service, whilst others (and especially youth services and the voluntary sector) are being given contracts to deal with those young people requiring intensive and specialist support. Furthermore, over and above the contract funding of these services, successful Connexions Partnerships have partnership agreements with a range of other service providers whose funding comes through other sources. For instance, one Partnership Board, with a budget for the Connexions Service of around £20m per year, has identified around £90m of services for young people being provided in the area. The Strategy thus covers a much greater range of services than the Connexions Service *per se*.

Several factors will be important as to whether Connexions will be a success. There can be little doubt that it aims to produce a radically different service, based upon a range of different professional 'disciplines' and combining these in multi-agency partnerships. Yet, building partnerships is not an easy business, especially when there is potential competition between partners for 'business'.

Key to doing this successfully will also be the knowledge, trust and experience gained by the new profession of personal advisers. Training, record keeping and information sharing will be crucial in this. Some of the training material being used is indicative of the range of issues now seen as the central components of 'welfare'. This covers 18 key areas and includes personal health factors (including emotional and mental health); social and behavioural development (including identity, self-image and risk of offending); family and environmental issues (including housing and income); as well as issues relating to education, skills and employment. The recommended method of assessing the needs of young people, for instance, covers 18 different aspects of a young person's life. The difficulties of doing needs assessments thoroughly and with due sensitivity is one area of criticism highlighted in the first OFSTED inspection of the Connexions pilots. Others include a lack of clarity about the role of personal adviser and how these are appropriately supported and managed (OFSTED, 2002). Area inspections also report inconsistencies in provision and patchiness of good practice, all suggesting that radical reform is not easy to deliver quickly (OFSTED, 2003).

Parallel to the development of Connexions has been a review of youth work provision. Youth work is concerned with the personal and social development of young people who engage with youth workers on a voluntary basis. It is delivered through a huge range of voluntary sector clubs and organisations as well as the statutory local authority youth services. Like Connexions, many youth workers target support for vulnerable groups sometimes operating through outreach and detached youth work as well as community based provision. Spending per head on youth services varies enormously between local authorities from under £30 to over £250 per young person (DfEE, 2001). *Transforming Youth Work* jointly published by the DfES and Connexions called on the statutory service to ensure more coherent service plans across all sectors. Youth Service Plans from 2003 onwards will be expected to ensure that together they meet the 'Pledge to young people' that there will be a 'safe, warm, well equipped meeting place within a reasonable distance of home', giving opportunities for personal and social development activities including arts, drama, music, sport, international experience and voluntary action (DfES, 2003). Under the reforms, youth work has specific targets and performance indicators (including work with the NEET group) and is to be subject to inspections by OFSTED with the threat that the co-ordination role of the LA youth service may be re-allocated if this is deemed unsatisfactory. The aim of the reforms is to signal 'a new beginning' for youth work working in the context of the Connexions Strategy.

Conclusions

This chapter has charted the re-configuration of welfare services for young people and reviewed the changing shape of 'youth' in the last quarter of a century. It has argued that, whilst the main youth transitions of the majority of young people have been extended, the policy agenda has been driven by the minority who experience 'failed' transitions and various forms of social exclusion. Partly fuelled by a realisation of the cost of policy failure and the 'joined up' nature of social exclusion, new approaches to youth policy and practice emerged at the beginning of the new century. A key role in this involves the Connexions Strategy, an attempt to build multi-agency partnerships to address the holistic needs of young people in a more coherent way. But partnership working, whilst it may sound to be based on common sense, is often fraught with difficulty – once described by a government minister as 'the suppression of mutual loathing in the pursuit of government money.' Whether the loathing can be either suppressed or replaced with mutual respect and effective teamwork, only time will tell. But, at the beginning of the twenty-first century, youth policy and a more holistic approach to welfare support for young people has at least begun.

Note

*The chapter is mainly based on developments in England.

References

For an overview of youth policy and provision see Bell, R. and Jones, G. (2000) *Youth, Parenting and Public Policy: a Chronology of Policy and Legislative Provision* and visit the website at http://www.keele.ac.uk/depts/so/research/youthchron.htm

Audit Commission (1996) *Misspent Youth: Young People and Crime*, London: Audit Commission.

Bentley, T. and Gurumurthy, R. (1999) *Destination Unknown: Engaging with the Problems of Marginalised Youth*, London: DEMOS.

Bignall, T. and Butt, J. (2000) *Between Ambition and Achievement: Young Black Disabled People's Views and Experiences of Independence and Independent Living*, Bristol: The Policy Press.

Biehal, N., Clayden, J., Stein, M. and Wade, J. (1995) *Moving On: Young People and Leaving Care Schemes*, London: HMSO.

Britton, L., Chatrik, B., Coles, B., Craig, G., Hylton, C. and Mumtaz, S. (2002) *Missing Connexions? The Career Dynamics and Welfare Needs of 16–17 Year Olds*, Bristol: The Policy Press.

Children and Young People's Unit (CYPU) (2002) *Building a Strategy for Children and Young People*, London: CYPU.

Coleman, J. and Hendry, L. (1999) *The Nature of Adolescence*, Third Edition, London: Routledge.

Coleman, J, and Schofield, J. (2003) *Key Data on Adolescence: 2003*, Brighton: The Trust for the Study of Adolescence.

Coles, B. (1995) *Youth and Social Policy: Youth Citizenship and Young Careers*, London: UCL Press.

Coles, B. (2000) *Joining-Up Youth Research, Policy and Practice: A New Agenda for Change?* Leicester: Youth Work Press–Barnardos.

Cutler, D. (2002) *Taking the Initiative: Promoting the Involvement of Young People in Public Decision making in the UK*, London: Carnegie Young People Initiative.

DfEE (2000) *Connexions: The Best Start in Life for Every Young Person*, London: DfEE.

DfEE (2001) *Transforming Youth Work: Developing Youth Work for Young People*, London: DfEE.

DfES (2003) *Transforming Youth Work: Resourcing Excellent Youth Services*, London: DfES.

Department of Health (DoH) (1999) *The Government's Response to the Children's Safeguards Review*, London: The Stationery Office, Cm 4105.

Furlong, A. and Cartmel, F. (1997) *Young People and Social Change: Individualization and Risk in Late Modernity*, Buckingham: Open University Press.

Howard, M. (2002) *Saving for a Foot on the Property Ladder*, London: The Future Foundation/ Egg.

Jones, G. (1995) *Leaving Home*, Buckingham: Open University Press.

Jones, G. and Bell, R. (2000) *Balancing Acts: Youth Parenting and Public Policy*, York: JRF.

Jones, G. and Wallace, C. (1992) *Youth, Family and Citizenship*, Buckingham: Open University Press.

Koprowska, J. and Stein, M. (2000) 'The mental health of "looked after" young people', in P. Aggleton, J. Hurry and I. Warwick (eds) *Young People and Mental Health*, Chichester: Wiley.

Matheson, J and Summerfield, C. (2000) *Social Focus on Young People*, London: The Stationery Office.

National Strategy for Neighbourhood Renewal (2000) *Report of the Policy Action Team 12: Young People*, London: The Stationery Office.

OFSTED (2002) *Connexions Partnerships: The First Year 2001–2002*, HMI 521, London: OFSTED.

OFSTED (2003) *Connexions: Coventry and Warwickshire*, London: OFSTED.

Robbins, D. (2001) *Transforming Children's Services: An Evaluation of Local Responses to the Quality Protects Programme*, London: Department of Health.

Shaffer, D. (2002) *Developmental Psychology*, Sixth Edition. London, Thomson Learning.

Social Exclusion Unit (SEU) (1998a) *Truancy and Exclusion*, London: The Stationery Office, Cm 3957

Social Exclusion Unit (SEU) (1998b) *Rough Sleeping*, London: The Stationery Office, Cm 4342

Social Exclusion Unit (SEU) (1998c) *Bringing Britain Together: a National Strategy for Neighbourhood Renewal*, London: The Stationery Office, Cm 4045.

Social Exclusion Unit (SEU) (1999a) *Teenage Pregnancy*, London: The Stationery Office, Cm 4342.

Social Exclusion Unit (SEU) (1999b) *Bridging the Gap: New Opportunities for 16–18 year olds not in Education, Employment or Training*, London: The Stationery Office, Cm 4405.

Utting, Sir William, (1997) *People Like Us: The Report of the Review of Safeguards for Children Living Away from Home*, London: The Stationery Office.

11
Education and Training Provision
For Young People: A New Era?

Stanley Tucker and Steve Walker

Education systems change over time and space (Archer, 1982). Nothing could be simpler or more obvious than that. But if we think about this assertion again, we will recognise that changes in the provision of education, schooling and training sometimes seem to be cosmetic refinements and at other times take the form of seismic reformations. Each one of them, however, has serious consequences for those working in schools and colleges – for students, for support specialists, for teachers and parents. To make sense of such transformations, therefore, we need to explore the nature, the motivation and the implications and consequences of change.

In this chapter we present a selective review of educational and training development in England since 1944. The reason for doing this is not merely a fascination with history. Rather, it is because we believe that it is through an understanding of the shifts and revisions in the schooling system in the second half of the twentieth century that we can move towards some understanding of policy for education and training in the first half of the twenty-first century.

Today's education system has its origins in the Church schools of the late nineteenth century, as structured by Acts of Parliament in 1870 and in 1902. Through these Acts emphasis was placed on developing clearly differentiated provision. On one hand, the intention was to provide a basic education grounded in social and moral conformity for the masses. On the other, the aim was to offer high culture, and academic training for the few lucky enough to be selected as embryonic, future 'leaders' of government, the professions and industry, after they had completed their largely private schooling and their University education. Many educational commentators (Archer, 1982; Bowles and Gintis, 1976; Dale, 1990; Young and Whitty, 1977) assert that this fundamental division, this *inequality of purpose and provision* has been a key feature of English education and training ever since.

'New lamps for old' – a social democratic settlement for education

After World War II, however, the first great educational revolution was enacted. The rebuilding of British society, which was required after the ravages of the war, is popularly referred to as the 'post-war, social-democratic settlement.' The settlement was an unwritten 'social contract' between the State and the citizen. In return for civic responsibility and a positive work discipline, citizens were guaranteed stable employment opportunities, economic growth and a free and comprehensive welfare provision – which included a right to quality education and training – the benefits of the Welfare State. A very significant element in the 'settlement' was the 1944 Education Act , which 'created a framework within which political equilibrium, economic activity and social improvement would be balanced.' (Middlemas, 1986).

The 1944 Education Act was the 'Butler Act' – named after R.A.B. Butler, the social democrat Minister of Education who designed the legislation. It provided both the ideological and the structural platform on which the provision of education and training was grounded for the ensuing 40 years. Under the provision of the Act, schooling for children between the ages of 5 and 14 (later extended to 15, then to 16, and now effectively to 17) was made universal, compulsory and free. The Act paved the way for the construction of the *tripartite* system for secondary education through a process of selecting pupils at the age of 11 for either grammar, modern or technical schools: pupils were to be educated 'according to their age, aptitude and ability'. The Act preserved an historic State-Church agreement under which Church-managed schools and colleges were funded by the State. It established a new contract between central government (which directed macro-education policies) and local education authorities (which managed micro-educational provision). The education system had a secure and solid foundation. Under the Labour government of Harold Wilson, the 1960s brought the re-organisation of secondary education under comprehensive lines (see Ball, 1990) but the basic structural features of the system remained intact.

It is worthwhile looking at certain principles in the 1944 legislation that shaped how education and training came to be executed in the post-war period. It is also worth considering whether or not these principles still underpin the provision for education and training in our 'modernised' system of the twenty-first century. Under the provision of the 1944 Act, school students with academic potential were held in higher status than those with either vocational or more diffuse talents. Only about 18% of children were 'selected' for the grammar school, which provided an educational pathway to university and for entry into the professions (Halsey, 1982). By the same token, vocational education was presented as the poor relation. The 'new' technical schools were few and far between. More importantly, the 'modern schools' – for so-called 'non-academic pupils' who had *failed* the scholarship examinations for 10 year olds, in English, Maths and General Intelligence – provided a lowly-rated general education. Importantly, however, the Act gave an enormous degree of freedom for schools, teachers and LEAs to devise and develop the curriculum, in both the primary and secondary sectors, in ways they thought relevant to the needs of the children in their educational care.

The 'Great Debate'

The first tremor to disturb the relative equilibrium of the system came from the Labour Prime Minister, the Rt. Hon. James Callaghan, in 1976. In a speech at Ruskin College, Oxford (ironically, the 'Trade's Union College'), Callaghan raised some questions about whether or not the education system as a whole was providing the State and society with what was needed, and in this speech Callaghan launched the 'Great Debate' about education. The debate significantly introduced a radical right-wing imagination and determination into educational discourse. The system for education and training was attacked by those who managed it for failing to prepare young people for the needs of industry, for failing to achieve high standards of learning and for allowing 'trendy, left-wing teachers and youth leaders' to nurture indiscipline and dissatisfaction in young minds. The solution was a turn to the Right. In their analysis of educational policy at this 1970s–80s roundabout, Walker and Barton (1987) identify the new radicalism being injected into educational thinking and into the practices introduced into schools and colleges:

> 'Current policy is radical', they contend, because it aims at establishing certain limited visions of what schools are designed to accomplish, at asserting certain educational priorities. In the vast majority of policy initiatives directed towards education since 1980, it is easy to detect the deliberate and determined application of a *'market ideology'* as the major perceptual framework for education planning and evaluation. This ideology is most obvious in the relentless drive to direct educational spending, the curriculum and teaching processes into explicitly vocational and instrumental pathways'.
>
> (Walker and Barton, 1987: xi)

In 1979, the Rt. Hon. Margaret Thatcher was elected as Prime Minister and began a series of reform projects that were to shake English education and training to their roots. Promising greater parental choice and more involvement in schooling by industrialists and agents from the private sector, the Thatcher administration embarked upon a series of 'modest reforms'. These included new entitlements for students with special educational needs in 1981, and the Assisted Places Scheme in 1985, through which working class pupils were sponsored to attend private schools. A new formal contract and specific conditions of service for school teachers was also introduced in 1986.

In the early 1980s, educational policy discourse was swamped with acronyms and neologisms. We were given TVEI the Technical and Vocational Education Initiative – to provide low-skilled work experience for those 14–16 year old students judged to be 'non-academic'. We were introduced to the MSC , the Manpower Service Commission – charged with linking schooling to industrial training. Other gifts from the government were YOPs and the YTSs, which were the Youth Opportunities Programmes and Youth Training Schemes aimed at bridging the gap between school and work for those without any worthwhile qualifications. There were many more – now dead on the files of the Department for Education and Science (DES) or the Department of Education and Employment (DfEE) as it became. This last shift in the nomenclature for the Ministry of Education gives us an important clue to a key element of the Thatcher project that was to be preserved and subsequently re-enforced by Prime Ministers Major and Blair.

On one hand, education and training were firmly separated by structural arrangements and through a differentiated curriculum in schools and Further Education colleges. Education equipped people for the professions and for the public services and training provided for those destined for low-skill, low status work in the ever-shrinking industrial sectors, or for unemployment. On the other hand, vocational education was relentlessly championed in policy speeches and innovations as the priority for developing and improving the secondary phase of schooling – especially refreshing those parts of schooling that were providing education or training for the 'less able'. This division continues to bind educational provision in the twenty-first century, as we will reveal shortly.

A New ERA?

1988 marked the dawn of the new era. Buoyed-up by a re-election in 1987, Margaret Thatcher and her New Right administration embarked on the most radical shake-up of the education system that could be imagined. Some think it was brave and innovative and some think it was a disaster and conservative – but it was certainly radical. The shake-up took the form of the Education Reform Act of 1988, an important piece of legislation in the New Right marketisation programme for the modernisation of the economy and of society in general. The legislation drove English education round a right-hand turn that was comprehensive and internally cohesive. The Reform Act introduced a National Curriculum for schools in England and Wales and a national 'testing' system. It provided for schools to control their own budgets, through the Local Management of Schools (LMS) initiative and it purported to increase parental choice of schools by ruling that all schools should enact a policy of 'Open Enrolment'. It introduced a system whereby schools could opt out of LEA control and receive funding directly from central government by becoming Grant Maintained or Foundation schools. It increased the representation and the roles of parents on school governing bodies. In what might be described as 'a fit of New Right revenge' on local politics, it abolished the Inner London Education Authority – hitherto the biggest and most influential educational management group outside government. And as a by-product, it spawned the creation of a new, non-elected regulatory body – the Office for Standards in Education (OFSTED) – charged with the responsibility to inspect, to guarantee and to improve national 'standards' of education performance in every school.

The National Curriculum, the centre-piece of the legislation, was made statutory in 1988, after a brief period of consultation between July and September, when most teachers and educators were on holiday. It is an awesome edifice, obliging schools, teachers and governors, by statute, to meet specific curriculum requirements. It is subject-based, distinguishing between Core subjects – English, Maths, Science and ICT – and the lower-status Foundation subjects. It is age-specific and assessment driven – dividing the learning careers of young people in school into four Key Stages and providing for nationally set and marked tests of attainment (SATs) at the end of each Key Stage for pupils at the ages of 7, 11, 14 and 16. It is centrally planned, written and managed. It has, more recently, been supplemented by National Literacy and Numeracy Strategies which not only prescribe what teachers should teach but the teaching techniques and methods that they should follow to 'deliver' the menu. Conformity is ensured by a rigorous regime of school inspection by OFSTED and the annual publication of the SATs results in the form of league tables showing school performance by rank. Thus, it represents the centralisation of educational management in its most extreme form.

By contradiction, many other aspects of the reform agenda are designed to inject 'market principles' into the running and regulation of schooling. Open enrolment means schools and colleges compete for 'clients' or 'customers' (in other words, children). Local Management of Funds means that schools buy from the private sector to run a public service and the publication of league tables is deliberately designed to allow parents to choose the 'best' schools, a choice often only available to those who can afford it. Such reforms represent the privatisation of educational provision in a very explicit form.

How can we explain the apparent contradiction between the two trends of increased centralisation and increased privatisation? A useful explanation is offered by Andrew Gamble (1989) in his analysis of the politics of Thatcherism:

> . . . the New Right has two major strands; a liberal tendency which argues the case for a freer, more open, and more competitive economy, and a conservative tendency which is more interested in restoring social and political authority throughout society.
>
> (Gamble, 1989: 29)

'Old/New Wine' – the 14–19 Programme

The 'Great Debate' begun by Prime Minister Callaghan rumbles on. Strains of the debate concerning the competitive edge of the UK economy and the skill and knowledge capabilities of the country's young people have emerged yet again in recent policy deliberations. Nowhere has this been more clearly illustrated than in discussions around the need to create specific 14–19 education and training initiatives aimed at upskilling young people – socially, vocationally and economically. Yet the drive to bring about significant change does not stop there, for this particular agenda is underscored by New Labour concerns about social exclusion and inclusion, about class driven advantage in terms of educational achievement and entry into higher education, and about the number of young people who enrol in further and higher education (*Guardian*, 2003).

Debates about the need to promote vocationally based education and training for working class youth (and working class young men in particular) have a long history in the UK. For example, Neary (1997) outlines how 'short courses' lasting between 5–12 weeks, 'Juvenile Instruction Centres' ('Dole Schools'), 'Juvenile Transfer Camps' and 'Juvenile Transfer Schemes' were introduced between 1918 and the mid 1930s to increase the 'adaptability' and employability of the young. Neary, using a quote from a Ministry of Labour report, captures the spirit of one such initiative thus:

> . . . the course of instruction is arranged with a view to improving their prospects of taking employment in the new area and includes organised games, gardening and instruction in woodwork and metal work.
> (Ministry of Labour, 1935, in Neary, 1997: 5556)

Over time then, government interest in youth training emerges and re-emerges as a consistent theme of political discourse. Sometimes that discourse is informed by concerns over high levels of youth unemployment and the need to 'soak up' surplus labour. At other times the debate has focused on the 'white heat of technology' and employer demands to refocus the curriculum development aspirations of both secondary and tertiary education. For example, during the 1960s the Federation for British Industry published its *Industry for Schools* (1965) report linking a failure to attract 'abler students' to the fact that 'schoolteachers neither knew nor understood the industrial and commercial environment in which most of their pupils would need to work' (Reeder, 1981: 192). The emphasis of the debate then, has reflected industrial concerns that the world of education does not understand its needs, with young people leaving school without the skill, aptitude and outlook required by employers. For the CBI (Confederation of British Industry) that requirement translated itself into the demand for a 16–19 curriculum that emphasised the need to develop a range of core transferable skills (CBI, 1993).

The challenge of producing such a curriculum has fermented over the last decade. Essentially the core skills debate has continued to occupy the thinking of policy makers and educationalists at all levels. Various groups and organisations from the Manpower Services Commission through to the National Curriculum Council, have pronounced on the need to define the nature of pre- and post-16 education and the requirement to promote a wider core skills agenda (see for example DES, 1989; NCC, 1990). So, it should come as no surprise to see the re-emergence of such ideas in recent New Labour policy developments.

Yet in one very specific way the agenda has changed. For the core skills debate has been rearticulated to embrace New Labour concerns about social inclusion, widening participation and justice. The 14–19 agenda for education and training is presented at a policy level as an attempt to enhance the employ-ability of young people while at the same time offering clear opportunities for progression from secondary to further and then on to higher education. There remains concern on the part of government that the participation rate in higher education is low when compared with the United States and other European countries. For example, the proportion of the population within the 25 to 65 age range educated to first degree level in the UK is 18% as compared to 28% in the US. There is also fear that unless young people are upskilled the significant expansion of higher education in the US as well as China and India will produce a widening of the 'competitive gap' in economic terms. Yet for the Secretary of State for Education this debate has to be linked back into wider concerns about class-based social exclusion:

> There is a big social issue here. The sad fact is that those from the top three social classes are almost three times as likely to enter higher education as those from the bottom three, and the gap has not narrowed – if anything it has widened.
> (Clarke cited in the *Guardian*, 2003)

In order to bring about change it is argued that both the systems and philoso-phies underpinning the development of 14-19 education have to radically change. Greater flexibility is required in terms of what is taught, approaches to learning and teaching, and the linking of secondary and tertiary provision. Specific courses and programmes of study need to be 'sold' to young people in terms of their relevance to the world of work. Approaches to curriculum devel-opment and assessment should foster the growth of key skills such as problem-solving and analysis. Specialising from the age of 14 should be encour-aged to allow young people to move on to higher level courses with the necessary amount of underpinning knowledge and skills.

Although these ideas are wrapped around with the discourse of New Labour in terms of the prominence given to matters of exclusion and social justice, many old themes dominate. The policy agenda is one that continues to be inspired by long-standing concerns about the 'deficiencies' of young people (Griffin, 1997). Disengagement from learning is portrayed in terms of 'low expectations', 'disaffection' and a failure to 'reach their full potential'. The learn-ing of a trade is still not valued. As part of the 'new/old' approaches to the development of education and training it is argued that emphasis should be placed on building on the English and Mathematics skills provided initially through primary schooling, the creation of an 'appropriate qualifications frame-work for the 14-19 phase', and more efficient approaches to the management of the education system (Full information on the proposals can be found at: www.dfes.gov.uk DfES, (2003c)). At the time of writing it is difficult to speculate what will happen in terms of the development of the 14–19 agenda, yet what does appear certain is that a new era of reform seems likely.

Trust the community – the management of schools

The election of a New Labour government in 1997 brought significant ideological challenges on how to improve the management of the education system. In many ways the agenda of the previous Conservative government in this area had been a radical one. This approach to educational management reflected wider political ambitions to 'roll back the state' and thereby reduce the influence of local government when it came to shaping educational policy (Johnson, 1991). In addition, the Conservative government looked towards overhauling the system of school governance by increasing parental and business involvement while at the same time decreasing the level of political nominations through local education authorities (LEAs). At one level the Conservative government agenda was self evident – to reduce the power of LEAs, particularly those in Labour controlled local authorities.

The dilemma facing New Labour was a complex one. A blueprint for school governance had been put in place that was largely popular. Parental involvement in particular fitted the wider concerns of the government to promote activities that would foster a strong sense of community development and extend opportunities for local decision making. Ringing in the ears of New Labour were also the media-sensitive activities of 'Labour-Left' local authorities and their concerns to promote equal opportunities through the education system. For example, there had been a sensationalised response to the banning of specific books and nursery rhymes in schools highlighted as carrying discriminatory messages (for further analysis see Gyford, 1985). Yet at the same time the government wanted to 'bring back into the fold' the former Grant Maintained schools, reassert at some level at least the importance of the co-ordinating and management functions of local education authorities and encourage the efficient management of resources through school governing bodies. These have all continued to be challenging areas for New Labour in terms of the development of educational policy.

Nowhere has the challenge been greater within educational policy making than in the area of school governance and the demand of the government to directly influence the constitution and management functions of governing bodies. School governors are being increasingly asked to enlarge the nature of their 'core business' activities; to transform themselves, for example, into 'Extended Schools' where 'extended activities and services' are offered for students, parents and carers, and members of the local community (DfES, 2003a). In order to make schools more representative in terms of those entitled to sit on governing bodies Statutory Guidance has recently been published in England to create a new framework for governance that provides parents on 'community school' governing bodies with 'at least one third' of the total representation available. Community and LEA appointed governors will share a similar proportion of representatives (one-fifth for both groups) and staff governance will include both teaching and support staff (DfES, 2003b). On top of all this, responsibilities for financial management, the appointment and discipline of staff, letting of tenders and the monitoring of curriculum developments has substantially increased. Governors are becoming increasingly accountable to bodies such as OFSTED for the efficient and effective management of their schools.

In many ways the government has taken its political inheritance from the previous Conservative administration and moulded it to suit its own agenda. Parental involvement and the promotion of 'parent power' remains a central theme in policy making terms. The mechanism of school governance is used to promote ideas of decentralisation and the enhancement of local decision-making through 'stakeholder' involvement. The stakeholders in this case being represented through the various parties sitting on a governing body. However, the role of political nominees in school governance appears to be decreasing.

A new era for young people?

Education systems change over time and place. We might expect then that, after 130 years of public education, the twenty-first century could herald the dawn of a new era for young people in Britain in the provision for them of their education and their training. But what is new? Sadly, current patterns of provision look remarkably similar to those in place at the end of the nineteenth century. A new era? We don't think so.

Note

The authors and editors with to acknowledge Ron Westerby's contribution to this chapter. Ron wrote a similar chapter for the first edition of this book.

References

Archer, M.S. (1982) *The Social Origins of Educational Systems*, London: Sage Publications.

Bowles, S. and Gintis, H. (1976) *Schooling in Capitalist America*, London: RKP.

Ball, S.J. (1990) *Politics and Policy-making in Education*, London: Routledge.

Confederation of British Industry (CBI) (1993) *Routes for Success. Careership: a Strategy for all 16–19 Year Old Learning*, London: CBI.

Dale, R.(1990) *The State and Education Policy*, Milton Keynes: Open University Press.

Department of Education and Science (DES) (1989) *Post 16 Education and Training, Core Skills: an HMI paper*, London: HMSO.

Department for Education and Skills (DfES) (2003a), *Spectrum Issue 65 May 2003*, Nottingham: DfES Publications.

Department for Education and Skills (DfES) (2003b), *Statutory Guidance on the School Governance (Constitution) (England) Regulations*, Nottingham, DfES Publications.

Department for Education and Skills (DfES). (2003c) *14–19 Opportunity and Excellence Summary*, DfES, Crown Copyright. www.dfes.gov.uk/14–19/whyreform.shtml

Federation for British Industry (1965) *Industry for Schools*. London: FBI.

Gamble, A. (1989) *The Free Economy and the Strong State: the Politics of Thatcherism*, London: Macmillan.

Griffin, C. (1997) ' Representations of the Young', in Roche, J. and Tucker, S. (eds) *Youth in Society*, London: Sage.

Guardian Newspaper (2003) 'An Ambitious Programme' The education secretary, Charles Clarke, outlines the government's proposals for 14–19 and higher education, the *Guardian*, 20 January 2003.

Gyford, J. (1985) *The Politics of Local Socialism*, London: Allen and Unwin.

Halsey, A.H. (1982) *Origins and Destinations*, Oxford: OUP.

Johnson, R. (1991) 'A Road to Serfdom, a Critical History of the 1988 Act', in *Education Limited, Schooling and Training and the New Right Since 1979*, Education Group 11, Department of Cultural Studies, University of Birmingham, London: Unwin Hyman.

Middlemas, K. (1986) *Power, Competition and the State*, London: Macmillan.

National Curriculum Council (NCC) (1990) *Core Skills 16–19: A Response to the Secretary of State*, York: NCC.

Neary, M. (1997) *Youth Training and the Training State*, London: Macmillan.

Reeder, D. (1981), 'A recurring debate: education and training', in R. Dale, G. Esland, R. Fergusson and M. MacDonald (eds) *Schooling and the National Interest*, Basingstoke: Falmer Press.

Young, M. and Whitty, G. (1977) *Society, State and Schooling*, Lewes: Falmer Press.

Walker, S. and Barton, L. (eds) (1987) *Changing Policies, Changing Schools: New Directions for Schooling?*, Milton Keynes: Open University Press.

12

Beyond Bricks and Mortar
Joe Oldman

This chapter discusses what we mean by homelessness and examines some of the causes of youth homelessness. It assesses the housing options available to young people and considers whether special initiatives can offer any long-term solutions. It then looks at the crucial role the benefits system has played and continues to play in affecting youth homelessness and poverty and the way in which resettlement services have attempted to break long-term patterns of homelessness. Finally, it examines some recent policy developments and their potential impact on young people.

During the late 1960s and early 1970s housing pressure groups, such as Shelter and CHAR (Housing Campaign for Single People), argued that homelessness was primarily caused by a decline in the availability of decent affordable housing, combined with rising unemployment and low income. The culmination of lobbying resulted in the Housing (Homeless Persons) Act 1977. This placed responsibility for specific categories of homeless people with local housing authorities, rather than social services. Today the majority of young people still need and desire a place of their own and a decent job. A Department of Environment survey found:

> Single homeless people felt that the problems of homelessness could only be solved by changes to housing and social security policies to improve housing opportunities to single people or by improved employment opportunities. (Anderson et al., 1993)

Is youth homelessness a problem associated with housing supply, employment and levels of income? The withdrawal of benefit from the majority of 16 and 17 year olds in September 1988 saw a visible increase in the numbers of young homeless people forced to sleep rough. The Children Act 1989 recognised that the causes and the consequent experience of homelessness leave young people prone and vulnerable on a number of levels. They are affected mentally, physically, and emotionally, and are exposed to drugs, petty crime, violence and sexual abuse. This demands a response that goes beyond a purely housing model.

Measuring youth homelessness

What is homelessness? The government has placed increasing emphasis on equating single homelessness with rooflessness, that is street homelessness. This definition provided the framework for a government initiative on homelessness, the Rough Sleepers Initiative (RSI), which directed resources into temporary and permanent accommodation for homeless people in Central London. Although rough sleeping is the most extreme form of homelessness it still represents only a small percentage of the total homeless population. The majority of young homeless people find themselves in hostels, bed and breakfast (B&B) hotels, squats, staying with friends, and other forms of temporary accommodation, rather than on the streets. By gradually shifting the definition of homelessness the government has claimed to be effective by tackling the most visible and popularly perceived manifestation of the problem. A more sensitive definition of homelessness encompasses factors concerned with a lack of decent, affordable, and secure accommodation. It would then include young people in poor, insecure, and overcrowded housing as well as those forced to stay with friends and relatives, whose homelessness tends to remain hidden. The adoption of this definition would have implications going far beyond one based simply on rooflessness.

Official homelessness statistics

The main source of homelessness statistics are the quarterly figures released by the Department of the Environment (DoE). These statistics are collected from housing authorities and monitor action taken by homeless people under the Housing Act 1985, Part III. They show the number of households who are accepted as homeless and who have demonstrated a 'priority need'. Those falling into the priority need category include households with children, but mostly exclude single people. Young people can be accepted as homeless if they are considered to be 'vulnerable' and are unable to fend for themselves. But individual local authorities vary in the interpretation of their obligations toward young people under the Housing Act and this has created contradictions in relation to their duties under the Children Act 1989. In addition to these legal filters there are also barriers relating to the administration of homeless persons units (who receive homeless applicants) and the quality of advice and assistance they are able to offer to young people. In 1992 housing authorities in England accepted 141,860 households as homeless. It was estimated that this represented in the region of 412,000 individuals which includes 200,000 children. These figures excluded the 250,280 households who applied as homeless but were turned away (Hutson and Liddiard, 1994). In 1994 acceptances fell to 122,660 households although no figures were provided for applications (Department of Employment, 1995). This decline can partly be explained by local authorities further restricting acceptances as housing resources diminish rather than any meaningful downward trend.

The government has also attempted to measure homelessness through the 1991 census. The census, with the co-operation of many housing agencies, counted the number of homeless people sleeping rough at 444 identified sites around the country, on a rainy night in April. It found 2,845 people sleeping rough in England and Wales, of which 1,275 were in London. This underestimated the problem because it failed to take account of long-term patterns and seasonal variations in levels of homelessness, and was unable to count people sleeping rough in derelict buildings, parks, and less visible or accessible sites. For example, in Birmingham the census found nobody sleeping rough, but a second study by the University of Central England, using a different methodology, found 61 people sleeping rough (Oldman and Hooton, 1993).

More recently the DoE commissioned a detailed report entitled simply *Single Homeless People* (Anderson et al., 1993), which involved a survey of 1,346 living in hostels or B&B for single homeless people, 351 users of day centres who were sleeping rough, and 156 users of soup runs who were sleeping rough. In regard to young homeless people its findings included the following:

1   Over two-fifths of young adults in hostels and B&Bs had slept rough in the previous 12 months. Seven out of ten were currently looking for accommodation.
2   A large minority of young adults in hostels and B&Bs, but particularly those aged under 18, had stayed at some point in a children's home or with foster parents.
3   A large minority of those aged between 18 and 24 had been in a young offenders' institution, prison or remand centre.

Generally official statistics have failed to recognise the problems of disadvantaged groups such as women and black and ethnic minority groups, whose homelessness often remains hidden. This is because young women are more likely to stay in unwanted relationships, or stay with friends and relatives. Young black people are also more likely to stay with friends and relatives in poor overcrowded accommodation rather than find themselves on the street, where they are more likely to be exposed to racism, harassment and violence.

Many local agencies working with young people do not collect statistics (although more are being compelled to do so through pressure from funders). Where agencies do collect statistics it is difficult to arrive at any aggregate figures because different agencies use different criteria and methodologies in collecting them. However, many agencies for young people, such as Centrepoint, have seen a dramatic increase in demand for their services. It has been reported that 'in 1994 over 1,400 young homeless people were admitted to Centrepoint hostels for the first time. Over 600 were under 18 years old.'

The causes of youth homelessness

Many young homeless people are forced to leave the parental home by a variety of 'push factors'. These may include violence, physical and sexual abuse, eviction, family breakdown, and arguments with step-parents. Research carried out by CHAR found that 4 in 10 young homeless women had been sexually abused. Changes in the payment of benefits to young people have placed a severe strain on families and are another contributory factor in pushing young people to leave home. The situation can be equally bleak for young people leaving care who may find they do not have the ability or skills to live independently, and without employment or support mechanisms they are much more likely to find themselves homeless. Many long-term homeless people have previously been in some form of institutional care and have found themselves isolated and lacking the social support provided by friends, relatives and work colleagues that is often taken for granted.

The main cause of youth homelessness is a lack of cheap housing combined with rising unemployment and low pay. Homelessness creates a vicious circle of no home no job, no job no home. A lack of economic power makes it difficult for young people to leave home at a time when it is natural for them to seek independence. Housing options for young people have become increasingly limited. Over the last 20 years there has been a steady decline in the construction of new local authority homes. Local authority house building figures have dropped from a peak of 105,200 in 1976 to 2,900 in 1992. This has been accompanied by a reduction in housing investment and financial restrictions that have stopped local authorities from reinvesting the income from the sale of council homes (under the Right to Buy) to replenish the housing stock.

In the past housing associations have been able to provide some housing to young single people but this has changed because of the increasing pressure on housing associations to cater for 'statutory' homeless people. Although the building of housing association homes has increased it has not compensated for the decline in local authority housing. In addition housing associations have been forced to secure a higher percentage of funding from private sources which has led to higher rents. These rents are difficult for low income groups to meet unless they receive full housing benefit.

The government has promoted the expansion of private rented accommodation as a significant source of accommodation for homeless people. Despite this there are many barriers to young people gaining access to the sector. Some landlords are reluctant to take on benefit claimants and usually ask for a deposit against property damage, and also rent in advance. Some local authorities and voluntary agencies have set up rent deposit schemes to get round this problem. The lack of mandatory regulations governing standards in private rented accommodation means that many vulnerable single homeless people find themselves in the poorest, most overcrowded parts of the sector. Restrictions in housing benefits are making this form of accommodation more difficult to sustain. Young black people face additional barriers as the result of prejudice and discrimination, and although the problem is more acute in the private rented sector it applies across all housing tenures.

Hostels and the 'foyer system'

Increasing numbers of young homeless people have little hope of finding permanent accommodation and find themselves trapped within the hostel system. Some young people are reluctant to use hostels for a number of reasons. These may range from poor standards, violence, restrictive regulations, and refusal to accommodate couples, to rules banning young people with dogs. Although proportionately there are more homeless young women compared with young men, this is not reflected in the availability of hostel bedspaces. Although some hostels set aside bedspaces for homeless women, they may not be prepared to use a mixed facility, especially if they have been exposed to male violence as part of their experiences of homelessness. There is also insufficient provision for gay men and lesbians who may have become homeless as the result of prejudice and discrimination. For all homeless people using the hostel system their concern is with having a self-contained room with some prospect of being resettled into permanent accommodation. As resources become more scarce hostels are restricting the client groups they are prepared to accommodate. They are more reluctant to accommodate young people with drink or drug problems or those with mental health or behavioural problems, who often end up on the streets.

The 'foyer' hostel is an idea that has been imported from the French hostel system for young people. Foyers are designed to provide cheap accommodation, in a communal setting, with the expectation that young people will follow employment and training schemes. It has been argued that foyers should provide a similar form of transition to independence offered to young people leaving home and entering higher education. The response to foyers has been mixed, partly because there is no clearly recognised definition of what they should offer. Greatest criticism has been directed at the concept of linking the provision of accommodation with the requirement to take up employment or training schemes. Centrepoint say: 'Foyers will only work if they are part of a range of options for young people. They are ill-equipped to deal with young people who have multiple problems to resolve before they begin work. Foyers should be slotted in at the preventative end of the scale' (Snape, 1992).

The emphasis on temporary accommodation may distract from the need for permanent long-term accommodation, although some form of supported hostel accommodation may provide a useful first step toward more permanent accommodation.

Rough Sleepers Initiative

The Rough Sleepers Initiative was set up in 1990 and provided £96 million over three years to supply temporary hostel places, and permanent move-on accommodation, to those with a history of rough sleeping. This was extended for a further three years in 1993 with the allocation of an additional £86 million. The government was placed under pressure to introduce the initiative by the rise in the numbers of young vulnerable people, as a result of benefit changes introduced in 1988, forced to sleep rough. The government has recently made a commitment to extending the Rough Sleepers Initiative outside London. Despite its limitations this extension at least recognises that street homelessness does exist outside London and the South East. A recent government White Paper on housing states the aim of eradicating street homelessness over the next 10 years, but it is still unclear how this can be achieved without reforms to the benefit system and a systematic programme of investment in the supply of affordable housing.

Impact of benefit changes

There have been a series of benefit changes since the 1980s that have systematically eroded the position of young people and directly contributed to an increase in youth homelessness. In September 1988 the government restricted the ability of 16–17 year olds to claim income support and introduced differential rates of benefit according to age. The introduction of these policies was based on the view that the benefits system encouraged young people to leave home, leading to the breakup of the family. In reality these policies had the opposite effect to their supposed intentions. By increasing the financial burden on the family they have created a greater likelihood of family disintegration. The government position seems to be based on a stereotypical view of young people that either ignores or misunderstands the true causes of their homelessness.

The majority of 16–17 year olds no longer receive income support. Instead they are expected to take up a Youth Training (YT) place with an allowance, and stay with their family or relatives. In reality, despite government promises to guarantee a place on a YT scheme, many young people have been unable to obtain a place. Young people in this position, or who have been forced to leave home, must show they are in 'severe hardship' before they can receive benefit. Severe hardship payments are discretionary, with no right of appeal, and mostly limited to eight weeks, after which an applicant must reapply. The system is complex and bureaucratic and young people are often dissuaded from applying: 78% of unemployed 16 and 17 year olds do not claim benefit (McCluskey, 1994).

The introduction of new restrictions in January 1996 means that housing benefit will no longer cover the payment of market rents. This is likely to result in evictions and a further reluctance by landlords to receive young people on benefits. Where full benefit is paid it does not cover fuel charges, cleaning, meals and furniture which must be paid for at the lower rate of income support. In some cases social services are compelled to pay top-up payments to allow young people to get by. There are often long delays in the payment of housing benefit which creates arrears and can also result in eviction. The rate at which housing benefit is withdrawn from young people who find employment creates a poverty trap because they may find themselves financially worse off than when they were claiming. These problems will be further compounded in October 1996 with proposals to introduce rules to restrict rates of housing benefit for young people to the level paid for bedsits and shared accommodation as opposed to self-contained accommodation. This will adversely affect many self-contained supportive schemes for young people and will place a greater financial burden on local services. Additionally in October 1996 the government will be introducing a lower rate of unemployment benefit (Job Seekers Allowance) for young people between 18 and 25.

Resettlement for young people

Resettlement is concerned with providing suitable accommodation, and attempts to provide support for the homeless young person. This support is provided within the context of allowing a young person to sustain a home rather than taking individual problems as the starting-point. The effects of homelessness may include mental and physical health problems, anxiety and depression, alcohol and drug misuse, involvement in crime or prostitution, loneliness or a lack of confidence. Resettlement attempts to address both the practical and the emotional issues that homeless people face, acting as a link service to put young people in contact with more specialist agencies such as drug or alcohol counselling.

Hostel providers often help with the resettlement process and may provide separate space within the hostel that helps young people to practise independent living skills. Alternatively there is increasing interest in 'floating support schemes'. This means that rather than resettlement being associated with a particular property or location it can provide support for homeless people in a variety of locations, allowing greater continuity in the support they receive.

Resettlement helps young people to gain and maintain accommodation, and through listening and negotiation it should identify and deliver individual support needs. Ideally it should offer a range from fully independent accommodation to that with a high level of support and special facilities. In general terms resettlement is a process which is able to offer young people ongoing support in securing a home and living independently. However, as housing options become more limited, resettlement is inevitably becoming more resource-led than needs-led.

Recent developments

The government is in the process of dismantling the existing homelessness legislation contained in Part III of the Housing Act 1985. These changes have been introduced against a background of Conservative Party attacks on young single parents accused of queue jumping on housing authority waiting lists. There is no evidence to support this position, and in fact government commissioned research has shown that 74% of those rehoused as homeless have already been on a waiting list. The changes will mean that any of those groups currently accepted as being in 'priority need' will only be offered temporary accommodation for 12 months, after which the local authority will review the case. It will mean that vulnerable young people will no longer have access to secure accommodation.

References

Anderson, I., Kemp, P. and Quilgars, D. (1993) *Single Homeless People*, Department of the Environment, London: HMSO.

Department of Employment (1995) 'Households found accommodation under the homelessness provisions of the 1995 Housing Act: England', DoE Information Bulletin.

Hutson, S. and Liddiard, M. (1994) *Youth Homelessness: the Construction of a Social Issue*, London: Macmillan.

McCluskey, J. (1994) *Breaking the Spiral: Ten Myths on the Children Act and Youth Homelessness*, London: CHAR.

Oldman, J. and Hooton, S. (1993) *The Numbers Game: Lessons from Birmingham*, London: CHAR.

Snape, V.B. (1992) *Foyers: What Young People Think*, London: Centrepoint and the Young Homelessness Group.

13
In and Out of Work? The Changing Fortunes of Young People in Contemporary Labour Markets

Harriet Bradley and Paul Hickman

Research into the labour market position of young people has highlighted dramatic changes over the past four decades. The pathways by which young school leavers enter the labour market are now more complex and varied. There has been a big fall in the numbers of young people in full-time employment and a massive growth in the numbers staying in full-time education. Youth unemployment has become a fact of life and a focus of social concern across Europe. Moreover, the prospects for young people entering the contemporary labour market are very different from those of their parents' generation. They are more likely to enter part-time or casual work, more likely to shift from job to job for many years and they enter new types of jobs. Where young men in the 1960s and 1970s often entered apprenticeships or took jobs as unskilled manual workers, their twenty-first century counterparts are more likely to go into catering, retail or other forms of unskilled service work. Young women may continue to enter some of the caring jobs that their mothers undertook, but those with qualifications are choosing to compete with their qualified male contemporaries for professional and managerial opportunities.

Lengthened transitions: The complex route from school to work

Thus, what youth researchers call 'the transition from school to work' has been transformed. An influential study published in the 1970s set out a model of three distinct pathways to employment. These were the 'extended careers' of those entering higher education prior to competing in the professional and managerial arena; 'short-term' careers available to lower middle and upper working class youths, and 'careerless' routes involving entry to unskilled jobs (Ashton and Field, 1976). Since the 1970s this pattern of transition has altered in two important ways. First, the *lengthened* nature of youth transitions has been highlighted by many commentators (for example, Hollands, 1990; Furlong and Cartmel, 1997). This is in part caused by the expansion of both higher and further education but is also due to the longer time it takes young people of all backgrounds to settle down into a steady 'career path'. For example, many students on completing undergraduate degrees will take temporary low-skilled employment in bars, restaurants and call-centres. This is sometimes as a way to make money for travel or further study and sometimes as a way to find out a little more about the world of employment and their own capacities before launching themselves into a more 'serious' career trajectory. Second, transitions have become more precarious and more complex. Young people's individual trajectories often take the form of movements in and out of various work statuses: study, temporary employment, unemployment, training, self-employment, part-time or full-time employment, 'fiddly jobs' in the unofficial economy (MacDonald, 1994). They may undertake several of these at once. Thus, there is no longer any sense of a simple linear pathway from youth to adult employment and economic independence.

Two decades of economic change

These changing prospects for young people in the labour market have to be understood within the context of major restructuring of the UK economy. Since the 1970s the proportion of jobs in manufacturing has declined sharply. In 1971 33.4% of employment was in manufacturing. By 2001 this had fallen to 16.6%, while over the same period employment in business and miscellaneous services had risen from 10.3% of total employment to 22.9% (Warwick Institute for Employment Research, 1995). This trend is continuing, with more new jobs being generated in services.

This pattern is typical of most of the highly developed economies of the West, and is often referred to as 'post-industrialism' (Bradley, 1996). Steady employment growth in the service sector is due to a number of factors. Heightened international competition and the availability of cheaper labour in other parts of the globe has led to the relocation of much industrial production to the developing societies. The ageing of the population, a common trend across Europe, brings increased demand for personal care services. There are also noticeable lifestyle changes, linked to the increasing employment of women and to higher levels of disposable income in some households. Activities such as eating out, holidays and sporting or leisure pursuits have become more widespread. Also, many aspects of services originally covered by the public sector have been reduced or privatised, leading, for example, to the development of private training agencies, care homes and nursery provision. Consequently, there has been considerable growth in caring professions, leisure industries, hotels and catering and business services.

The application of new forms of sophisticated technology, especially that based on computers, has precipitated the need for more technically based experts. Indeed another term which has become a popular description for contemporary change is 'the knowledge-based economy' (Leadbeater, 1999). This idea has been taken up by the New Labour government and is the basis of their policy thinking on education, training and skills. It is believed that the UK suffers from a lack of highly trained people skilled in the new technology (Bradley et al., 2000). The resultant change in the occupational structure is shown in Table 13.1.

Young people then, are entering into what has been termed the 'new economy'. Many new jobs are seen to offer less good conditions and prospects than the jobs of the post-war economy. Part-time employment has increased steadily over the past 20 years and working patterns have become more diverse and flexible (among others, see Beatson, 1995). It is estimated that 65% of all jobs in retailing and 55% in hotels and catering are part-time (that is, under 30 hours per week). Where employees have part-time contracts their employment rights are curtailed. As a result many commentators take a sceptical view of the 'new economy' believing that flexibility in the labour market results in the rise of 'McJobs', the loss of 'jobs for life' and fragmented employment histories, with people having to spend more time out of the labour market. Some see these changes as positive, offering more choice, variety and 'empowerment' to employees (Handy, 1994; Leadbeater, 1999), while others believe that they lead to stress, illness and instability, along with tightened managerial control and what Richard Sennett has called the 'corrosion of character' (Aronowitz and DiFazio, 1994; Sennett, 1998). Whichever interpretation is chosen, it is clear that young people in particular are at the sharp end of these changes and are acting as pioneers in these new economic arrangements.

Growth in the service sector, traditionally a site of 'women's work', has changed the gender profile of the workforce. A disproportionate number of these jobs will be part-time, meeting both the needs of employers and women with child care responsibilities. Some employers see women as more suitable for jobs calling for 'customer service skills' and the ability to communicate, as women are considered better at 'people skills' than male workers. Sylvia Walby (1987) has celebrated what she calls a 'gender transformation' in women's lives as they escape from the domestic fate of their mothers' generation and use qualifications to compete with men for the best opportunities. The press often present this as men 'losing out', given the increase in male unemployment; Table 13.1 indicates how some areas of the economy have been feminised over the past decades, with women now making up nearly half of the total workforce. But it is important not to overestimate the effects of feminisation on young women's lives (Bradley et al., 2000). A study of young adult workers carried out in Bristol$_1$ showed that women in the age-group 20–35 earned less than men, were more likely to be in part-time employment, were still inclined to sacrifice their careers to raise children, and did more of the housework.

Unemployment and the decline in youth employment

A key feature of this epoch has been the increase across Europe of unemployment, sometimes long-term in nature. From the 1970s UK unemployment rose

Table 13.1 Occupational structure 1981–2001

	Managers and administrators		Professional occupations		Associate professionals and technical occupations		Clerical and secretarial occupations		Craft and skilled manual occupations		Personal and protective service		Sales occupations		Plant and machine operatives		Other occupations		Total	
	000s	%	000s	%	000s	%	000s	%	000s	%	000s	%	000s	%	000s	%	000s	%	000s	%
Employment Levels																				
1981	2,932	12.1	1,890	7.8	1,743	7.2	4,201	17.4	4,229	17.5	1,668	6.9	1,657	6.9	3,090	12.8	2,742	11.4	2,415	100.0
1991	4,114	16	2,262	8.8	2,283	8.9	4,241	16.5	3,750	14.6	2,211	8.6	1,878	7.3	2,670	10.4	2,247	8.8	25,655	100.0
1994	4,282	17.2	2,291	9.2	2,342	9.4	3,951	15.9	3,418	13.8	2,271	9.1	1,854	7.5	2,453	9.9	1,982	8	24,843	100.0
2001	4,916	18.5	2,710	10.2	2,677	10.1	3,860	14.6	3,325	12.5	2,825	10.7	1,973	7.4	2,451	9.2	1,779	6.7	26,517	100.0
Females as % total employment by occupation																				
1981		23.6		34.2		45.4		72		10.9		62.9		60.7		23.4		50.9		40.5
1991		32.7		39.4		50.3		77.2		11		67.7		65.1		22.3		51.6		45
1994		34.7		41.6		51.6		78.4		12.1		68.9		65.9		22		50.8		46.3
2001		39.4		42.9		53.1		79.7		12.7		71.1		67.2		20.9		47.0		47.9

Source: Review of the Economy and Employment – Occupational Assessment 1995. Institute for Employment Research, University of Warwick

from around half a million in the mid 1970s to over 3 million during the 1980s with the number of young people in employment declining even more sharply. Moreover, youth employment failed to recover during the economic boom of the 1980s and remained high across Europe in the 1990s as Table 13.2 shows.

Table 13.2   *Unemployment rate (%) among under 25s in the EU in the 1990s*

	1990	1991	1997	1998
Austria	–	–	6.7	6.6
Belgium	15.3	14.9	23.0	22.1
Denmark	11.4	11.6	8.4	7.4
Finland	9.2	16.2	25.2	23.5
France	19.3	21.5	29.1	26.6
Germany	–	5.9	10.8	9.8
Greece	21.5	22.9	30.8	29.8
Ireland	19.4	22.4	15.3	11.5
Italy	27.4	26	33.1	33.2
Luxembourg	3.8	3.2	8.1	6.9
Netherlands	8.6	8.3	9.6	7.8
Portugal	10.0	8.8	15.1	10.6
Spain	32.2	31.1	39.1	35.3
Sweden	4.4	7.6	20.6	16.7
UK	10.8	14.4	14.2	13.6

Source: Eurostat, 2000: 148.

Economic improvement in many countries has led to some decline; but although the UK economy has recently demonstrated considerable stability, unemployment among those under 24 is higher than within other age groups. In 2002 rates for the18–24 age group were 12.2% for men and 8.8% for women.

The fall in the numbers of young people going into full-time employment has a number of explanations. At the level of individual firms, the employment prospects of young people have diminished because strategies to cope with difficult conditions in the global market have reduced the demand for young workers. During recessions employers tend to cut back the number of trainees they take on. Since a large proportion of young people enter the labour market as trainees this has a big impact. Another problem is that young people do not have the necessary experience to compete effectively against adults.

At a macro-economic level, they have been victims of the economic and occupational restructuring discussed in the previous section, with formerly full-time occupations replaced by part-time jobs and a rise of all forms of non-standard employment contracts (sub-contract, temporary, seasonal, agency-based working).

The other side of the coin has been the creation of new places in education and training for young people, which has had the effect of delaying their entry into the jobs market. The delegation of budgets through local management of schools has pressured schools to retain students in order to secure funding. The expansion of further and higher education can be seen as making a virtue out of declining youth employment, enabling young people to build up their level of skills and qualifications in order to meet the demands for upskilling in many occupations.

There are considerable ethnic variations in staying-on rates. The Fourth National Survey of Ethnic Minorities in Britain found that all major minority groups were more likely to stay on in full-time education, a trend particularly marked in the 16-24 age group as Table 13.3 shows.

Table 13.3 *Participation in full-time education, 16–24 year olds (percentage in age group) by ethnicity*

	White	Caribbean	Indian/AfricanAsian	Pakistani/Bangladeshi
Men	7	18	38	31
Women	12	18	25	19

Source: Modood et al., 1997

Youth unemployment has unsurprisingly, been highest amongst the most disadvantaged and the least qualified young people who have suffered most from the decline of unskilled manufacturing jobs. Notably, unemployment rates are significantly worse for all minority ethnic 16–24 year olds regardless of their qualifications: 36.9% for Bangladeshis, 24.9 % for Pakistanis, 23.7% for Black Caribbeans, 24.1% for Black Africans and 18.4% for Indian people, compared to 10.9% for white people (Office for National Statistics, 2002).

The least well-qualified young people have also experienced more intense competition from their better-qualified contemporaries who have 'traded down' to the bottom end of the labour market, filling jobs for which they would previously have been considered over-qualified. Whether this loss of employment opportunities has resulted in the growth of an unemployed or underemployed 'underclass' is not a debate that will be entered into here. This trend does, however, raise questions about the growth of the alternative or unofficial economy. Many officially out of work young people may find a source of income in 'fiddly jobs', criminal activity and, particularly, in Britain's thriving drugs sub-culture. Low-level self-employment is another option. There has been a rise in street selling (especially common in Europe among young legal or illegal immigrants) and in craft markets. Young people may also work the popular music festival scene, selling refreshments and New Age artefacts.

Government policy

Governments over the past decades have seen youth unemployment especially among young men, as a threat to social security and stability and have responded with a variety of policies. The Thatcher government, with its commitment to unfettered market forces, believed that young people were pricing themselves out of work by excessive wage rates which had been artificially inflated above the market rate through trade union negotiation and legislative measures. By encouraging lower rates of pay the government believed that employers would be better able to afford to employ more young people. Consequently, between 1982 and 1988 the Young Workers Scheme and the New Workers Scheme offered subsidies to employers who took on young people at rates of pay below the average for that age group. In 1986 young people were removed from the protection of the wages councils that set minimum wages in industries where trade unions were weak.

There is evidence that subsequently the gap between youth and adult earnings has widened. In 1979, 16–17 year old men in full-time work could expect to earn 63.6 % of the wage rate of adult men. By 1995 16–17 year olds were earning 33.9% of the adult wage rate and 18–20 year olds 48.9% (Department of Employment, 1995). In 2001 the average gross weekly wage for full-time workers was £444 (£490 for men and £366 for women). A survey of young adult workers aged 20–34 carried out in the same year in Bristol, a fairly affluent city, revealed that 81% earned less than £444. Moreover nearly half of them (48%) were living on less than £12,000 per year. This reflects the mix of activities people in this age group are doing: low-paid jobs, part-time and casual work, studying and training, relying on benefits. All this suggests that young people find themselves in a precarious economic environment, which certainly makes it difficult to 'settle down and start a family'.

The rise of a low-wage youth economy however, did not bring unemployment to an end. The New Labour government took a different track, focusing on training and the acquisition of skills. They brought back the minimum wage (which many young people are now paid) and started up a series of programmes, starting with the New Deal, designed to help young people into employment. Research suggests that a smooth transition into the labour market is a strong predictor of subsequent labour market stability. The latest programme designed to help young people out of school into employment, education and training, Connexions, deals with 13–19 year olds especially those deemed to be 'failing'. It includes a system of designated personal mentors, working to produce plans tailored to individual needs, and computer tracking of individuals' progress. While it is a universal guidance service for the whole age group, it is targeted especially at those designated as 'at risk'. This is a European trend, with provision increasingly targeted at excluded groups.

An adaptable generation? young people's attitudes and aspirations

How, then, are young people themselves dealing with the problems associated with more precarious, complex and lengthened transitions? Research has shown that most, especially those from disadvantaged class and ethnic groups, still have conventional aspirations for their futures: a steady job, a house, a car and a family (McDowell, 2001; Allatt and Dixon, 2001).

Writing in the mid 1990s, Kenneth Roberts provided a definitive picture of youth employment and unemployment at the time (Roberts, 1995). Noting the trends discussed above, he also drew attention to a significant change in young people's attitudes linked to the increased participation in higher education and to the rise of individualisation, speaking of 'a widespread change . . . the raising of young people's ambitions above their actual employment opportunites' (1995: 105). As young people received more training and qualifications, they expected to find jobs at an equivalent level, but Roberts noted the dearth of 'quality jobs'. He found that young people were increasingly accepting personal individual responsibility for how they got on in life, blaming themselves if they failed to gain their objectives (1995: 116). An individualized stance to life often involves establishing goals and then planning the steps needed to take them. Since these goals were often unrealistic there was a danger of young people being disappointed and frustrated. As Wallace and Kovatcheva observe (1998), young people now tend to attribute failure to lack of training or of diligence. However, Roberts also noted the acceptance of precarious transitions:

> Uncertain futures and risk-taking are also becoming just parts of life for today's youth. That is not to say that many would not prefer greater security, more rapid transitions and better jobs than are actually available. It is simply to note that these problems are now normal
>
> (1995: 122).

Roberts's ideas are supported by the 'Winners and Losers' study[1] which was carried out in Bristol in 2000–2 by Fenton et al., (2002). The young adults in the study had work histories that revealed the precariousness of their situation. Some had held many jobs; others were persistently moving between jobs, study, unemployment and self-employment. Those who chose what the team termed 'alternative careers', for example as creative artists, in the media, in computer design or in the clubbing/DJ scene, were particularly vulnerable, and, as noted above, very few of the young adults earned high salaries. The exception was a minority of about 10%, mainly white men from middle class backgrounds, who were employed in more traditional careers (law, medicine, engineering). But despite this picture of uncertainty, the young adults in the study displayed high levels of satisfaction about their lives and extraordinary optimism about their futures. Acceptance of the value of education and training was also widespread and many young Bristolians were engaged in taking degrees and courses, often at the same time as working.

The researchers suggested that their attitudes could be characterised as 'internal flexibility'. Through their schools, the media, their home lives, they had been prepared for the climate of uncertainty and change. The difference from Roberts's account is that this was not simply a matter of grudging acceptance; many young adults positively embraced the notion of flexibility. They believed that the idea of a 'job for life' was a feature of their parents' generation, and many stated that they would find it boring to stay in one job for years. Even those in the established professions spoke of moving between organisations in order to 'fulfil their potential' and build careers. The findings of the Bristol study indicate that young people are creatively addressing the opportunities as well the pitfalls of flexibility; they may be seen as constituting an 'adaptable generation'.

Conclusions and future prospects

What, then, can today's young people expect from their working lives? As we have seen they are entering more flexibly constructed labour markets and may expect some experience of casual, temporary and part-time jobs. They are likely to have a more fragmented work history than the previous generations, moving between different jobs and occupations, with spells of training and withdrawal from the labour market.

The majority of young people will not enter full-time work until their early 20s, having spent their immediate post-16 years in full-time education or training. Many will work part-time while they study. The minority who enter full-time work will find that in general they will experience low rates of pay.

While these are general trends across the age group, it is important to stress that the fortunes of young people will vary strongly according to gender, ethnicity and class. The trend towards greater participation of women in paid work is well established and is likely to continue as young couples find that two incomes are necessary to maintain a desired lifestyle, particularly in view of the hyper-inflation of the housing market which puts a mortgage beyond the reach of a single low-wage earner. Well-qualified females will have greater opportunities to move into management and professional occupations.

Young people who are not well qualified will have the greatest difficulty in finding full-time employment. They will make up the peripheral workforce in insecure, temporary low-paid employment or will be forced into the twilight world of the alternative economy. The 'Winners and Losers' study demonstrated that class is still the major determinant as to whether young people stay on at school or leave early. Early leavers in the study went on to experience more job changes, lower wages and less skilled work than those who stayed on (Fenton et al., 2002).

Among the most disadvantaged are those from black minority ethnic groups. Although they are as well as if not better qualified than their white counterparts, they face racial discrimination when they seek employment. Graduates take longer to find jobs and there are difficulties in achieving promotion. However, the experiences of Indian young people appear to be closer to those of white youth, suggesting a subtle interplay of class and ethnicity. Across Europe, minority ethnic young people are seen to be over-represented at the bottom of the hierarchy, being unemployed or performing unqualified and sometimes illegal work (Wallace and Kovatcheva, 1998).

The picture then is a complex one, with both negative and positive features. In some respects old hierarchies are being dismantled with young women and some minority ethnic young people, especially the women, improving their labour market positions. But class divisions remain securely entrenched (Fenton et al., 2002). Young people do appear to face more turbulent work histories and lengthened transitions in comparison to their parents, and the picture of the flexible labour market and its insecurities seems bleak. However, the Bristol respondents were facing up to flexibility with resourcefulness and good humour. This it seems *is* an adaptable generation, learning to take advantage of training resources to weave ways in and out of the labour market.

Notes

The author and editors are grateful to the late Paul Hickman who wrote the first version of this chapter for the first edition of this book. Some of his work is included in this chapter.

1   ESRC Grant no R000238215, *Winners and losers in changing labour markets*, Research team: Steve Fenton, Harriet Bradley, Jackie West, Will Guy and Ranji Devadason.

References

Aronowitz, S. and DiFazio, W. (1994) *The Jobless Future*, Minneapolis: University of Minneapolis Press.

Allatt, P. and Dixon, C. (2001) '"Learning to labour": how 17 year old A-level students manage part-time jobs, full-time study and other forms of work in times of rapid social change', *ESRC Youth Citizenship and Social Change Newsletter* 4.

Ashton, D. and Field, D. (1976) *Young Workers*, London: Hutchinson.

Beatson, M. (1995) 'Progress towards a flexible Labour Market', *Employment Gazette*, February.

Bradley, H. (1996) *Fractured Identities*, Cambridge: Polity.

Bradley, H., Erickson, M., Stephenson, C. and Williams, S. (2000) *Myths at Work*, Cambridge: Polity.

Department of Employment (1995) New Earnings Survey, London: DoE.

Eurostat (2000) *Eurostat Yearbook 2000*, Luxembourg: Office for Official Publications of the European Communities.

Fenton, S., Bradley, H., West, J., Guy, W. and Devadason, R. (2002) *Winners and Losers in Changing Labour Markets*, Report to ESRC.

Furlong, A. and Cartmel, F. (1997) *Young People and Social Change*, Milton Keynes: Open University Press.

Handy, C. (1994) *The Empty Raincoat*, London: Hutchinson.

Hollands, R. (1990) *The Long Transition*, London: Macmillan.

Leadbeater, C. (1999) *Living on Thin Air*, London: Viking.

MacDonald, R. (1994) 'Fiddly jobs, undeclared working and the something for nothing society' Work, *Employment and Society*, Vol 8(4): 507-30.

McDowell, L. (2001) *Young Men Leaving School*, Leicester: Joseph Rowntree Foundation/Youth Work Press.

Modood, T., Berthoud, R., Lakey, J., Nazroo, J., Smith, P., Virdee, S. and Beishon, S. (1997) *Ethnic Minorities in Britain: Diversity and Disadvantage*, London: Policy Studies Institute.

Office for National Statistics (2002) *Annual Labour Force Survey 2001–2*, London: ONS.

Roberts, K. (1995) *Youth and Employment in Modern Britain*, Oxford: Oxford University Press.

Sennett, R. (1998) *The Corrosion of Character: the Personal Consequences of Work in the New Capitalism*, London: W.W. Norton.

Walby, S. (1987) *Gender Transformations*, London: Routledge.

Wallace, C. and Kovatcheva , S. (1998) *Youth in Europe*, London: Macmillan.

Warwick IER (1995) *Review of the Economy and Employment*, Warwick: Institute for Employment Research, University of Warwick.

14

Youth Justice: Responsibilisation and Rights

John Muncie

For much of the past century the virtues of adopting a welfare based approach to young offenders has been an almost taken for granted idiom of youth justice. The establishment of juvenile courts, probation, care orders, individualised treatment and rehabilitation programmes and separate custodial regimes have all been heralded as evidence of 'acting in a child's best interests'. The conventional wisdom is that such welfarism dominated youth justice until at least the 1970s. However it has always had to sit alongside a prior and counter discourse that all offenders must be held responsible and punished for their actions no matter what their age and circumstances. As a result academics, policy makers and practitioners have been embroiled in making sense of the contradictions involved in the simultaneous delivery of welfare *and* punishment.

Welfarism promises a focus on meeting needs and seeking rehabilitation through treatment, whilst a neo-conservative framework of moral culpability and punishment focuses on deeds and seeks individual accountability and retribution. However this debate has come to be realised as particularly shortsighted as neither model has ever been fully realised in practice. Rather, youth justice tends to act on an amalgam of rationales, oscillating around, *but also beyond*, the caring ethos of social services and the legalistic ethos of responsibility and punishment. Such uncertainty tends to be resolved by a continual expansion of the remit of the system – both in sentencing powers and system reach. Youth justice is not simply concerned with the offender but with those 'at risk' or thought likely to offend. Similarly, whilst problems of control and order have always been central to youth justice discourses, they have also been underpinned by concerns for vulnerability and protection (Muncie and Hughes, 2002).

This chapter explores how New Labour has responded to such ambiguities through its 'root and branch' overhaul of the youth justice system in England and Wales since 1997. It should be noted that the rest of the UK, and Scotland in particular, has developed somewhat different trajectories to that described here. Although jurisdictions other than England and Wales are drawn on for comparative purposes they are not the main focus of this chapter.

New Labour: New youth justice

New Labour attempted to overcome, or bypass the philosophical disputes of welfare/punishment by reformulating the purpose of youth justice in England

and Wales to that of *preventing* offending by children and young people in which there would be 'no more excuses' (Home Office, 1997). The sheer volume and speed of pilot schemes and legislative activity since 1997 has indeed been remarkable. They include:

> The 1998 Crime and Disorder Act
> The 1999 Youth Justice and Criminal Evidence Act
> The 2000 Criminal Justice and Court Services Act
> The 2000 Powers of Criminal Courts (Sentencing) Act
> The 2001 Criminal Justice and Police Act
> The 2002 Criminal Justice Bill
> The 2003 Anti-Social Behaviour Bill

Collectively these initiatives have been heralded as marking the most radical 'shake-up' of the youth justice system in a century. For Goldson (2000a) they amount to the construction of a 'new youth justice'. The main reforms (enacted and proposed) are outlined below.

Cautioning, reprimands and final warnings

The 1998 Crime and Disorder Act replaced the previous practice of police cautioning with a system of reprimands and a final warning. A first offence can be met with a reprimand, a final warning or criminal charges depending on the seriousness of the offence. In 1994 guidelines had already been issued to discourage the use of second cautions even though they had been successful in diverting many young people out of the system altogether. Now on a second offence a final warning (akin to caution plus schemes that had previously operated in some parts of the country) will usually involve some community based intervention. The offender is referred to a youth offending team for assessment and allocation to a programme designed to address the causes of offending, even though no formal prosecution has taken place. Non-compliance with a programme may be announced in court on the committal of future offences. Further, the 2002 Criminal Justice Bill proposes a new 'street bail' with arrested persons being interviewed and processed without going to a police station.

Fines, compensation and reparation

For those under the age of 16 fines are usually made against a parent or guardian. Compensation orders may relate to injury, loss or damage and are designed to provide recompense to victims, rather than to punish the offender. In addition the 1998 Act introduced the reparation order which requires the young offender to make reparation to a victim or to the wider community by, for example, apologising personally, writing a letter of apology, cleaning graffiti or repairing damage. Breach may result in a £1,000 fine or the court can re-sentence for the original offence.

Referral orders

Introduced by the 1999 Act, referral orders are a *mandatory*, standard sentence. They are imposed on all offenders, no matter how relatively minor the offence, as long as they are under 18 years old, have no previous convictions, and plead guilty. Following pilots in 11 areas, referral orders went national in 2002. Offenders are referred to a youth offender panel (made up of local volunteers) to agree a programme of behaviour to address their offending. There is no provision for legal representation. It is not a formal community sentence but does require a contract to be agreed to last from a minimum of 3 months to a maximum of 12. The programme may include victim reparation, victim mediation, curfew, school attendance, staying away from specified places and persons, participation in specified activities, as well as a general compliance with the terms of the contract for supervision and monitoring purposes. Failure to agree a contract or breach of conditions results in the case being referred back to court to sentence the young offender afresh.

Parenting orders

Since the 1991 Criminal Justice Act parents and guardians can be ordered to exercise proper care and control over young offenders in their charge. In addition the 1998 Act introduced new powers to require a parent or guardian of a convicted young person to attend counselling or guidance sessions and to comply with certain specified requirements (such as ensuring the child goes to school each day and is indoors by a certain hour in the evening). Breach is a criminal offence with a liability of up to a £1,000 fine. In addition the 2001 Act extended magistrates' powers to deal with a new offence of 'aggravated truancy' which carries a maximum fine of £2,500 per parent and three months in prison for failing to ensure their children regularly attend school.

Community sentences

Five new community based orders have been added to the pre-existing attendance centre orders, supervision orders, probation (now renamed as community rehabilitation orders) and community service (now renamed as community punishment orders):

Action plan orders   These have been described as a short intensive programme combining punishment, rehabilitation and reparation to change offending behaviour and prevent further crime. The court specifies the particular 'tailor-made' requirements which may include specified activities, attendance centre, school attendance and reparation. Originally each order was prescribed for a fixed term of 3 months but the 2002 Criminal Justice Bill proposes an extension to 12 months.

Curfew orders   Powers to impose a curfew on offenders aged 16 and above were introduced in the 1991 Criminal Justice Act but are only available in those areas where monitoring arrangements, for example through electronic tagging, have been established. A curfew of different places or different periods can be made for a maximum of 6 months and between 2 and 12 hours a day. Powers to extend electronic monitoring to 10 to 15 year olds were introduced in 2001.

Drug treatment and testing orders   These may be imposed on offenders aged 16 and over where the court decides that the offender is dependent on, or has a propensity to misuse, drugs, that such misuse is related to the offence and that the offender is susceptible to treatment. The order can only be made with the offenders consent to undergo treatment (as an outpatient or resident in a hospital or clinic) and to submit to further testing of drug usage during the course of the order. Such an order can last between 6 months and 3 years.

Exclusion orders   Introduced by the Criminal Justice and Court Services Act 2000, these prohibit the subject from entering specified places for a period of 3 months if under 16 and for 2 years if over 16. Compliance can be monitored electronically.

Intensive supervision and surveillance programmes   These were launched in 2001 as part of a pilot 'zero tolerance of yob culture' campaign, largely aimed at those 15 and 16 year olds with a prior record of offending and as a last community based resort before custodial sentencing. They are not a court order as such but can be added to a supervision order, community rehabilitation order or to bail. They typically involve 24 hours a day electronic monitoring together with training, offending behaviour work and reparation. They are planned to be available nationwide by 2004. In 2003 a further *intensive control and change programme* for 18 to 20 year olds was unveiled combining curfew, community work and compensation.

Custodial sentences

Following the 1994 Criminal Justice and Public Order Act the maximum sentence of detention in a young offender institution was increased from 12 to 24 months. The same Act also introduced secure training orders for 12 to 14 year olds who had been convicted of three or more offences which would be imprisonable in the case of an adult. By 2003 three such centres were available. However the 1998 Crime and Disorder Act abolished these separate sentences and replaced them with a generic detention and training order (DTO). This came into force in April 2000 and, significantly, extends the custodial option to 10 year olds. A DTO can be given to 15 to 17 year olds for any offence considered serious enough to warrant a custodial sentence; to 12 to 14 year olds who are considered to be 'persistent offenders'; and to 10 and 11 year olds at the discretion of the Home Secretary. The orders are for between 4 and 24 months. Half of the order is served in the community under the supervision of a social worker, a probation officer or a member of a youth offending team. A custodial sentence of detention (without the training component) is now restricted to those aged 18, 19 and 20. However in cases of homicide, causing death by dangerous driving and other 'grave' crimes, the youth court can pass its jurisdiction to the Crown court. Under the powers of Sections 90–92 of the Powers of Criminal Courts Act 2000 (which consolidated those of Section 53 of the 1933 Children and Young Persons Act) 10 to 17 year olds can be detained for a longer period than the normal maximum of 2 years, at the discretion of the Home Secretary, either in a local authority secure unit or a prison service establishment. In addition the 2001 Act extended the reasons for giving custodial remands from 'protecting the public from serious harm' to 'preventing the commission of future imprisonable offences'.

Preventive measures

One of the most radical initiatives of New Labour's reforming agenda was the availability of new civil orders and powers that can be made other than as a sentence following conviction. Child safety orders, Local child curfews and Anti-social behaviour orders for example do not necessarily require either the prosecution or indeed the commission of a criminal offence. *Child safety orders* can be made by a family proceedings court on a child below the age of criminal responsibility if that child is considered 'at risk'. Justified as a 'protective' measure it places the child under the supervision of a social worker or a member of a youth offending team for a period of up to 12 months. The court can specify certain requirements such as attending specified programmes or avoiding particular places and people. Breach may result in the substitution of a care order under the powers of the 1989 Children Act. In addition local authorities can, after consultation with the police and local community, introduce a *local child curfew* to apply to *all* children under the age of 10 in a specific area. This places a ban on unsupervised children being in a specified area between 9 pm and 6 am. The 2001 Act extended the reach of curfews to 15 year olds, although it remains significant that by 2003 no local authority had ever evoked such a power. Similarly an *anti-social behaviour order* is a civil order which can be made by the police/local authority on anyone over the age of 10 whose behaviour is *thought likely* to cause alarm, distress or harassment. The order lasts a minimum of 2 years and breach is punishable by up to 5 years imprisonment. Though justified as a means to control 'nuisance neighbours' there is increasing evidence that ASBOs are primarily targeted at youthful 'rowdy and unruly' behaviour. The 2003 White paper – *Respect and Responsibility* (Home Office, 2003) – extends police and local authority powers to confiscate stereos, to criminalise begging, to give fixed penalty fines for 'disorderly' 16 and 17 year olds and to ban the sale of spray paints and fireworks to those under 18.

Responsibilisation strategies

It is increasingly difficult to 'read' these measures through the traditional lens of welfare and punishment. Rather a discourse of *responsibility* seems to lie at the heart of New Labour's reforming programme. It carries three separate but related arguments:

1   communities should take primary responsibility for crime prevention.
2   individuals should be held responsible for their own actions.
3   families, in particular parents, have a responsibility to ensure their children do not develop anti social tendencies.

Community responsibility

Garland refers to a community responsibilisation strategy involving 'central government seeking to act upon crime not in a direct fashion through state agencies (police, courts, prisons, social work, etc.) but instead by acting indirectly, seeking to activate action on the part of non-state agencies and organizations' (1996: 452). For example, from the mid 1980s onwards numerous campaigns (such as Neighbourhood Watch), organizations (such as Crime Concern) and projects (such as Safer Cities) were established to encourage interagency co-operation and local initiative. The message was that all of us – from property owners to manufacturers to school authorities, families and individuals – have a responsibility to reduce criminal opportunities and increase formal controls. The state may issue directives, but responsibility for their enactment is passed down to local bodies and ultimately individuals themselves (Crawford, 1997). In the field of youth justice this has developed into a simultaneous devolution and centralisation of youth justice policy.

By the late 1990s all local authorities in England and Wales were given the statutory duty to 'prevent offending by young people'. All aspects of their work have become infused with crime prevention and crime reduction responsibilities. For example, by 2000 all 154 local authorities had formulated and implemented an annual youth justice plan setting out how youth justice reform was to be funded and put into operation and had established a YOT (youth offending team), consisting of, on a statutory basis, representatives from each of social services, probation, police, health and education authorities. These agencies are designed to 'pull together' to co-ordinate provision, ensure each agency acts in tandem and to deliver a range of interventions and programmes that will ensure that young people 'face up to the consequences of their actions'. What were formerly youth *justice* teams (designed to divert young people from court and custody) have been replaced by youth *offending* teams (designed to directly intervene in all aspects of criminal, anti-social and disorderly behaviour). In effect the YOT displaces the statutory child care operations of social services departments (Goldson, 2000b). But each YOT plan also has to be submitted to a national body – the Youth Justice Board – for approval which, by 2000, had formulated a set of practice criteria to act as national standards (Youth Justice Board, 2000). Moreover, their work is constantly scrutinized through budgetary planning and auditing for cost and effectiveness. The youth justice plan enables local agencies to be held to account for their 'success' or 'failure'. Local ownership is circumscribed by national standards, performance targets and statutory limits (Vaughan, 2000; Muncie, 2002).

However, whatever the rhetoric of government intention, the history of youth justice is also a history of active and passive resistance from pressure groups and from the magistracy, the police and from youth justice workers through which such reform is to be effected. At one level this is reflected in the wide disparities between courts in the custodial sentencing of young people. These range from 1 custodial sentence for every 10 community sentences in the South West to 1 in 5 in the West Midlands and the North West. On another level it is reflected in the haphazard implementation of national legislation and youth justice standards in different localities (Holdaway et al., 2001). Indeed Cross et al. (2003) have begun to detect divergences between policy and practice in Wales and in England. Significantly the Welsh Assembly decided to locate youth justice services in the portfolio of Health and Social Services rather than Crime Prevention thus prioritising a 'children first' rather than an 'offender first' (as in England) philosophy. There is also always a space to be exploited between written and implemented policy. The translation of policy into practice depends on how it is visioned and reworked (or made to work) by those empowered to put it into practice. As a result youth justice practice may well continue to be dominated, not by *national* homogeneity, but by a complex of *localised* rehabilitative 'needs' and responsibilised 'deeds' programmes.

Individual responsibility and restorative justice

Much has been made of the principles of restorative justice – restoration, reintegration as well as responsibility – that ostensibly underpin some of the new legislative initiatives. Within restorative justice the talk is less of formal crime control and more of informal offender/victim participation and harm minimisation. These initiatives in part draw upon notions of informal customary practices in Maori, Aboriginal and Native American indigenous populations. They have come to find practical expression in various forms of conferencing in Australasia, in healing circles in Canada and in the processes that underpin the work of the Truth and Reconciliation Commission in South Africa. Both the United Nations and the Council of Europe have given restorative justice their firm backing for its potential to achieve participative justice and to reduce the recourse to youth imprisonment. The often quoted reference point is the experience of Family Group Conferences (FGCs) pioneered in New Zealand in 1989 and based on traditional systems of conflict resolution within Maori culture. FGCs involve a professional co-ordinator, dealing with both civil and criminal matters, who calls the young person, their family and victims together to decide whether the young person is 'in need of care and protection' and if so what should be provided. The outcome is usually some form of apology or community work. The key element of progressive restorative practice is that the offender is not marginalised but accepted as a key contributor to decision making (Morris and Maxwell, 2001).

In England restorative principles are typically cited as being present in referral, reparation, final warning programmes and action plan orders (Dignan, 1999; Crawford and Newburn, 2003). Scotland's 30 year old experience of Children's Hearings has also been borrowed by England to inform its referral orders and youth offender panels (though in turn it should be noted that Scotland is piloting the return of the youth court for 16 and 17 year olds). The Northern Ireland criminal justice review (O'Mahony and Deazley, 2000) advocates youth conferencing to be at the heart of its new approach to juvenile justice. There is little doubt that restoration holds the potential for a fundamental overhaul of policy and practice. Some radical advocates, for example, speak of replacing legal definitions of crime and formal procedures with processes of reconciling conflicting interests and of healing rifts (De Haan, 1990; Walgrave, 1995).

Current practice in England and Wales, however, appears rather more partial and circumspect. They are additions to, rather than core defining components of, a system that is built around and acts upon notions of punishment and retribution (Gelsthorpe and Morris, 2002). Reviews of restorative practices, and in particular the implementation of referral orders for almost all first offenders, have lauded the more positive lines of communication that have been opened up between offenders, parents, victims and communities. Yet they lament its coercive nature, problems of low victim participation, blurred lines of accountability and a general failure to provide offenders with the socio-economic resources necessary for them to develop a 'stakehold' in community life (Crawford and Newburn, 2003; Gray, 2003). The danger remains that any form of compulsory restoration may degenerate into a ceremony of public shaming and degradation, particularly when it operates within a system of justice whose primary intent is the infliction of further harm (as currently seems to be case in England and Wales). It also tends to merely reinforce notions of individual responsibility rather than those of social inclusion and social justice. The burden of responsibility falls on individuals to atone or change their behaviour, rather than on the state to recognise that it also has a responsibility (within UN conventions and rules – see below) to its citizens.

Family responsibility and the parenting deficit

A major preoccupation with the family and anti-social behaviour has dominated Labour's legislative initiatives. The centrality of family responsibility is found in the prevailing contention that crime runs in certain families and that anti-social behaviour in childhood is a predictor of later criminality. Such notions have opened the door to a range of legislative initiatives targeted at 'disorderly' as well as criminal behaviour. It has also drawn numerous aspects of social policy – housing, income support, youth inclusion programmes, family support, New Deal employment schemes and Sure Start nursery programmes – into a broader criminal justice agenda. As a result children below the age of criminal responsibility have been drawn into formal networks of social control. For example the Youth Justice Board announced in 2002 that new *youth inclusion and support panels* will target those as young as 8 if they are considered 'at risk of offending'. In this way social policy and welfare are becoming indistinguishable from criminal justice. Much of this early intervention is justified through notions of 'child protection' or 'nipping crime in the bud' or 'zero tolerance'. This rather narrow interpretation of crime causation is in no small part derived from multivariate correlational analyses, which have identified poor parenting, family breakdown, low intelligence and school failure as the key 'risk factors' in the onset of offending (Farrington and West, 1990; Utting, 1996; Graham, 1998). In this logic strong families fit the traditional image of conjugal, heterosexual parents with an employed male breadwinner. Single parenting and absent fathers are key harbingers of social disorder. Parental responsibility and moral obligation continually resurface in the new reforming agenda.

In practice family responsibilisation has been realised through a series of programmes which seek either to remove young people from the street or to provide them and their parents with coercive 'retraining'. A range of behavioural and cognitive interventions are considered to be most effective – in contrast, counselling, therapy, shock incarceration and corporal punishment are deemed 'not to work' (Audit Commission, 1996; Goldblatt and Lewis, 1998). In this way the targets of early intervention have invariably become individualised and behavioural. Throughout lies the objective of compelling parents to take 'proper' care and control of their children, whilst by the age of 10 children will be held fully responsible themselves (Goldson, 1999).

Authoritarianism and the Abrogation of Rights

As we have seen, the 1998 Crime and Disorder Act promised to break with 'past failures' and to open up a new era in youth justice based on the primary aim of *preventing crime and disorder*. It has been used as a means of justifying a wide range of social, health and employment as well as criminal justice policies. The evocation of prevention is present not only in such programmes as parenting classes or drugs education but also in containment in secure environments. The mood was best captured by Prime Minister Tony Blair in his edict that we should not be surprised if 'the penalties are tougher when you have been given the opportunities but don't take them'. As a result despite the (re)emergence of restoration, there is also contrary evidence to suggest that the custodial function of youth justice has never been seriously questioned. The detention and training centre, young offender institution, detention centre, youth custody centre, borstal, approved school, reformatory or youth prison have always formed the cornerstone of youth justice against which all other interventions are measured and assessed (Goldson, 2002). A vociferous ideology of 'popular punitiveness' continues to maintain that youth crime is caused by simple wickedness and that the only real effective action is that which involves punitive incarceration. England and Wales now lock up more young people than any other country in Europe: 4 times that in France, 12 times that in the Netherlands and 160 times that in Norway, Sweden and Finland (Muncie, 2003); and often in conditions condemned by the Chief Inspector of Prisons as 'utterly unsuitable' and as 'unworthy of any country that claims to be called civilised' (Children's Rights Alliance, 2002). With reconviction rates of ex-prisoners as high as 88% and increasing evidence of inappropriate and brutalising regimes characterised by bullying, self harm and suicide, it is clear that child incarceration is an expensive failure. Nevertheless it continues apace (Goldson and Peters, 2000; Goldson, 2002). Custodial sentences rose from 4,000 in 1992 to 7,600 in 2001 with a growing tendency to incarcerate the under 15s, ethnic minorities and young women being most notable.

In 1989 the United Nations Convention on the Rights of the Child established a near global consensus that all children have a right to *protection*, to *participation* and to basic material *provision*. The only countries not to have ratified are Somalia and the USA. The Convention built upon the 1985 UN Standard Minimum Rules for the Administration of Youth Justice (the Beijing Rules) which recognised the 'special needs of children' and the importance of dealing with offenders flexibly. It promoted diversion from formal court procedures, non-custodial disposals and insisted that custody should be a last resort and for minimum periods. In addition the Rules emphasised the need for anonymity in order to protect children from lifelong stigma and labelling. The Convention cemented these themes in the fundamental right that in all legal actions concerning those under the age of 18, the 'best interests of the child shall be a primary consideration' (Article 3.1). Further it reasserts the need to treat children differently, to promote their dignity and worth with minimum use of custody and that children should participate in any proceedings relating to them (Article 12). In 1990 the UN guidelines for the Prevention of Juvenile Delinquency (the Riyadh guidelines) added that youth justice policy should avoid criminalising children for their minor misdemeanors. Yet, in the gamut of New Labour youth justice reforms no directive has ever been given to the courts or youth offending teams that child welfare should be of 'primary consideration'. The UN has, first in 1995 and again in 2002, advised the UK to raise its age of criminal responsibility but New Labour has stubbornly refused to do so. Indeed somewhat perversely it has instead moved in the opposite direction by abolishing the principle of *doli incapax* which for centuries had established that 10 to 14 year olds cannot always be presumed to be fully responsible for their actions (Bandalli, 2000). England and Wales, Northern Ireland and Scotland have the lowest ages of criminal responsibility in Europe. The UN Convention stipulates that children should be protected from custody whenever possible and when deprived of liberty should be treated with humanity. In England age reductions in the detention of young people coupled with increases in maximum sentence appear directly at odds with the UN Convention on the Rights of the Child. This states at Article 37 that imprisonment of a child 'shall be used only as a measure of last resort and for the shortest appropriate period of time'. Moreover as there are no separate young offender institutions for girls, they are held in adult prisons often sharing the same facilities as adults. The Detention and Training Order (DTO) raises the possibility that 12 to 14 year old girls could now also find themselves in adult jails. Again this is in contravention of the UN Convention that states that 'every child deprived of liberty shall be separated from adults unless it is considered in the child's best interests not to do so' (Howard League, 1999). The UN's 2002 observations on the UK's implementation of the Convention repeated the concern at the increasing numbers of children in custody, at earlier ages for lesser offences and for longer periods, together with custodial conditions that do not adequately protect children from violence, bullying and self harm.

Article 6 of the European Convention on Human Rights, which was incorporated into UK law by the Human Rights Act 1998, provides for the right to a fair trial with legal representation and a right to appeal. The introduction nationwide of referral orders with lay youth offender panels deliberating on 'programmes of behaviour' with no legal representation would appear to be in denial of such rights. Article 8 confers the right to respect for private and family life and protects families from arbitrary interference. Parenting orders, child curfews and anti-social behaviour orders, in particular, would again appear to be in contempt (Freeman, 2002). More seriously, many of the principles of restorative justice which rely on informality, flexibility and discretion sit uneasily against legal requirements for due process and a fair and just trial. Rights may be given to the victim or the community to receive reparation, but juridical rights guaranteeing restraint against the child offender may be removed. This is compounded by preventive early interventions directed at those thought to be 'at risk'. Prevention, especially in the guise of 'zero tolerance' seems to have no boundaries and makes the system insatiable. But in response to the UN Committee on the Rights of the Child in 1999, Labour has claimed that early intervention is an 'entitlement' and that such pre-emptive policies contribute to 'the *right* of children to develop responsibility for themselves'(UK Government, 1999: para. 10.30.2, italics added). In these ways a discourse of rights is appropriated to justify degrees of authoritarianism that are far removed from UN intentions. Clearly it is possible to claim an adherence to the principle of rights whilst simultaneously pursuing policies which exacerbate structural inequalities and punitive institutional regimes. The development of a positive rights agenda remains at best limited, at worst non-existent (Scraton and Haydon, 2002).

Conclusion

It is clear that any number of inclusionary and exclusionary practices can be legitimated within the general rubric of crime prevention. Criminal justice is being increasingly turned to for the resolution of social problems. New Labour has ultimately conspired to promulgate the familiar story that crime, however complex, is to be blamed on the moral failure of culpable individuals, families and communities. Its obsession with risk factors and evidence-based analysis fails to address the complex interrelated problems of child poverty, urban degeneration and social exclusion. It continually seeks new disciplinary techniques rather than developing a political commitment to forge new routes to an active citizenship based on tolerance, mutual respect and entitlement (Pitts, 2001). As a result the goal of securing welfare, justice or rights for young people has become increasingly obscured. Above all the numbers of young offenders incarcerated continues to grow thereby undermining any commitment to promoting rehabilitation and preventing re-offending. All of this seems far removed from the principles of crime prevention and restorative justice. It is more a reflection of how youth justice policy is driven by short-term pragmatism and political expediency and ever-desperate measures to placate tabloid and mid-market newspaper law and order campaigns. As a result, whilst there have been important shifts in discourse and practice, the dominant terms of the political debate over crime and punishment have not been disrupted. New Labour's 'modernization' of youth justice amounts to an institutionalisation of intolerance (Muncie, 1999). Youth justice reform has been legitimated in the name of rebalancing the system in favour of victims and community empowerment. In reality it is the state that has greatly increased its power and its reach. And as Lee Bridges (2003) has concluded, it is those very same families in disadvantaged communities that already endure the greatest victimisation that now face the brunt of the new authoritarianism.

References

Audit Commission (1996) *Misspent Youth*, London: Audit Commission.

Bandalli, S. (2000) 'Children, responsibility and the New Youth Justice', in B. Goldson (ed.) *The New Youth Justice*, Lyme Regis: Russell House.

Bridges, L. (2003) 'New Labour and new authoritarianism in criminal justice' www.irr.org.uk/2003/January.

Children's Rights Alliance (2002) *Rethinking Child Imprisonment*, London: Children's Rights Alliance.

Crawford, A. (1997) *The Local Governance of Crime: Appeals to Community and Partnership*, Oxford: Clarendon Press.

Crawford, A. and Newburn, T. (2003) *Youth Offending and Restorative Justice*, Cullompton: Willan.

Cross, N., Evans, P. and Minkes, J. (2003) 'Still children first? Developments in youth justice in Wales', *Youth Justice*, 2 (3): 151–62.

De Haan, W. (1990) *The Politics of Redress*, London: Unwin Hyman.

Dignan, J. (1999) 'The Crime and Disorder Act and the prospects for restorative justice', *Criminal Law Review,* January, 48–60.

Farrington, D. and West, D. (1990) 'The Cambridge study in delinquent development', in H.J. Kerner and G. Kaiser (eds) *Criminality: Personality, Behaviour and Life History*, Berlin: Springer-Verlag.

Freeman, M. (2002) 'Children's rights ten years after ratification', in B. Franklin (ed.) *The New Handbook of Children's Rights*, London: Routledge.

Garland, D. (1996) 'The limits of the sovereign state: strategies of crime control in contemporary society', *British Journal of Criminology*, 36 (4): 445–71.

Gelsthorpe, L. and Morris, A. (2002) 'Restorative justice: the last vestiges of welfare?', in J. Muncie, G. Hughes and E. McLaughlin (eds) *Youth Justice: Critical Readings*, London: Sage.

Goldblatt, P. and Lewis, C. (eds) (1998) *Reducing Offending*, Home Office Research Study, no.187, London: HMSO.

Goldson, B. (1999) 'Youth (in)justice: contemporary developments in policy and practice', in B. Goldson (ed.) *Youth Justice: Contemporary Policy and Practice*, Aldershot: Ashgate.

Goldson, B. (ed.) (2000a) *The New Youth Justice*, Lyme Regis: Russell House.

Goldson, B. (2000b) 'Children in need or young offenders?', *Child and Family Social Work*, 5: 255–65.

Goldson, B. (2002) 'New punitiveness: the politics of child incarceration' in J. Muncie, G. Hughes, and E. McLaughlin (eds) *Youth Justice: Critical Readings*, London: Sage.

Goldson, B. and Peters, E. (2000) *Tough Justice*, London: The Children's Society.

Graham, J. (1998) 'What works in preventing criminality', in P. Goldblatt, and C. Lewis (eds) *Reducing Offending*, Home Office Research Study no.187, London: Home Office.

Gray, P. (2003) *An Evaluation of the Plymouth Restorative Justice Programme*, University of Plymouth: Department of Social Policy and Social Work.

Holdaway, S., Davidson, N., Dignan, J., Hammersley, R., Hine, J. and Marsh, P. (2001) *New Strategies to Address Youth Offending: The National Evaluation of the Pilot Youth Offending Teams*, Research Directorate Occasional paper no. 69, London: Home Office.

Home Office (1997) *No More Excuses: A New Approach to Tackling Youth Crime in England and Wales*, cm 3809, London: HMSO.

Home Office (2003) *Respect and Responsibility: Taking a Stand Against Anti-Social Behaviour*, cm 5778, London: HMSO.

Howard League (1999) *Protecting the Rights of Children*, London: The Howard League for Penal Reform.

Morris, A. and Maxwell, G. (eds) (2001) *Restorative Justice for Juveniles*, Oxford: Hart.

Muncie, J. (1999) 'Institutionalized intolerance: youth justice and the 1998 Crime and Disorder Act', *Critical Social Policy*, 19 (2): 147–75.

Muncie, J. (2002) 'A new deal for youth?: early intervention and correctionalism', in G. Hughes, E. McLaughlin, and J. Muncie (eds) *Crime Prevention and Community Safety: New Directions*, London: Sage.

Muncie, J. (2003) 'Youth justice: globalisation and multi-modal governance', in T. Newburn, and R. Sparks, (eds) *Criminal Justice and Political Culture*, Cullompton: Willan.

Muncie, J. and Hughes, G. (2002) 'Modes of youth governance: political rationalities, criminalisation and resistance', in J. Muncie, G. Hughes, and E. McLaughlin (eds) *Youth Justice: Critical Readings*, London: Sage.

O'Mahony, D. and Deazley R. (2000) *Juvenile Crime and Justice: Review of the Criminal Justice System in Northern Ireland*, Research Report no. 17, Belfast: Northern Ireland Office.

Pitts, J. (2001) *The New Politics of Youth Crime: Discipline or Solidarity?*, Basingstoke: Palgrave.

Scraton, P. and Haydon, D. (2002) 'Challenging the criminalisation of children and young people: securing a rights based agenda', in J. Muncie, G. Hughes, and E. McLaughlin (eds) *Youth Justice: Critical Readings*, London: Sage.

UK Government (1999) *Convention on the Rights of the Child: Second Report to the UN Committee on the Rights of the Child by the United Kingdom*, London: HMSO.

Utting, D. (1996*) Reducing Criminality among Young People: a Sample of Relevant Programmes in the UK*, Home Office Research Study, no.161, London: HMSO.

Vaughan, B. (2000) 'The government of youth: disorder and dependence', *Social and Legal Studies*, 9 (3): 347–66.

Walgrave, L. (1995) 'Restorative justice for juveniles: Just a technique or a fully fledged alternative?', *Howard Journal*, 34 (3): 228–49.

Youth Justice Board (2000) *National Standards for Youth Justice*, London: Youth Justice Board.

15
Youth Cultures and Sub-Cultures

Daren Garratt

The notion of 'youth', and the culture and sub-cultures it creates and claims for itself, has proved to be a constant source of bewilderment, fear, and possibly envy, for adult society. But why is it that, once young people form themselves into highly visible groups, they are suddenly seen to be 'problematic'?

Through media manipulation and, somewhat ironically, commercial exploitation, adult society is continually kept informed of the shifting trends and movements of young people, and the sub-cultures that then arise. History shows, however, that as soon as a new sub-culture is seen to emerge, its members can become transformed into modern 'folk devils', and a 'moral panic' can ensue (Cohen, 1972). What Cohen means by this is that when a highly visible youth group emerges, the media stereotypes that follow it ensure it will come to be seen as a threat to society. The resulting flurry of activity will see society's 'moral thinkers' (politicians, tabloid newspaper editors) putting everyone on their guard as they spout forth reasons and solutions to curb this rising 'problem'.

But what exactly is the 'problem' here? Is it young people themselves, or adult society that *perceives* them as a threat, vilifying them accordingly? For most young people, sub-cultures are probably, at best, nothing more than a means to create and establish an identity in a society where they can find it difficult to locate a *sense of self*. At worst, subcultures prove to be *'symbolic challenges to a symbolic order'* (Hebdige, 1979, own italics), because by the style that sub-cultures adopt, they *represent* that not *all* young people are willing to be moulded into what adult society considers the norm. They are *symbolic* because these 'challenges' offer no real danger to a social 'order' that is based purely on aesthetics and fashion. They are gestures and, like all communicative gestures, they offer an *indication*. In this case, they indicate that the young people involved have their own values and their own lives, and that these should be recognised and accepted by the rest of society.

For adults working with young people, sub-cultures should be understood as young people understand them, and not as 'respectable' adult society would have them portrayed. This chapter offers a *framework to* assist in identifying and overcoming any preconceptions or prejudices that may still arise from a primarily media-based image of youth.

Notions of 'culture', 'youth', and 'sub-culture'

Culture is a complex notion. To some it is a standard of artistic and aesthetic refinement and excellence. It is an expression of respectability. That is why, in many circles, going to the opera is *cultured*, but going to a rave is uncouth and, as we shall explore later, *deviant*. There is a different notion of culture, however, which sees it as, quite simply, 'a way of life', characterised by the *relationships* between all the different elements of society. 'Culture' has nothing to do with concepts of 'highbrow' and 'lowbrow' but instead relies on the *interaction* of all of society's components; art, learning, institutions and ordinary behaviour. This understanding of 'culture' was expanded by Hall et al. (1976) who agreed that not only is culture the level at which different groups develop patterns and relationships, but more importantly, it is how these experiences are *expressed*. That is, we can see culture as a means of social interaction and expression.

And what of 'youth'? To merely see it as the period between the ages of 12 and 20 is both misleading and inadequate. 'Youth' goes some way towards bridging the gap between the dependency of childhood and the independent 'freedom' of adulthood, and in order to combat the marginal social status and sense of powerlessness attributed to 'youth', it becomes its own social institution with its own codes and cultural claims. As a result, it poses a threat to the accepted *norms* of adult society. 'Youth' is, therefore, the point where the dominant culture loosens the control of its young, and 'youth culture' is the result.

And, as it is on the streets that most young people make themselves visible in their attempts to express their independence from adult society, it is 'the streets' that enable the creation of these cultural activities. This 'culture' *interacts* on the streets, and finds its *expression* in the style it adopts. The high visibility of a group of young people with shared musical preferences, fashion ideals, and beliefs leads to the creation of a 'sub-culture'.

The main characteristic of any emerging sub-culture is that it captures the social, political and economic spirit of the time. Its members translate whatever is going on around them into the music, fashion and behaviour they use to identify themselves. Punk, for example, 'dramatised rage' (Coon, cited in Lydon, 1993: 79). Whether this was rage against the existing musical establishment or rising unemployment, didn't matter. It was a *feeling* that was being expressed.

This also may be why Punk affiliated itself closely with Rastafarians. Here was another sub-cultural group of alienated working class Britons experiencing unemployment and trouble with authority, but on an undoubtedly larger scale. And like Punk, the style the Rastas adopted declared an objection and resistance to *white* adult society. British Rastas took the original Jamaican Rastafarian image, but stripped it of its religious connotations, incorporating instead more militaristic overtones.

Rastas (in crude simplistic terms) wanted to return to the mythical Africa that filled the white Caribbean colonialists with such dread that they pronounced it *the forbidden land* (see Hebdige, 1979).

The white man's Bible, with its history of racist colonialism and economic exploitation, was easy to see through and subvert, and from this grew the realisation that only by overthrowing the oppression and servitude of living in a white man's Babylon could the black races be delivered and return to Africa, *the promised land*. Little wonder, then, that a style that embodied the struggle to overcome and infract white control and oppression was so appealing to the black youth of the 1970s.

Fundamentally, though, where Punks and Rastas differed most was that whilst Punks were happy to *symbolise* the alienation they felt, and *dramatise* their subsequent rage, the *real* anger felt by many young blacks occasionally spilt over into fully fledged riots.

This notion of sub-cultures being a 'thermometer' for a society's political climate is perhaps most effective when considering the only really major youth movement of the 1980s – Acid House. Acid House offered a new take on sub-cultural politics and resistance, in that it wasn't visible. The emphasis was not on individual spectacle, like Punk, but on anonymity. As a result, it allowed people to dance to non-specific music in a uniform of their own choosing (the only concession being the adoption of the 'Smiley' logo as a secret sign of 'membership'); they could interact and express their individuality, but at the same time they could 'disappear'. Thus, an ironic subversion of the existing political climate took place: Thatcherism concerned itself solely with notions of the *self*, and a new, hedonistic, youth-dominated group emerged full of solitary individuals with no visible identity.

A brief history of sub-cultural theory

The first major work to look at the notion of 'youth' as its own creative movement was *The Teenage Consumer* (Abrams, 1959). Prior to this, all major studies of the concept of 'youth' had focused upon the delinquent, anti-social 'problem' of young people, as opposed to their essential role *within* society (see Burt, 1925).

Abrams was the first to identify the rise of 'youth' as a consumer group. This was, after all, the period of post-war affluence, the 'you've never had it so good' era of disposable income, and the resultant goods aimed specifically at a teenage market. Young people became set apart simply by their market choices, and were defined in terms of leisure and leisure goods. This *aspiring culture* was predominantly white, male and working class, and this emerged as the most affluent sector of society, as they were seen to have the greatest amount of disposable income and the widest range of 'specialist' goods to spend it on.

But something else was happening to further set white working class youth apart from the rest of society. In the mid to late 1950s, the working class community underwent a process of fragmentation and polarisation (Hebdige, 1979). All aspects of life saw cultural change – in the family, school, workplace, and leisure pursuits – and, as was pointed out earlier, if *culture* changes, it then follows that the interactions and forms of expression that help create it must also change. This change was most visible in young people, as this was also the era of Britain's first, truly visible 'spectacular sub-culture': the Teds.

Rock 'n' roll, and the idols who personified it, emerged as the means by which young people could articulate their new-found freedom, or generational consciousness. Style became the expression of independence. Soon, all over Britain, gangs of teenagers could be seen in their newly adopted style of clothes, previously attributed to Edwardian 'gentlemen' (hence *Teddy* boys). By adopting a visual style outside of its immediate environment and class restrictions, and awarding it a new 'secret' meaning, the Teds defied what was expected of them, just as the utilisation of safety-pins and bin-bags did with the Punks 20 years later.

By wanting to act and dress differently to their peers, and therefore set themselves apart, they unconsciously offended the dominant culture's mythical vision of unity and cohesion. But were they actually doing anything wrong?

The reactions of adults to each subsequent sub-culture has often given them greater significance and prominence than they have had in the lives of the young people involved (see Widdicombe and Wooffitt, 1995). What to the majority of young people is no more than a naive, stylistic expression of independence becomes, especially in the hands of the media and academics who are often the first to publicly voice concern about the nation's youth, a *problematic* social phenomenon, created to *understand* something that is increasingly alien and closed to them.

The problematic of youth

Hebdige (1979) sees that one of the core qualities of 'sub-culture' is the suggestion of 'secrecy, Masonic oaths, an underworld'. That is, in the eyes of the adult world, not only are youth sub-cultures somewhat impenetrable and beyond comprehension, but they are also fundamentally corrupt (an underworld). In short, they are *deviant*. 'Deviant', in this context, *should* only imply distinction and 'anything that differs from what is most common' (Becker, 1973), but there is a definite stigma about the term in adult society, and this often leads to a misconception about what deviant sub-cultures actually are.

It is common to see 'deviance' as dysfunctional, for another definition of the term is 'the failure to obey group rules'. In wider social terms, the *group rules* of a culture are, generally, the rules of the dominant adult society. Therefore, if we apply this theory to the post-war spectacular sub-cultures that we understand and encounter, it is adult society that creates these deviants, simply because they have broken no rule other than that which we see as the accepted dominant rules of style, behaviour and expression. Youth sub-cultures give easily identifiable teenagers a means to rebel, but it is through *style* not crime. This is less direct and understandable as a means of deviance, and is therefore *more* threatening to adults. Also, just as a problematic view of 'youth' is often built around their 'deviance', it is possible that the term 'sub-culture' can also imply negative qualities.

In its most common usage, the prefix *sub* has an inherent meaning: it implies a below-average worth or quality. Therefore, simply by labelling a group of young people as a *sub*-culture', society infers its negativity or '*sub*versive' qualities. And, because our expectations aren't being met, it follows that the sub-cultural group is '*sub*standard'. This notion was probably best illustrated with the Punk phenomenon, which adopted an expressive style so alien to all understanding of fashion, and so oppositional to all concepts of decency, that in order to be justified its members *had* to be '*sub*normal', or even '*sub*human'. These are largely subconscious, socially ingrained associations, *but*, by constructing the label 'sub-culture', adult society also constructed an unprovoked perception and reaction.

Another major factor in problematising the phenomenon of 'youth' (and upholding those associations outlined above) is the role of the *media*. When the first rumblings of a 'youth movement' were heard in the mid 1950s, it coincided with the arrival of the concept of 'mass culture' which was seen to be no more than the *manipulation* of people by big business. It was exploitative. People became nothing more than consumers, and as television and cinema increasingly took a hold, 'authentic artistic culture' (Willis, 1990) was seen to be degraded.

And in the midst of all this was 'youth'. Mass culture relied on their exploitation to exist, so a whole influx of youth-specific goods flooded the market (rock 'n roll movies, records, pop magazines and TV shows), and as a result, young people were blamed, and even envied, by adult society for their loss of cultural dominance. The media has continually portrayed the young as something to be feared and envied.

A 'new' sub-culture is always attractive to the media because of the stylistic 'innovations' it shows on the streets, and is generally reported in terms of creativity. However, any deviant acts that are then 'discovered' by the moral lobbyists of a society TV watchdogs, police, politicians) are *used* to explain why these subversions of *accepted* style happened in the first place (Hebdige, 1979). The resulting media coverage that seeks to justify these fears ensures that a few isolated incidents are applied to the *whole* sub-culture. A process of self-perpetuation then emerges, as the sub-culture is suddenly seen to possess additional subversive qualities that its members never knew about. In the instance of Punk, once the *media image* of Punk was crystallised as a group of foul mouthed, violent, moronic yobbos, then it wasn't long before emergent Punks thought that this was how they *should* behave. Once again, a hedonistic group of bored teenagers with shared interests became, in the hands of the media and the subsequent reaction of adult society, a deviant sub-culture. The result of this is an *understanding* of a sub-culture far removed from its initial ideal, and this is perhaps best illustrated in the case of Mods and Rockers.

The running gang battles along Brighton beach in the mid 1960s gave Britain a reason to fear its young again (there had been a relative lull after the storm of the Teds died down in the late 1950s). But, it later emerged that a lot of the press reports of these 'riots' were mainly over-reactions to minor incidents. The skirmishes that did happen were generally between the teenagers and the *locals*, many of whom, it was rumoured, would not let anyone who *appeared* to be a Mod or a Rocker into their establishment. Once in the hands of the press, though, these became uniformed battles, and from that moment these two small groups became national sub-cultures, with their identities and subversive qualities secured (Cohen, 1972). But, once society has created the problem of youth sub-cultures, how does it then find a solution?

More often than not, a 'solution' is found simply within the limitations of a sub-culture thriving on media exploitation. Firstly, the various products that are designed for 'youth' often seek to portray the phenomenon as something alien and trivial in order to placate the adult population (after all, who is the media run by if not other adults?). That is, adults' fears are immediately put to rest by the portrayal of 'youth' as being largely risible and ineffectual. The other point to be raised here is that simply by pouncing upon any sub-cultural innovation, and incorporating it into the mainstream, the movement is immediately robbed of its 'secret' appeal.

The money-making power of any new spectacular sub-culture was so firmly established that, throughout the 1980s, every indication of an emerging *musical* scene was smothered by big business and packaged as the next big youth movement, thus starving the young people involved of any creative, personal input. Even the Acid House movement with its emphasis on anonymity was finished when the once secretive 'Smiley' logo was denounced as 'evil' in the tabloid press, and subsequently emblazoned across T-shirts on every street corner.

But the main 'solution' to a sub-culture is, by and large, out of adult society's hands. Once a movement is felt to have lost its creative qualities and become a commercially governed fashion, then like all fashions it isn't long before its members get bored and subscribe to something else. After all, effective sub-cultures are the creation of young people, and they serve a purpose for young people.

The role of sub-cultures in the lives of young people

In the days before sub-cultures were thought of purely as undesirable, commercial products, they were seen to be the result of a group of like-minded individuals establishing a set of standards in order to overcome shared social conditions (Cohen, 1955). That is, for young people perhaps the easiest, most effective way to achieve an identity in a culture that increasingly marginalises and disregards them is to *change* their cultural world. By making themselves *visible*, young people show that they will not merely exist passively in a world that is not their own. They create their own identity, and therefore their own culture, refusing to be seen and treated as 'young adults'.

The fact that all post-war spectacular sub-cultures have a coexisting soundtrack (Elvis, the Who, the Sex Pistols, Prodigy) often helps distract from their importance, and trivialises their impact. But, the truth is, the most influential movements are the ones that society doesn't fully perceive until they are already established, and their musical flags are already flying above the commercial media. We come into contact with their commercialisation and not their formation.

So, although it is indisputable that the white working class teenagers of 1956 heard Elvis and acted upon the freedom of finally being spoken to (as opposed to *at*), this doesn't explain why Teds made their entrance, and were attracting considerable attention as early as 1953. The music has always been adopted by the initial sub-cultural style, it has never started the movement. This is because sub-cultures are not preconceived. Instead, they are a reflection of what is happening in society, and they provide a temporary, yet essential, means of expressing and dealing with those problems. The majority of young people, though, don't become aware of a sub-culture until it has been absorbed and become a pop/fashion movement. What, then, does a specific sub-culture 'do' for them?

The Teds, for instance, gave working class kids the chance to simply enjoy themselves before settling down. Rigid social conventions were still upheld by late 1950s youth, but before they did what was expected of them they had a glamorous, delinquent image on offer. The Mods, by their seemingly reactionary though stylistically modified appearance, managed to bridge their social and working lives. Most Teds, and more obviously Punks, could only adopt their sub-cultural uniform *outside* of the workplace. 'Hard-core' Mods, though, lived the 'Mod life' continually.

Perhaps most important is the impact and influence of Acid House. The current dance culture that it has evolved into is a racially unified experience shared by all generations and all classes (Hills, 1996). It is no longer enjoyed by a minority but by a significant cross-section of people, and any communal acts that are seen to occur in our increasingly fragmented society should not be dismissed out of hand.

To summarise, sub-cultures give young people the chance to express their difference from the rest of society, yet coexist within it. More importantly, they enable young people to find their own *individual* identity, yet still have the support of *group* solidarity (Brake, 1980).

Conclusion

The fear and envy that adult society has of its young are given a visible expression when a spectacular sub-culture emerges. Any 'respectable fears'

(Pearson, 1983) that we may have about trends within society are transformed into Cohen's 'moral panics' when a group of teenagers rebel against our *stylistic* conventions. Once new groups appear on the streets, then doubts about the future of 'respectable' society dominate the media. Creative expressions of individuality, once in the hands of adults, become problems simply because, for the first time, young people have taken control of an aspect of their lives. The safety-pin, or the Edwardian drape jacket, gets removed from its traditional role and reapplied. Style becomes unconventional and, it is argued, if each successive generation isn't socialised into having conventional, 'respectable' outlooks, then society as we know it simply can't continue (Brake, 1980).

Yet something here is being overlooked, and that is the *importance* of sub-cultural developments in the lives of young people. Sub-cultures are not a threat to adults. They are an effective means for some young people to bridge the dependency of childhood and the 'freedom' and 'responsibility' of adulthood. Through stylistic innovation they assist a young person in forming an identity, and because the mechanics of that process get lost as adulthood progresses, the fixation with the period intensifies. As a result, the theories that emerge about sub-cultures are often far removed from the realities of a sub-culture on the day-to-day life of the young person involved.

References

Abrams, M. (1959) *The Teenage Consumer*, London: Routledge & Kegan Paul.

Becker, H.S. (1973) *Outsiders: Studies in the Sociology of Deviance*, London: Collier Macmillan.

Brake, M. (1980) *The Sociology of Youth Culture and Youth Subcultures*, London: Routledge & Kegan Paul.

Burt, C. (1925) *The Young Delinquent*, London: University of London Press.

Cohen, A.K. (1955) 'A general theory of subcultures', in D.O. Arnold (ed.) (1970), *Subcultures*, Berkeley, CA: Glendessary Press.

Cohen, S. (1972), *Folk Devils and Moral Panics*, London: MacGibbon & Kee.

Hall, S., Clarke, J., Jefferson, T. and Roberts, B. (eds) (1976) *Resistance through Rituals*, London: Hutchinson.

Hebdige, D. (1979) *Subculture: the Meaning of Style*, London: Methuen.

Hills, G. (1996) 'Rave new world', *The Observer Preview*, 4–11 February.

Lydon, J. (1993) *Rotten: No Irish, No Blacks, No Dogs*, London: Hodder & Stoughton.

Pearson, G. (1983) *Hooligan: a History of Respectable Fears*, London: Macmillan.

Widdicombe, S. and Wooffitt, R. (1995) *The Language of Youth Subcultures*, Hemel Hempstead: Harvester Wheatsheaf.

Willis, P. (1990) *Moving Culture*, London: Calouste Gulbenkian Foundation.

16

Black Adolescent Identity and the Inadequacies of Western Psychology

Lena Robinson

The field of child and adolescent research is based largely on white middle class children and adolescents, and its findings are assumed (or defined as) normative and generic to all children and adolescents. The behaviours and patterns of development in non-white children and youngsters are then viewed comparatively against this 'norm' and defined as 'exceptions' or 'deviations from the norm'. Black psychologists (mainly in the USA) have presented alternative perspectives on black child development. However the research of black scholars, who have unique insights into the problems of minority children and adolescents, has been largely neglected by mainstream developmental psychology (Spencer, 1988).

The issues discussed in this chapter are offered as the beginning steps toward an understanding of one aspect of black adolescence – black identity development. The topic of black identity has been of concern to psychologists and youth workers for decades. Low self-esteem, self-hatred, and a negative racial identity have been the characteristics traditionally attributed to black children and adolescents. This chapter argues that the model of psychological nigrescence is more relevant to the psychological life experiences of black adolescents in Britain than the more traditional psychological theories. It will enable us to gain a better understanding of the difficulties experienced by black adolescents in Britain.

The term 'black' in this chapter is used to describe people from South Asian, African and Caribbean backgrounds. Black identity has been discussed extensively in the social science literature using various terms and measures. According to Looney, 'Black identity deals specifically with an individual's awareness, values, attitudes, and beliefs about being Black' (1988: 41). It can also be viewed as 'an active developmental process which is exposed to various influences within and without, and [which] can be selective and/or adaptive' (Maxime, 1986: 101). We will use these definitions as our 'operating definition' in our discussion of black identity development.

Inadequacies of Western psychology

The conventionally accepted paradigms and discoveries of Western psychology do not provide an understanding of black adolescents. Even a casual observation of the history of psychology will demonstrate that psychological literature over the last 100 years has been based on observations primarily on Europeans, predominantly male and overwhelmingly middle class. The formulations of notable thinkers who have shaped the thought of Eurocentric psychology, such as Sigmund Freud and Carl Jung, have all directly or indirectly asserted the superiority of European races over non-European races. Despite the diversity of the various schools of Western psychology, they seem to merge unequivocally in their assumption of the Eurocentric point of view and the superiority of people of European descent. It is not surprising, therefore, that the conclusions reached from the application of their concepts and methods are invariably of the inferiority of non-European peoples (Robinson, 1995).

Professionals in Britain and the USA have been influenced greatly by the psychoanalytic approach. This approach is based on Sigmund Freud's work, but has been developed by neo-Freudians (for example, Erikson, Melanie Klein, and Jung). The psychoanalytic approach has been influential in accounts of adolescent development (for discussion, see Bateman and Holmes, 1995).

In contrast to the critiques of Freud for sexism (Frosh, 1987; Mitchell, 1974), the racism of the psychoanalytic approach is relatively unknown. Mama criticises Freudian psychoanalysis for 'its universalism and ethnocentrism. A theory which takes sexual repression and taboo as the bedrock of "civilisation" is also highly culture-bound' (1995: 127). Fernando notes that Freud 'envisaged the development of civilisation being dependent on suppressing instinctual behaviour under the guidance of the super-ego, elaborated into a "cultural super-ego"; it was natural for him that the "leadership of the human species" should be taken up by "white nations" (Freud, 1930), and that "primitives" have a lower form of culture' (1991: 41). In his book *Totem and Taboo*, Freud (1912–13) refers to the practices and behaviours of African peoples as 'savage' or 'primitive'. However, 'although Freud adhered to racist thinking, it was Jung who integrated racist ideas more fully into psychological theories' (1991: 42).

Carl Jung (at one time Freud's star pupil) has been referred to as the father of 'transpersonal psychology'. He believed that certain psychological disorders found among Americans were due to the presence of black people in America. He noted that: 'The causes for the American energetic sexual repression can be found in the specific American complex, namely to living together with "lower races, especially with Negroes"' (1950: 29). Jung identified the modern African as 'primitive' in every sense of the word. Dalal (1988) maintains that Jung considered black people to be inferior and not just different. Dalal discusses how Jung explicitly equates:

(1)   The modern black with the prehistoric human
(2)   The modern black conscious with the white unconscious
(3)   The modern black adult with the white child.

It is this that constitutes the racist core of Jungian Psychology on which all else is based. (1988: 263)

Erikson's (1968) psychoanalytical theory focuses on one distinctive feature of adolescence – the development of a sense of identity. He proposed a process whereby adolescents begin with an unclear sense of their identity, experience a 'crisis', and achieve a clear sense of their identity. He felt that 'identity crisis' was normative to adolescence and young adulthood. Erikson (1964) spoke of ethnic self-doubt and a pathological denial of one's roots as being seminal to Negro identity. He could not conceive that, for some individuals, their colour may actually be a source of pride. In an article 'Memorandum on identity and Negro youth', he states: 'A lack of familiarity with the problem of Negro youth and with the actions by which Negro youth hopes to solve these [identity] problems is a marked deficiency in my life and work which cannot be accounted for by theoretical speculation' (1964: 41).

Models of black identity development

A perspective that has largely been ignored by traditional Eurocentric psychology is the research on the psychology of nigrescence (the 'process of becoming black'). The traditional psychological literature on black identity tended to have children as subjects (for example, the doll studies), whereas the nigrescence approach studies black identity in adolescents and adults. Parham considers that: 'The process of psychological Nigrescence is a lifelong process, which begins with the late-adolescence/early-adulthood period in an individual's life' (1989: 194–5).

Nigrescence models tend to have four or five stages – and the common point of departure is not the change process *per se* but an analysis of the identity to be changed. These models are useful as they enable us to understand the problems of black identity confusion and to examine, at a detailed level, what happens to a person during identity change. Perhaps the best known and most widely researched model of black identity development is Cross's (1971; 1980; 1991) model of the conversion from 'Negro' to 'black'.

Cross suggests that the development of a black person's racial identity is often characterised by his/her movement through a five-stage process, the transformation from pre-encounter to internalisation-commitment. In the first stage, *pre-encounter*, the black person is likely to view the world from a white frame of reference (Eurocentric). The person accepts a 'white' view of self, other blacks, and the world. The person has accepted a deracinated frame of reference and, because his or her reference point is usually a white normative standard, he or she develops attitudes that are very pro-white and anti-black. The person will also deny that racism exists.

In the second stage, *encounter*, some shocking personal or social event makes the person receptive to new views of being black and the world. The person's Eurocentric thinking is upset by an encounter with racial prejudice which precipitates an intense search for black identity. The encounter stage involves two steps. The first is experiencing and personalising the event, during which the person realises that his or her old frame of reference is inappropriate, and he or she begins to explore aspects of a new identity. The second is portrayed by Cross et al. 'as a testing phase during which the individual [first] cautiously tries to validate his/her new perceptions' (1991: 324), then definitively decides to develop a black identity.

The third stage, *immersion-emersion*, is the period of transition in which the person struggles to destroy all vestiges of the 'old' perspective. This occurs simultaneously with an intense concern to clarify the personal implications of the new-found black identity (Cross, 1985). An emotional period ensues where the person glorifies anything black and attempts to purge him or herself of the former world view and old behaviour. The person tends to denigrate white people and white culture. Hence, the demonstrations of one's blackness are high – for example, black clothes and hairstyles, linguistic styles, attending all-black functions, reading black literature. The person does not feel secure about his/her blackness. He/ she can be vicious in attacks on aspects of the old self that appear in others or her/himself, and he/she may even appear bizarre in his/her affirmation of the new self.

In the fourth stage, *internalisation*, the person focuses on things other than himself/herself and his/her ethnic or racial group. He/she achieves an inner security and self-confidence with his/her blackness. He/she feels more relaxed, more at ease with the self. The person's thinking reflects a shift from how one's friends see him/her (am I black enough?) toward confidence in one's personal standards of blackness. The person also exhibits a psychological openness and a decline in strong anti-white feelings. The person still uses 'blacks as a primary reference group, [but] moves toward a pluralistic and nonracist perspective' (Cross, 1991: 326). This stage and the next are characterised by positive self-esteem, ideological flexibility and openness about one's blackness.

In the fifth stage, *internalisation-commitment*, the person finds activities and commitments to express his/her new identity.

There is an extensive empirical literature that confirms Cross's model of black identity development (see Cross, 1971; Hall et al., 1972). Although Cross's identity development model has been developed with African-American samples in the USA, it is argued by various authors (for example, Sue and Sue, 1990; Maxime, 1986) that other minority groups share similar processes of development. In Britain, Maxime (1986) has used Cross's model in the understanding of identity confusion in black adolescents.

Parham (1989) has expanded Cross's nigrescence model. He integrates Cross's (1971) model into three developmental stages: adolescence, middle adulthood, and late adulthood. He argues that it is during adolescence and early adulthood that a person might first experience nigrescence, and after this first experience, the likelihood of experiencing nigrescence is present for the rest of a person's life.

Implications for youth workers

How does one rear a black child to have a positive identity in a predominantly white society? Youth workers, teachers and social workers who work with black children and young people should attempt to answer this question. Discrimination can have damaging effects on the psychological adjustment and self-esteem of young children and adolescents. In particular, through racial prejudice the black adolescent in Britain is subjected to derogatory views and negative self-images projected not only by the media, but also by teachers, parents and the wider society. Early in life, the child acquires knowledge of how the black person is viewed in society. Youth workers need to be aware that raising children in a white-dominated society places special pressures on the black parent. Comer and Pouissant propose various ways in which black parents can promote racial pride in their children. They suggest that 'parents can discuss color and race-related issues in a natural way' (1992: 17). Other important tools in combating poor racial identity are talk (open acknowledgement of racial issues), positive modelling, and reinforcement of a child's cultural heritage (blackness) (Powell-Hopson and Hopson, 1990). These techniques could be employed by youth workers involved in working with black adolescents who experience difficulty in maintaining a positive black identity.

Although most black adolescents in Britain 'possess the survival skills necessary for the development of a positive racial identity [there are those] who experience difficulty in maintaining a positive sense of racial identity' (Maxime, 1986: 101). Youth workers will need to have an understanding of Cross's model of racial identity development in order to work effectively with black adolescents who experience identity confusion. In working with this group of adolescents the issue of race must always be addressed. A youth worker should listen for cues about the role of race when asking the young person about peer relationships, school life, struggles with independence, occupational choices, and parental relationships. To deny the significance of the race of a black person as an important part of identity is to deny an important and overriding aspect of his/her being. The youth worker needs to help the adolescent in recognising the denial of his/her identity by helping him/her question and confront his/her perceptions and his/her use of denial. He or she must assist the young person in uncovering and examining the fears etc. underlying this defence. Black youth need to understand and re-evaluate negative images of their own group. This process can be expected to lead eventually to a more secure sense of self and more healthy adjustment. Cross's model is useful in mapping out the process by which black youth achieve a positive racial identity. Racial identity models have helped mental health professionals in understanding the psychological aspects of racial identity development. Pre-encounter attitudes have been linked to high levels of anxiety, psychological dysfunction, depression (Carter, 1991; Parham and Helms, 1985), and low self-regard and self-esteem (Parham and Helms, 1985). Young people's perceptions of the worker are likely to be influenced by their racial identity development. Young people at the pre-encounter stage are more likely to show a preference for a white worker over a black worker. An encounter client is likely to seek a black worker, believing that their shared racial group membership will increase understanding.

In Britain, Maxime (1986) has used Cross's (1971) model in the understanding of identity confusion in black adolescents and adults. Maxime cites the case of a girl who had been in a children's home for nine years. She was described by her social worker as 'a well-adjusted, obedient little girl who will fit nicely into a family'. However, Maxime discovered that the girl was 'unable to accept herself [as black] and hold positive feelings about herself' (1986: 103). An understanding of Cross's model should sensitise youth workers to the role that oppression plays in a black individual's development. The model will help youth workers in recognising differences between members of the black group with respect to their racial identity. It serves as a useful assessment tool for youth workers to gain a greater understanding of black youth (Helms, 1985).

Youth workers, teachers and social workers need to also understand and analyse their own biases, assumptions, values, and feelings before any help can be given to black adolescents.

References

Bateman, A. and Holmes, J. (1995) *Introduction to Psychoanalysis*, London: Routledge.
Carter, R.T. (1991) 'Racial identity attitudes and psychological functioning', *Journal of Multicultural Counselling and Development*, 19: 105–15.
Comer, J.P. and Pouissant, A.F. (1992) *Raising Black Children*, New York: Plume.
Cross, W.E. (1971) 'The Negro to Black conversion experience: towards the psychology of Black liberation', *Black World*, 20: 13–27.
Cross, W.E. (1980) 'Models of psychological nigrescence: a literature review', in R.L. Jones (ed.), *Black Psychology*, 2nd edn, New York: Harper & Row.
Cross, W.E. (1985) 'Black identity: rediscovering the distinction between personal identity and reference group orientation', in M.B. Spencer, G.K. Brookins and W.R. Allen (eds) *Beginnings: the Social and Affective Development of Black Children*, Hillsdale, NJ. Erlbaum.
Cross, W.E. (1991) *Shades of Black: Diversity in African American Identity*, Philadelphia: Temple University Press.
Cross, W.E., Parham, T.A. and Helms, J.E. (1991) 'The stages of Black identity development: nigrescence models', in R.L. Jones (ed.), *Black Psychology*, 3rd edn, Berkeley, CA: Cobb & Henry.
Dalal, F. (1988) 'The racism of Jung', *Race and Class*, 29 (3): 1–22.
Erikson, H. (1964) 'Memorandum on identity and Negro youth', *Journal of Social Issues*, 20 (4): 29–42.
Erikson, H. (1968) *Identity: Youth and Crisis*, London: Faber.
Fernando, S. (1991) *Mental Health, Race and Culture*, London: Macmillan.
Freud, S. (1912–13) *Totem and Taboo*, Harmondsworth: Penguin.
Freud, S. (1930) 'Civilization and its discontents', in J. Strachey (ed.), *The Standard Edition of the Complete Works of Sigmund Freud*, vol. 21, trans. J. Riviere, London: Hogarth.

Frosh, S. (1987) *The Politics of Psychoanalysis*, London: Macmillan.

Hall, W.S., Cross, W.E. and Freedie, R. (1972) 'Stages in the development of a black identity', ACT Research Report no. 50, Research and Development Division, American Testing Program, Iowa City.

Helms, J.E. (1985) 'Cultural identity in the treatment process', in P.B. Pedersen (ed.), *Handbook of Cross Cultural Counselling and Therapy*, Westport, CT: Greenwood Press.

Jung, C. (1950) 'On the psychology of the Negro', in W. McGuire (ed.), *Collected Works of Carl Jung*, vol. 18, Princeton, NJ: Princeton University Press.

Looney, J. (1988) 'Ego development and black identity', *The Journal of Black Psychology*, 15 (1): 41–56.

Mama, A. (1995) *Beyond the Masks*, London: Routledge.

Maxime, J. (1986) 'Some psychological models of black self-concept', in S. Ahmed, J. Cheetham and J. Small (eds), *Social Work with Black Children and their Families*, London: Batsford.

Mitchell, J. (1974) *Feminism and Psychoanalysis*, London: Allen Lane.

Parham, T.A. (1989) 'Cycles of psychological nigrescence', *The Counselling Psychologist*, 17 (2): 187–226.

Parham, T.A. and Helms, J. (1985) 'Relation of racial identity to self-actualization and affective states of black students', *Journal of Counselling Psychology*, 28 (3): 250–6.

Powell-Hopson, D. and Hopson, D.S. (1990) *Different and Wonderful: Raising Black Children in a Race Conscious Society*, New York: Prentice-Hall.

Robinson, L. (1995) *Psychology for Social Workers: Black Perspectives*, London: Routledge.

Spencer, M.B. (1988) 'Self concept development', in D.T. Slaughter (ed.), *Black Children in Poverty: Developmental Perspectives*, San Francisco: Jossey-Bass.

Sue, D.W. and Sue, D. (1990) *Counselling the Culturally Different*, New York: Wiley.

17
Technologies of the Self

Maria Pini

Technologies of the self . . . permit individuals to effect by their own means or with the help of others a number of operations on their bodies and souls, thought, conduct and way of being, so as to transform themselves in order to attain a certain state of happiness, purity wisdom, perfection or immortality.

Michel Foucault, 'Technologies of the Self'

One of Foucault's major contributions to academic thinking was his foregrounding of the human body as the site of power operations. What his work directs us towards is a recognition that power does not exist 'outside of' or separately from the individual body, as an oppressive or repressive constraint. Rather, power is the complex and ever-present force which enables us to become human subjects in relation to other subjects within the wider organisation we call society. To say that power works directly upon bodies means thinking about the 'self' and 'identity' as always embodied. Traditionally, the 'self' has been seen as some kind of inner 'essence' or 'mental' phenomenon which exists 'inside of' the body. Foucault's work and those who have drawn upon it seek to challenge this, arguing that the physical body has to be seen as the primary surface upon which our selves are constructed. This means thinking about our 'selves' as produced out of the many ways in which our bodies are classified, managed, disciplined and regulated by others and also by ourselves.

To understand this proposal, it is important to grasp Foucault's basic idea of the relations between power and knowledge. For him, these terms are inseparable. Where there is knowledge, there is power. 'Knowledge' of ourselves and of others is never simply a neutral or objective 'understanding'. Rather, this knowledge is always bound up with our specific historical and cultural location. One of Foucault's key examples in demonstrating this argument comes from his analysis of the history of sexuality, which shows how, within different cultural and historical contexts, particular ideas about sexuality emerge – ideas which function as 'truths'. Therefore, what we 'know' about sexuality and how we experience this are inextricably bound to our historical and social position. Something as 'objective' sounding as the statement 'I am gay' or 'you are straight' is then always the product of a particular history which makes the statement meaningful. In his analysis of sexuality, therefore, Foucault illustrates how something which is considered one of the most private, most personal and most fundamental aspects of our being is the product of a wider network of disciplinary practices. This network is shown to have a specific history and race, sex, sexuality, and so forth, are meaningful only in as much as they are part of this wider classificatory system.

In one sense, Foucault's model of power/knowledge seems to offer a rather pessimistic view of our being in the world. We can never escape the workings of power because it is only through power/knowledge that we can come to be who we are. Further, these power/knowledge processes are tied into a drive to discipline and regulate. However, just as Foucault argued that where there is knowledge there is power, he also argued that where there is power there is resistance. If the body is seen as the primary target of power, then it can also be a site of resistance. Bodies can 'resist' their particular classification by 'speaking out' in ways which challenge or 'upset' established order, in ways deemed 'inappropriate'. Foucault was therefore interested in seeing what he called 'subjugated' (or censored) voices 'speak out' in resistance to their regulation. He pointed, for example, to the gay liberation movement, which developed what he called a 'reverse discourse' which sought to legitimise itself. Hence the human, embodied subject is not simply a passive recipient of a wider disciplinary drive. S/he can appropriate her/his own power through creating her/his own oppositional knowing and naming. However, oppositional practices and discourses, once established, also become bound up within their own power/knowledge systems. Feminist politics provides a clear example of this. Feminism developed out of a drive to resist what were seen as men's definitions of women. However, and as many non-white and working class women have argued, it also developed its own definitions of 'proper' feminist activity and its own classifications of 'right' and 'wrong' action. As a result, it can therefore be seen to have developed its own disciplinary practices – practices which might involve 'correcting' other women, or 'keeping a check' on one's self. Hence, from a Foucauldian perspective, there is no completely unregulated space, no space which is ever free from the workings of power and its attendant regulatory drive. Even oppositional struggles can be seen to involve their own regulatory mechanisms. What is important, however, is the wider effect of such struggles. So, to return to the examples of the feminist and gay liberation movements, one can acknowledge the challenges posed by such movements whilst at the same time recognising that such movements also involve their own means of regulating subjects.

A further important feature of 'oppositional' or 'reverse' discourses is that these discourses do not come from 'outside' of the system they seek to challenge. Often, these oppositional movements use the *same* language which previously functioned to problematise them. Clear examples come in the recent gay reappropriation of the term 'queer' and contemporary black film-makers' reappropriation of the term 'nigger'. Alternatively, one might think of certain brands of radical feminism which take on the discourse of a 'natural' and essential difference between men and women (a discourse which traditionally casts women as 'naturally' inferior) in order to make claims for men's 'naturally' more aggressive characters. So, the important thing about these discourses is who is using them, and why and where they are being used.

Power, bodies and resistance

Having outlined some of Foucault's central arguments, I now want to briefly consider how this work can be applied to an understanding of certain contemporary youth practices. What is the value of all of this work to those working with young people today? What does it tell us about youth practices, and most importantly what is its use 'in the field'? To recap:

1   Selfhood or subjectivity is produced out of the many ways in which our bodies are classified, managed, disciplined and regulated by others and by ourselves.
2   Power works through this 'management' of bodies.
3   The individual body is not 'passive' but can also be a site of resistance.

What is fundamental to Foucauldian thinking, and indeed to what we call 'poststructuralist' thinking in general, is the argument that selves (which are always considered embodied) are socially constructed. What this means is that our selves do not emerge 'naturally' but are produced within a wider historical and social context. Embodied selves, however, are not seen as simply being passive within these processes. So, how do we negotiate a sense of self? If 'experts' (doctors, social workers, psychiatrists, judges and so forth) have their own professional criteria by which the population is classified, then how do we – as individuals relate to these criteria? What is the work that we do in the process of identity formation? To return to the quote which opens this chapter, Foucault formulates the concept 'technologies of the self' to get at the many ways in which we create or transform our own selves – our own 'bodies and souls', as he puts it. These 'technologies of the self', or what we might call 'modes of enselfment' (ways of becoming a self), include all the different ways in which we 'work upon' our bodies so as to become a self and achieve a sense of fulfilment. However, these 'technologies of the self' are always related to our specific historical and social location – and so too are the particular senses of 'freedom', pleasure and so forth we strive towards. If the eighteenth century Catholic sought a sense of purity and freedom through the processes of confessing, then how do we seek such senses today, and what particular pleasures do we look for? To put this another way, by what means are contemporary bodies transformed in their quests for fulfilment?

To begin, it is possible to argue that within the conditions of economic hardship facing most young people in Britain today, the physical body has become one of the main places where control can be exerted. In a moment where most young people can 'manage' little else, the body provides one important site for management and also becomes the primary vehicle for the achievement of pleasure. Clearly, for young people the developing adult body has always provided one of the primary sites for the execution of control. The use of drugs, cigarettes, alcohol etc. and the cultivation of a particular fashion for oneself can, in this context, all be seen as attempts to stake out an independence from the parental and societal regulation of these bodies. In other words, they can be seen as attempts to explore the pleasuring and management of one's self. However, we can find this stress on self-pleasuring reaching an extreme within today's youth practices. Examples of this suggestion are all around us, in the growth of body-building; in the increase of interest in 'new age' notions of achieving 'higher' states of awareness and fulfilment through meditation or 'trancing'; in the ever-growing use of drugs such as 'ecstasy'; in the popularity of dance-based music scenes; in the spread of body-piercing and other forms of body decoration. The physical body has become *the* major source of pleasure. Where job prospects and long-term planning become increasingly dismal, immediate bodily pleasure has arguably replaced far-sightedness. Raving, for instance, and the large amounts of money and time invested in this, can be seen as a form of 'resistance' to this wider economic and social depression. Further, it is easy to read rave culture as a mass attempt on the part of young people both to resist their wider regulation as subjects and to create for themselves a more collective world wherein individuals can gain a sense of oneness with others. Within rave and post-rave dance cultures emphasis has largely moved away from sexual pick-up, and been replaced by a 'pleasuring' of the self. Song and DJ lyrics tell ravers to 'work your body', 'take it higher' and so forth. Some have related this absorption in one's own body to the wider spread of HIV and AIDS and have argued that perhaps dance has replaced sex as a means of interpersonal physical contact. Angela McRobbie suggests that in this climate of economic depression and ever-growing fears about the 'dangers' of sex, one can find in rave the development of a 'hyper-sexual' feminine appearance in the form of scanty dresses (and one could point to the more recent cultivation of a 'Barbie doll' look) which can be seen as an 'empty signifier'. What this means is that the 'look' is there without its traditional connotations and in this sense it can be seen as a form of 'reverse discourse'. This reading highlights how young people can take on and subvert conventional signs, and so create for themselves 'oppositional' identities and hence a sense of control over the meanings of their own bodies (McRobbie, 1994).

Clearly, it is not only Foucault's work which makes us rethink how young people work upon their bodies in the construction of their (often oppositional) identities. Hebdige illustrates the many ways in which young people can take certain objects, words or symbols and re-create the meanings of these in order to 'resist' and assert some control over their own destiny. He takes the example of the Punk girl's laddered stockings, exaggerated eye make-up and bin-liners in posing a challenge to conventional understandings of femininity (Hebdige, 1979). In a similar way, it is possible to read the rave girl's 'babe' presentation of herself as a form of challenge. McRobbie reads further into this 'look' and sees within it a form of 'escape' back into childhood which she claims is one way of managing the body within a wider climate of depression, threat (environmental, sexual, economic etc.) and general hopelessness and 'resisting' this hopelessness.

To return to Foucault's conception of 'technologies of the self' which permit us to reach a state of happiness, we find, within rave culture, enormous stress on 'taking the self higher'. It is through drugs, music, and dance that the particular self of rave is produced. The raver strives to move 'beyond' the confines of the individual body and become part of something 'bigger'. Ravers' accounts of events and the use of 'E' repeatedly stress a sense of 'losing oneself' to a bigger body of rave. This body is seen as a wider 'spiritual' body wherein participants all feel 'connected' with one another (Pini, 1996). Arguably, this is one way in which young people today actively cultivate a sense of belonging and unity within a culture wherein these features are quickly being eroded. On the other hand, the practices of rave (such as dancing all night on appetite-suppressant E or speed) also go hand in hand with a wider stress for women on remaining thin. Hence, something which on the one hand represents a form of 'resistance', can also be seen to represent a collusion with a wider disciplining of the female body. This alerts us to the complicated nature of both power and 'resistance'.

Another significant factor which emerges from looking at raving is the extent to which the raver very much regulates her/his self. For many, raving is associated with ultimate freedom; the freedom to – in rave terms – 'go mental'. This apparent freedom is seen by certain authorities as posing a threat to established order and to the 'safety' of the young. However, when we look more closely at what is involved in the processes of reaching the 'peak' state which the raver strives towards, what is clear is the amount of hard work (many stress that they have to 'push it' to reach a 'peak'); self-monitoring (many stress the constant 'checks' kept on the self to 'keep at bay' the potential 'paranoia' which threatens to disturb the 'peak'); self-classifying (in terms of 'coming up', 'coming down', 'rushing' etc.); self-regulating (by coming to know what drugs, in what quantity and so on, are best suited to one's personal body, and what kinds of music are needed to reach the proper 'peak': for some it is 'Jungle' whilst for others it is 'Trance'); and self-management (the management of drug effects by drinking enough water to avoid dehydration). Hence what is obvious is the extent to which these young people regulate and manage *themselves*. This clearly carries implications for traditional perceptions of the young as simply 'victims' in need of interventionist 'care'. For those working with the young, this highlights the extent to which these people develop their *own* strategies of 'care' and self-management. Hence, these young people, far from being in need of external control and regulation, devise their own means of managing themselves, assessing and limiting potential risks.

The fact that young people, far from passively adopting the latest fashion, or 'unthinkingly' aligning themselves with particular sub-cultures, ongoingly negotiate these identities for themselves, forces us to rethink traditional perceptions of the young as either the victims or the perpetrators of particular social 'problems'. That aspects of power, control and subjectivity formation are central in young people's management of their bodies is clear. Just as wider bodies like school, work, parents, social work etc. are active in attempting to regulate young people, the young themselves develop strategies to command control over their definition and their bodies. One might point to the growing number of (largely working class) teenage mothers who, in becoming pregnant, pose a challenge to wider attempts at regulating them. Similarly, anorexia (traditionally seen as the young girl's passive adoption of societal definitions of beauty) can be read as an attempt to assert control over a body which is not only surrounded by fears of the 'uncontrolled' feminine, but which is also rapidly changing and growing. Likewise, the young man who 'works out' every day represents a clear illustration of the management of the physical in the constitution of identity. Also, to reiterate, we can think of the recent cultivation on the streets and in the clubs of a female 'Barbie doll' look (one which in feminist terms might be seen as retrogressive), which has subsequently been taken up within TV programmes like 'The Girlie Show' or 'God's Gift' and which signals an arguably 'resistant' image of femininity, one which poses in the attire traditionally associated with passivity and availability but which redefines this in terms of assertiveness and active desire.

For those working with the young, poststructuralism illustrates the complex power relations involved in the management and regulation of bodies and the negotiation of identities. Hence, it is important not only to see how the physical body is constructed within the disciplinary practices of health, law, schooling and so forth, but also to see how young people themselves negotiate their bodies. It is important to recognise, therefore, that regulation does not simply come 'down' on young people from above. They regulate and manage their own bodies, experiencing them as sites of both pleasure and resistance – sometimes with the effect of producing the selves expected of them, sometimes with the effect of challenging these expectations.

References

Foucault, M. (1976) *The History of Sexuality*, vol. 1, London: Peregrine.

Foucault, M. (1988) 'Technologies of the self', in L.H. Martin, H. Gutman and P.H. Hutton (eds), *Technologies of the Self*, London: Tavistock.

Hall, S. (1996) *Race as a Floating Signifier*, talk given at Goldsmiths' College, 29 February 1996.

Hebdige, D. (1979) *Subculture: the Meaning of Style*, London: Routledge.

McRobbie, A. (1994) *Postmodernism and Popular Culture*, London: Routledge.

Pini, M. (1996) 'Women and the early British rave scene', in A. McRobbie (ed.), *Back to Reality: the Social Experience of Cultural Studies*, Manchester: Manchester University Press.

18
Sexuality

Tim Edwards

Sexuality, as practice and as identity, for young people today appears increasingly complex and difficult to control. More recent concerns over contraception and pregnancy, the age of consent for male homosexuals, sex education and AIDS/HIV transmission, appear to compound older issues such as economic dependency and the struggle to define oneself outside of parental or state interference. The state, in particular, appears increasingly intrusive, involving itself in everything from education to housing and care, and from contraception to consent. It is, then, my primary purpose in this chapter to try to unpack and explore exactly what is new or at issue here and what perhaps represents a more historically common set of interests. The chapter has three sections: the first looking at more theoretical concerns and in particular social construction; the second addressing the question of gender; and the third applying the first two to contemporary sexual issues of importance to young people.

The social construction of sexuality

At its simplest, social constructionist theory states that sexuality, far from being inevitable or biologically driven, natural or normal, is socially constructed, that is to say shaped, controlled and subject to social, economic and political developments and circumstances. The perspective developed primarily out of opposition to essentialist viewpoints which see sexual identity and practice either as the result of genetics and instincts, as in the case of sociobiology; or as the outcome of unconscious drives and family formations, as in the example of psychoanalytic theory. The primary criticism of these essentialist perspectives is that they see sexuality as a uniform, fixed and unchanging phenomenon, a point that is often refuted in historical and anthropological findings (Greenberg, 1988).

As a consequence, social constructionist theory asserts that sexuality, as identity and as practice, varies from time to time and from place to place. For example, sexuality is neither seen nor practised in the same way in Africa or North America as it is in the UK, or in previous centuries or even the 1950s as it is now. However, a key division occurs around the distinction of sexual acts from sexual identities. Sexual acts are relatively universal, as, for example, heterosexual intercourse takes place in all societies at all times; whilst sexual identities are relatively new overall and often specific to Western societies, though not exclusively. This point is applied particularly vociferously to homosexuality, as, whilst homosexual acts are seen as relatively universal, the homosexual identity is seen as primarily a modern and Western phenomenon (Plummer, 1981; 1992; Weeks, 1985).

Social constructionist theorists vary according to the degree of construction involved and what they perceive as the main causes or mechanisms of change and development. For example, for some so called 'soft' constructionists it is only the societal reaction to sexuality which is primarily socially shaped; whilst for so-called 'hard' constructionists it is the very concept and practice of sexuality itself that is constructed (Vance, 1989). Similarly, for some theorists, most particularly Jeffrey Weeks, it is developments in the economy of industrial capitalism, the rise of the state and the creation of a modern sexuality in tandem with the formation of modern society which is at issue; whilst for others it is the individual learning of sexual identities and roles which is the key factor in the social construction of sexuality (see Plummer, 1975; 1995; and Weeks, 1977; 1981; 1985 particularly).

Many of Jeffrey Weeks's ideas are directly derived from the work of Michel Foucault, perhaps the most influential of all theorists of sexuality in recent times. In the introduction to his three-volume work *The History of Sexuality* (1978), Foucault overthrows the myth of the 'repressive hypothesis', namely the idea that Victorian society repressed all forms of sexuality, and asserts to the contrary that the same period saw an unprecedented 'production' of sexual discourse, of talk concerning sexuality, and the creation of a whole series of sexual categories and types from homosexuality to sadomasochism (Foucault 1978; 1984a; 1984b). In short, the *repression* of sexuality was the *production* of sexuality.

The key motor in this 'production' of sexuality was the rise of the modern state, defined in the widest sense to include medicine, psychiatry and similar professions which sought to control, regulate and categorise, as well as treat and cure, the sexual individual.

Numerous criticisms have since followed Foucault's assertions, not least of all the absence of a more gendered sense of power, a point put forcibly by some feminists whose work I wish to explore more later. Foucault's perspective upon sexuality is essentially a macro or wide-view one, often encompassing several centuries or countries at a time. As such, it contrasts sharply with other forms of social constructionist theory as explored through interactionism, a micro or small-scale perspective (see Plummer 1975; 1981). Plummer sees sexuality as understood and learned in interaction with the wider society as part of an individual's or group's own developmental process. This applies particularly well to 'coming out' and similar sexual 'stories' and, more recently, he has also applied the model to issues of sexual exploitation and rape (Plummer, 1995).

To sum up, there is clearly a series of contradictions at work in social constructionist theory, as for more historical social constructionists, like Foucault or Weeks, the answers lie in the wider society and the processes of history itself; whilst for more interactionist social constructionists, like Ken Plummer, the solutions lie at a more individual level. More recently, some critics have also pointed to the empirical weaknesses of the perspective, pointing out that there is a neglect of the continuities, as opposed to changes, in societal reactions towards sexuality across time and space (Greenberg, 1988).

The gender factor

So far I have considered sexuality in a gender neutral way, that is to say without regard to differences according to sex. This is clearly incorrect, as the experience of boys and girls as they become young men and young women are not the same and are, in particular, gendered or shaped in relation to their sex. For young men growing up, issues tend to centre upon questions of sexual access and prowess as the development of their sexuality is often tied up with the formation of their masculinity or manhood; whilst for young women, sexuality is often inherently more risky with concerns centring upon contraception, sexual exploitation or self-protection.

One particular and common concern is the so-called double standard which comes into play as boys and girls reach puberty. Whilst promiscuous boys are often praised for their prowess or merely seen as reckless youths, girls behaving in similar ways are often castigated as sexually depraved and deserving of all that comes to them. More recent concerns in relation to the transmission of AIDS and HIV have often done little to alter this situation as girls carrying condoms are often seen as 'loose' whilst boys, following the liberation of the contraceptive pill, still have problems in seeing contraception as part of their responsibility (Holland et al., 1991; 1992; Wight, 1993; 1994).

Many of these problems, as well as the more general importance of gender in relation to sexuality, have of course been raised by feminist theorists, some of whom have been severely critical of the often gender blind or sexist nature of much of the social constructionist theory mentioned earlier (Jeffreys, 1990; Stanley, 1984). Nevertheless, like social constructionists, feminist theorists vary in their perspectives upon sexuality. Some still primarily align themselves with social constructionism and see gendered differences in sexuality as a result of the same processes that shape all aspects of modern sexuality including the formation of the modern state and industrial capitalism (Segal, 1987; Vance, 1984). For others, though, the gendered differences in sexuality are not explained so simply and more attention is necessarily paid to the question of gender itself. For some feminists, the concept and practice of sexuality are inherently 'masculine' or controlled and designed to support men's power over women. For example, the contraceptive pill, often seen as part of the modern emancipation of women, is seen alternatively as a source of free sexual access for men (Jeffreys, 1990). Most importantly, many feminists have highlighted the important part sexual exploitation from harassment to rape plays in shaping and controlling women's lives (Brownmiller, 1975; Hanmer and Saunders, 1984; Morgan, 1977; Russell, 1984). Similarly, some feminists have also highlighted the significance of pornography and the misrepresentation of women's sexuality more generally as causal of women's oppression (Dworkin, 1981; Mackinnon, 1987).

The clear difficulty for these perspectives lies in making such important points square with the empirical reality that individual situations are necessarily more varied whilst retaining the significance of underlying gendered mechanisms. Some feminists have also pointed to the importance of reclaiming sexuality as a site of pleasure for women as well as protecting them from sexual danger (Vance, 1984; Rubin, 1984; Segal, 1987; 1994). The very clear difficulty of providing a safe space for women to explore their sexual pleasures separate or free from sexual exploitation and violence, though, is not easily resolved and is a point which feminists continue to wrestle with today. To summarise, gender is of clear importance to our understanding of the differing sexual experiences of young men and young women and yet this can easily slide into over-generalisation, and the difficulty of recognising its significance as well as its complexities remains.

Power, control and responsibility

In this next section, I wish to consider some of the issues raised in the previous two sections in relation to a selection of contemporary concerns to young people, in turn connected to questions of power, control and responsibility.

One of the primary and increasing concerns to young people today is their sexual learning or sex education. Sex education is traditionally secondary to all other forms of education inside and outside of schools. This is often due to the assumption that sexuality is not something one is taught and therefore needs to learn, rather 'it just happens'. This point echoes the tension of constructionist and essentialist viewpoints outlined earlier, as does the associated criticism that sex education 'puts ideas in young people's heads'. Despite the point that it is difficult to conceive of even the most sheltered adolescent not having the idea of sex in their head already, this viewpoint derives from the essentialist 'domino theory' of sexuality where, like dominoes in a line, if one knocks down one defence then all defences against 'an unruly tide of sexuality' are apparently lost.

The contrary point that young people know of sexuality already, and therefore need educating appropriately, is premised on an entirely different notion of childhood, that of knowingness as opposed to innocence, which curiously still echoes the same essentialist–constructionist tension: if children know of sexuality *prior to* learning it, then *how* do they know it? The resolution of sorts lies in the reality that many young people learn sexuality outside of school, and frequently outside of the family as well in talking with friends, finding sexually explicit materials perhaps accidentally or more intentionally, and most widely through the media. In addition, young people learn sexuality through experimentation, or trial and error, that often takes years to develop.

If one accepts, and plenty do not, that there is a need for some kind of sex education to help young people through the wilderness of their early experiences, then the next question centres on the form and content that the education should take. Sex education in the past has traditionally centred upon physical or medical concerns and has left out social or personal questions such as contraception, exploitation and the myriad of potential emotional impacts opened up through sexuality. Part of the difficulty clearly is that the variety of individual circumstances and experiences is simply too vast to fit into the curriculum; the other part of the difficulty is the profound discomfort we still feel when talking openly of sexuality. Most importantly, the whole question of the content of sex education is politically controlled. For example, where more social aspects of sexuality are included in the curriculum, this is frequently in conservative terms of heterosexual and loving couples, leaving out advice concerning casual relationships and homosexuality. As a result of all of these factors, sex education is located in a force-field of politics and power relations, often involving the state, which echo Foucault's earlier concerns with sexual control.

The recent increase in concern over sex education has tended to stem from other contemporary concerns and particularly contraception and the AIDS/HIV crisis. The concern over contraception has centred upon the apparent and comparative explosion in rates of teenage pregnancy. The primary point to make here is that whilst rates have increased over recent decades, rates have also started to level off and fall in some cases (Central Statistical Office, 1995). These issues then tap into increasing paranoia concerning the changing form of family life and the family itself. For example, the anxiety over contraception for girls under the legal age of sexual consent not only opens up questions to do with the legitimation of sexuality, but also raises issues to do with support for alternative lifestyles and, within this, the sexual autonomy of young women.

The importance of the legitimation of sexuality *per se* has applied more directly to discussion of the AIDS/HIV crisis. AIDS as a sexually transmitted and currently terminal medical condition has shaken Western society with anxiety since its discovery in the early 1980s. However, its more specific impact upon young people was of less concern until more recently. More particularly, it was the awareness of rising rates of seroconversion among young people, stemming from social research as well as epidemiological studies, which stimulated discussion and controversy. Young people were clearly acting upon their sexuality earlier, and studies such as Project SIGMA, for example, demonstrated that young gay men in particular were taking serious risks in having unprotected intercourse (Davies, 1993; Remafedi, 1994; Rotherhan-Borus et al., 1995). Similarly, the difficulties for often powerless young women in protecting themselves from sexually transmitted diseases were also increasingly more apparent (Richardson, 1987). Whilst safer sex campaigners and charities asked for increased access and resources to produce more sexually explicit educational materials, they faced a Conservative government clamp-down on funds and access alike, most notoriously in Section 28 which sought to outlaw local authority 'promotion' of homosexual lifestyles and similar 'pretend' families. At stake was a concern not to legitimate any form of sexuality, let alone gay sexuality, in apparent contradiction with the increasing complexity of its experience.

Despite this, I would argue that the most major concerns to young people here do not centre upon sex education; they are rather located in the wider context of power relations. Young people are traditionally not only inexperienced, they are economically dependent upon their families and the state and, most importantly, they are tied up in the myriad of messages from home, school and media which provide a confusing array of signals as to how to handle their sexuality. In short, they are relatively powerless. Whilst sex education is potentially one form of empowerment, it is the wider context in which young people live that truly puts them at risk and which needs to accommodate them. The position for young men in this respect is particularly difficult, for traditional male roles are losing relevance as unemployment looms and young women decreasingly depend upon men economically or emotionally. Young women are conversely faced with an increasing array of confusing and partially legitimated options as traditional roles for women are similarly undermined.

In this last section, I wish to concentrate upon some of the most contentious issues surrounding young people and sexuality, particularly homosexuality and institutional care. Since the late 1960s, gay sexuality has increased in its status as an alternative lifestyle, tolerated in some sectors of society and certainly more visible, but it remains a deeply stigmatised identity where the twin threats of social castigation and institutional discrimination remain. In addition, for young people growing up aware early of their homosexuality, the lack of positive support and guidance for their development often increases their sense of isolation and decreases their sense of self-worth, whilst the formal and informal pressures to conform to heterosexual norms are often immense. This amounts to what has been called 'compulsory heterosexuality', a term initially applied to women yet which applies equally well to men. Social policy, particularly Section 28, has attempted to completely annihilate the potential of putting homosexuality in the school curriculum, whilst peer groups often apply the most pressure in stigmatising homosexuality through everything from name-calling to complete ostracism. All of this then compounds to hinder not only a young person's coming-out process, or disclosure of their sexuality to themselves, others and society at large, but rather their entire psychosexual development.

In addition, continuing confusion centres on the conflation of male homosexuality and paedophilia, or sexual relations of adults with children. Concerns raised during the campaign to lower the age of consent for gay men exemplified this process as claims were made repeatedly that young men, uncertain of their sexual orientation, were open to the lures and corruption of older men. Similarly, many recent concerns centring upon the sexual exploitation of young people in institutional care perpetuated the stereotype of the homosexual paedophile preying on young people.

Despite the sensationalism of the mass media, most cases of sexual exploitation of young people involve heterosexually identified perpetrators, even when homosexual acts are involved. The distinction of acts from identities is thus critical here, as it is often not the self-identified gay man who is at fault but, rather the heterosexually identified man seeking to satisfy and legitimate his secret homosexual practices. Fears concerning sexual exploitation in institutional care, whilst clearly an important issue, also mask wider questions to do with the sexual exploitation of young people and children that is conducted within the parental home or the confines of the family. It is often at this level that conflicts of 'family versus state' occur, echoing earlier concerns with the powerlessness of young people, the power of the state and the fundamental importance of the family. Following on from this, then, the need to distinguish fact from fiction and to develop an awareness of differing implications in terms of gender and sexual orientation is of paramount importance.

Conclusion

Throughout this chapter, I have emphasised the importance of social construction in shaping young people's sexual experiences. In particular, I have also highlighted the significance of gender and sexual orientation in understanding the often dual role of the state in simultaneously attempting to ameliorate and control young people's experiences of sexuality. In the final analysis, though, it is the role of social constructionist theory in separating fact from fiction, myth from reality, that is of primary importance in understanding and improving the often uneasy relationship of youth and sexuality. Solutions to the difficult situations that develop, though, do not lie solely in a reconstitution of the role of the state: rather they are located in a wider sense of understanding of the overall position of young people today. Their dependency upon the family and the state, in an era of educational expansion, high unemployment, sexual risk and contradictorily increasing pressures from all forms of the media for their sexual, emotional and economic independence, is quite unprecedented and requires a radical rethinking of young people's empowerment in a social, economic and political context which seemingly disempowers them at every turn. In short, if we expect young people to act like adults, then we need to provide the conditions for them to do so; this involves giving them the same rights and responsibilities that we expect ourselves.

References

Brownmiller, S. (1975) *Against Our Will; Men, Women and Rape*, New York: Simon & Schuster.

Central Statistical Office (1995) *Social Trends*, London: HMSO.

Davies, P. (1993) *Sex, Gay Men and AIDS*, London: Falmer Press.

Dworkin, A. (1981) *Pornography: Men Possessing Women*, London: Women's Press.

Foucault, M. (1978) *The History of Sexuality. Vol. One: An Introduction*, Harmondsworth: Penguin.

Foucault, M. (1984a) *The History of Sexuality. Vol. Two: The Use of Pleasure: The History of Sexuality*, Harmondsworth: Penguin.

Foucault, M. (1984b) *The History of Sexuality. Vol. Three: The Care of the Self*, Harmondsworth: Penguin.

Greenberg, D. (1988) *The Construction of Homosexuality*, London: University of Chicago Press.

Hanmer, J. and Saunders, S. (1984) *Well Founded Fear: a Community Study of Violence to Women*, London: Hutchinson.

Holland, J., Ramazanogla, C., Scott, S., Sharpe, S. and Thomson, R. (1991) 'Between embarrassment and trust: young women and the diversity of condom use', in P. Aggleton, G. Hart and P. Davies (eds), *AIDS: Responses, Interventions and Care*, London: Falmer Press.

Holland, J., Ramazanogla, C., Scott, S., Sharpe, S. and Thomson, R. (1992) 'Pressure, resistance, empowerment: young women and the negotiation of safer sex', in P. Aggleton, P. Davies and G. Hart (eds), *AIDS: Rights, Risks And Reason*, London: Falmer Press.

Jeffreys, S. (1990) *Anticlimax: a Feminist Perspective on the Sexual Revolution*, London: Women's Press.

Mackinnon, C. (1987) *Feminism Unmodified: Feminist Discourses on Life and Law*, Cambridge, MA: Harvard University Press.

Morgan, R. (1977) *Going Too Far*, New York: Random House.

Plummer, K. (1975) *Sexual Stigma: an Interactionist Account*, London: Routledge & Kegan Paul.

Plummer, K. (ed.) (1981) *The Making of the Modern Homosexual*, London: Hutchinson.

Plummer, K. (ed.) (1992) *Modern Homosexualities: Fragments of Lesbian and Gay Experience*, London: Routledge.

Plummer, K. (1995) *Telling Sexual Stories: Power, Change and Social Worlds*, London: Routledge.

Remafedi, G. (1994) 'Predictors of unprotected intercourse among gay and bisexual youth: knowledge, beliefs and behaviour', *Paediatrics*, 94 *(2):* 63–198.

Richardson, D. (1987) *Women and the AIDS Crisis*, London: Pandora.

Rotheran-Borus, M., Reid, H., Rosario, M. and Kasen, S. (1995) 'Determinants of safer sex patterns among gay/bisexual male adolescents', *Journal of Adolescence*, 18 (1): 3–15.

Rubin, G. (1984) 'Thinking sex: notes for a radical theory of the politics of sexuality', in C. Vance (ed.), *Pleasure and Danger: Exploring Female Sexuality*, London: Routledge & Kegan Paul.

Russell, D. (1984) *Sexual Exploitation: Rape, Child Sexual Abuse, and Workplace Harassment*, Beverly Hills, CA: Sage.

Segal, L. (1987) *Is the Future Female? Troubled thoughts on Contemporary Feminism*, London: Virago.

Segal, L. (1994) *Straight Sex: the Politics of Pleasure*, London: Virago.

Stanley, L. (1984) 'Whales and minnows: some sexual theorists and their followers and how they contribute to make feminism invisible', *Women's Studies International Forum*, 7 (1):53–62.

Vance, C. (ed.) (1984) *Pleasure and Danger: Exploring Female Sexuality*, London: Routledge & Kegan Paul.

Vance, C. (1989) 'Social construction theory: problems in the history of sexuality', in D. Attman (ed.), *Which Homosexuality? Essays from the International Scientific Conference on Lesbian and Gay Studies*, London and Amsterdam: Gay Men's Press and Uitgeverij Andekker Schorer.

Weeks, J. (1977) *Coming Out: Homosexual Politics In Britain from the Nineteenth Century to the Present*, London: Quartet.

Weeks, J. (1981) *Sex, Politics and Society: the Regulation of Sexuality since 1800*, London: Longman.

Weeks, J. (1985) *Sexuality and Its Discontents: Meanings, Myths and Modern Sexualities*, London: Rouledge & Kegan Paul.

Wight, D. (1993) 'Constraints or cognition? Young men and safer heterosexual sex', in P. Aggleton, P. Davies and G. Hart (eds), *AIDS: Facing the Second Decade*, London: Falmer Press.

Wight, D. (1994) 'Assimilating safer sex: young heterosexual men's understanding of "safer sex"', in P. Aggleton, P. Davies and G. Hart (eds), *AIDS Foundations for the Future*, London: Taylor & Francis.

19
Constructing a Way of Life

Rex Stainton Rogers

> I would there were no age between sixteen and three-and-twenty, or that youth
> would sleep out the rest; for there is nothing in the between but getting wenches
> with child, wronging the ancientry, stealing, fighting.
>
> Shakespeare, *The Winter's Tale*

Sounds familiar doesn't it? This speech, which Shakespeare puts into the mouth
of 'an old shepherd' (much as a soap-opera writer today might have used a
'pensioner'), encapsulates a way of talking about youth which was already
ancient as he wrote. Similar views can be traced in many other cultures and they
persist in our own to this day. What the quotation brings to light for us is that
youth, as a supposed time of troublesome behaviour, was not 'discovered' by
social scientists or social workers – professions unknown in Shakespeare's day –
but predates them. However, what is certainly true is that we have views on this
portrayal of 'troublesome youth' which were unheard of in the London of James
the First.

From that time to our own, our resources for thinking about our world have
expanded. It isn't that people have got brighter, it isn't even a simple matter of
more and wider education (though we have that). The crucial shift has been in
the 'tools' we have available for understanding. This is obvious, of course, in a
literal sense: think of the kinds of equipment used to make *things*. Any trip to a
museum or historical theme park can make that point, as we compare an adze to
a power plane or an embroidery frame to a programmable sewing machine.
What is harder to illustrate are the less tangible changes that have taken place in
the ways in which we make *sense of things*. Yet, clearly, the tools we now employ
to construct a sense of, say, youth, make use of concepts that would have seemed
in 1610 as magical as electronic technology.

To give some idea, right from the start, about how resources for thinking have
expanded, we could do worse than look at what a modern audience might hear
about young people. The example I have chosen is an interesting one because it
concerns a reworking of another image of youth from Shakespeare, that of young
lovers. Youth, as social histories have recently made very clear, already had many
meanings, of which writers like Shakespeare made full use. Many – like that of
a time of 'hot' sexual pairing – still entertain (and, perhaps, trouble) us today. In
1957 the 'hit' musical was *West Side Story*, a *Romeo and Juliet* tale set in modern
New York. At one point in the action, gang members taunt the police with how
JDs (juvenile delinquents) are portrayed:

Dear kindly Sergeant Krupke,
You've gotta understand It's just our bringin' upke
That gets us outta hand.
Our mothers all are junkies,
Our fathers all are drunks,
Golly Moses – natcherly we're punks.
Gee Officer Krupke, we're very upset;
We never had the love that every child oughta get.
We ain't no delinquents,
We're misunderstood,
Deep down inside us there is good!

What Stephen Sondheim's lyrics put to his audience is not just observation or jibe, but expands into a whole range of *theories* about youth. These theories, the song suggests, are not just some kind of professional property but have become part of ordinary understanding: they are, for example, the kind of material the tabloids can confidently assume readers will recognise. What is more, they are also known to, and employed by, the young people that are supposed to be explained by them.

It is these theories of social life – tools for thought – that did not exist in Shakespeare's time – which help to construct our realities as surely as the new technologies that have shaped the New York in which *West Side Story* is set. Writing, in the broad sense of the word, is not just something writers do: it relies on communication between writers and audience. That, in turn, depends on the resources both sides have to shape their perceptions and their experience. It isn't that Shakespeare (or his first audiences) lived in a world free of street gangs (far from it – his contemporary Kit Marlowe died in a tavern brawl). But what they did seem to inhabit was a world largely empty of any profound need to 'understand' them or take informed action about them. Youth, as we might now see it, had not yet been shaped by the tools that today help to construct it as a *social issue*.

You have, of course, been set up. Set up to pose questions about why things have changed. Set up also to be drawn into an argument about *knowledge as a social issue*, in particular, our knowledge of what shapes us, of development. When Shakespeare wanted to explore developmental ideas he often resorted to magic and mystery (as he did, say, through the monster Caliban in *The Tempest*). Nearly two centuries on, towards the end of the eighteenth century, a new dimension had been added to our resources for exploring what we can know of the social world: science. In seeing how this happened, we will move from the fictional (however factive) output of Shakespeare and into a new reality of 'social facts' (the kinds of things that informed Sondheim). We will do so by looking at an event which more or less coincides with the emergence of social science around the end of the eighteenth century.

In 1799, a so-called wild (feral) boy, of perhaps 11 or 12, was captured by hunters in the woods of La Bassine, southern France. He was put into the care of a widow and escaped after eight days. Moving 'territory', he reached the Aveyron region, where he occasionally went to farms to be fed. On 8 January 1800 he entered a dyer's workshop and from there came to the attention of a local government officer Constans Saint-Estève, who committed him to an orphanage. Later that year he finished up in Paris where, as the *Sauvage de l'Aveyron* (or as we know him, the wild boy of Aveyron), he 'was to help answer the central question of the Enlightenment, what is the nature of Man [sic]' (Lane, 1977: 19).

Of course, the answers that investigators like Itard, who studied him, came up with were not definitive. Nor, by the way, were they much more clarified nearly two centuries later when a 'wild girl' of 13 – this time a victim of severe social isolation in her own home – was brought into a welfare office in Los Angeles and fell into the hands of present-day developmentalists. In my view, the story of Genie (Rymer, 1993), no less than that of the wild boy of Aveyron, tells us more about the social science mentality of those who used and abused them than it does about the human nature of the subjects of these studies. Yet, over the last two centuries, both these young people (and many like them) became cases and case studies in an argument about the roles and relative importance of the 'forces' of nature and nurture in shaping development.

Although the fine-grain theorisation of this debate has been refined over the last two centuries, its essentials have not. What French 'experts' were arguing in 1800, is still argued now: what is it that shapes us and how can we intervene upon it? The 'natural experiments' provided by wild children seem, to some, an ideal route to answers. The 'facts' seem obvious enough: 'wild children' are very odd, they don't behave like 'normal' teenagers in the most fundamental ways, and most obviously their language performance is absent or rudimentary. Sometimes, intervention can make a profound difference. But are such cases really testbeds from which to explore the well-springs of 'human nature' in general?

To take it for granted that they are, is to assume that when we look at anything young people do (say, being in the gangs Sondheim describes in *West Side Story*) we are seeing some kind of interplay between nature ('deep down inside us we are good') and nurture (something that stems from their 'bringin' upke'). Social constructionists like me regard such analyses as employing just one conceptual tool-box from a range of alternatives. We are not, in general, arguing against the idea that this particular tool-box is one which works well in the material world of objects (including the objects we call bodies). It has, for example, enabled us to discriminate between causes of diseases that are inherited (say like the Huntington's chorea which killed folk-singer Woody Guthrie) and acquired conditions like the AIDS which killed Freddie Mercury. It will also eventually provide the knowledge that will bring effective treatments for these conditions: in the material world, studying *causes* can lead to effective *interventions*. But are the Jets talking about causes in the same kind of sense when they tease Officer Krupke that they may be 'psychologically disturbed' or that 'Juvenile delinquency is purely a social disease'?

Many social scientists and social practitioners seem to subscribe to the idea that cause in the laboratory sense and cause in the social sense refer to effectively the same kind of agency. However, along with that way of thinking which is concerned with uncovering causes as a route to social engineering, there has been another tradition in thought over the last two centuries – *critique*. An important current trend in critical social analysis is social constructionism. We could sum up the distinction like this: if science begins with questions, critique begins by questioning those questions.

I admit to finding critique the more interesting of the two, but when I apply it to 'real life' issues like 'child abuse' (Stainton Rogers and Stainton Rogers, 1992) I often face the reaction: 'all very interesting but . . .'. The 'but' is often directed to practical concerns like: 'how does it help in this concrete situation I face?' I'm increasingly coming to respect that response: being a parent myself helps! But I'm also 'learning to listen' because I hear it more and more applied to mainstream social analysis as well. What I think is slowly percolating through is that just under 200 years of social science and social intervention have left us with precious little that could be called effective practical knowledge of human development.

One important reason why this is so can be expressed quite easily: *what most often concerns us about developments in human behaviour, and the developments that most concern us, are the result not of causes but of human actions (and inactions).* Unlike the movement of planets or the growth of trees in a virgin forest, social life is neither lawful nor brought about by simple forces. Of course, I'm not trying to deny facts about bodies as such – for example, that young people get hot and dehydrated dancing or that, should a fire break out, we need enough fire doors to rush bodies of certain sizes and mobility through. But what I do argue is that an interest in 'hops' or 'raves', a taste for 'winkle-pickers' or 'Dr Martens', are not primarily markers of some strange force of development but, rather, are matters that we as a society (and particularly young people as consumers) bring into being. Furthermore, what comes to be constructed in the social world (or discarded, like last year's fashion) is seldom the result of clear and straightforward plans and, even where it is, the outcomes are seldom exactly what we expect. They cannot be, in our sort of society anyway, because we live in a set of rapidly changing systems.

As those systems change, so too do our concerns. Few social scientists, if any, predicted the fall of the Soviet Empire, the emergence of the HIV, the transformation of Ecstasy into a major social drug, or the present highlighting of child sexual abuse. Yet each has had major effects on young people. However, our social soothsayers are often very good at being 'wise after the event'! Social constructionist Kenneth Gergen (1973) argues that being 'out of date' is inevitable: our social sciences will always be historical disciplines in disguise. 'Youth culture', including the idiom in which it is expressed, is not a thing but a living and changing way of life (which is what culture means in this context). Another reason for bringing you into the world of Sondheim's Jets is to allow you to savour just how ancient it all sounds! Today, we might feel a concern not only about how it portrays gender (we have, for example, the Jets and 'their girls', one of whom is unselfconsciously called 'Anybody's'!) but about what it fails to portray, 'girl gangs' in their own right.

The ironic result of the argument we have just been through is that the most predictable social worlds and the clearest examples of 'causes' that we can find lie outside of, or on the fringes of, our social-science-informed society. We can easily enough point to communities where young people are to a fair extent model and modelled citizens. They exist as small pockets in the industrialised world (usually in tight, well-regulated and somewhat 'time-frozen' religious sects like the Amish – featured in the movie *Witness*) and existed (at least until quite recently) in surviving hunter-gatherer communities like the !Kung of the Kalahari desert (once called 'Bushmen') or the Inuits ('Eskimos') you can see in the work of the old documentary film-maker Robert Flaherty *(Nanook of the North)*. In general, extremes of socialisation, from the massive social isolation experienced by Genie to the 'hot-house' families like that of John Stuart Mill (who is said to have been got into Ancient Greek at the age of three), can be dramatic in some of their effects. However, in the very large middle range our knowledge remains, at best, gross and based on past patterns which may not extrapolate into the future. It is, if you like, akin to the football pools: today's teams may have the same names as they did last season but they are not the same units; we cannot use past performance as an effective guide to predicting today's outcomes at any useful level.

Yet, as a culture, we continue to believe that there *are* patterns out there in the middle range to discover: for example, that there *are* best ways to educate within a given budget, or that there either is or is *not* a direct link between unemployment or poverty and crime. The fact that these usually turn out also to be *political* arguments does little to change the way statistics and counter-statistics are used to make the respective cases. One value of critique is that it explores why this is. The first part of the argument suggests that the kinds of government and policies (governance) that countries like the UK have increasingly adopted over the past two centuries are enmeshed with the idea of the value of pure and applied social science (scientism). One result is that we are inundated with information which is employed both to warrant policy and to implement it – in other words, to winkle out of the tight purses of both government and ordinary individuals (as 'donations') resources to meet these documented needs. Constructionists are not arguing for 'turning back the clock' to a time when we didn't have this sort of information, but they are arguing for looking at it *critically*. Crucial in that is recognising the socially constructed character of both our concerns about young people and the information we employ to warrant those concerns.

What constructionists claim here is that the conviction that social science can enable us to build up an objective picture of what young people are 'really' like or 'really' experience or 'really' need is misguided: there are no direct ways to know 'the truth'. There are two main threads to this challenge. The first is conceptual. Like any other belief system, social science directs our attention, highlighting some things and leaving others in the shadows. In fact, it does more than that. The tools of social science (research, field experience) construct what we perceive of young people as surely as a *son et lumière* show uses its tools (sound and light) to conjure up an illusion of the past. The second line of argument is that of recognising that 'information' is never simply a matter of 'facts'. Information is a commodity. It is bought (as when you purchase a book, a journal, a private or a governmental report) and sold (by researchers to grant-giving bodies, or by witnesses to newspapers). What is more, the law recognises the need for this trade to be regulated. A politician or civil servant, for example, is prevented by law from selling or trading information about upcoming contracts ('insider dealing'). Less tangible 'goods', like academic reputations, are also bought for and sold as information. The message that comes from this is obvious: *caveat emptor* (let the buyer beware).

To take a few examples, such 'information' as:

> 43% of young people sometimes have unprotected sex
> 38% of young offenders need psychotherapy
> 61% of university students are living in poverty
> 70% of young people distrust politicians

are better seen not as statements of objective fact but as moral or political rhetoric. (These are, as it happens, figures I have 'plucked out of the air'.) Their function is to persuade, either to consolidate what is already the case, or to produce changes of view and changes in action. Needless to say, what is implicitly being advocated (respectively: more sex education; a less punitive approach to young offenders; more financial support for students; a sense of 'how right they are') may seem to you a worthwhile objective. The catch is that the more it does, the less easy it is to recognise the social construction of knowledge involved. Yet in each case, the link between the supposed information and the objective is tenuous. The kinds of questions that perhaps should be provoked are:

1   Who says? (What is their vested interest?)
2   Are the terms clear and unambiguous? (What is 'sometimes'? What is a 'need'? What do we mean by 'poverty'? What is a desirable level of distrust of politicians?)
3   Does the claim actually warrant one specific form of action? (Is sex education the best route to 'safer sex'? Does anybody need psychotherapy? How best should study be funded, if at all? Is it better to distrust politicians or change them?)

All of this paves the way to the largest critical question of all: what are young people; and do we need specific responses to them at all? My response here would be first to argue that there is no once and for all social scientific way of defining young people. There is no age at which one objectively stops being a child or starts being completely 'adult' (Stainton Rogers and Stainton Rogers, 1992). What we have (and all we have) are local and contingent markers, set up in current law, guidance and practice, that simply have to be made to work until the next set of changes. In other words, because they have been put there and, in many cases, either exclude younger and older persons or operate in a different way for those other than 'young people,' we need specific responses for young people. And, of course, we also need responses that vary according to the complex set of laws and rules our society has within the category 'young people'.

However, if these responses are guided by purported 'facts' and so-called 'scientific theories' which are better seen as disguised politics and ethics, we may be a good deal better off if we remove the disguise and admit that what we are operating are politico-moral endeavours. Not the least likely beneficiaries of such a critical unmasking are young people themselves. Who knows, we might even start to move towards giving young people a defined position as co-players in the game? Perhaps some recent changes in law and practice are moving in that direction, but we are still a long way from a serious societal acknowledgement of young people as first and foremost people, citizens in a common endeavour and deserving of equal rights within it.

References

Gergen, K.J. (1973) 'Social psychology as history', *Journal of Personality and Social Psychology*, 26: 309–20.

Lane, H. (1977) *The Wild Boy of Aveyron*, St Albans: Granada.

Rymer, R. (1993) *Genie: Escape from a Silent Childhood*, London: Michael Joseph.

Stainton Rogers, R. and Stainton Rogers, W. (1992) *Stories of Childhood: Shifting Agendas of Child Concern*, Hemel Hempstead: Harvester Wheatsheaf.

20
Friends and Lovers

Harriette Marshall and Paul Stenner

The briefest glance at cultural and academic representations of 'young people' reveals that they are very rarely portrayed or talked about as alone. Relationships – whether friendly or romantic – feature recurrently, whether in talk of the effects of 'peer pressure'; of an epidemic of teenage pregnancies and terminations; of the danger of youth cultures such as the 'rave scene'; of networks of illegal drug takers; and so on. The main audience-grabbing story-lines in popular soap operas inevitably seem to concern young people's relationships. A theme that runs through much of this 'talk' and 'representation' is a tension between the two poles of *independence* and *(inter)dependence*. Young people are portrayed as having to negotiate a hazardous voyage through which they have to learn life lessons about how to be together whilst managing to stay together as or in themselves. This theme finds a clear reflection in the social science literature. The chief reason for this is that young people are seen to represent a point of transition between childhood and adulthood. Hence:

> During adolescence, peer relations become more intense and extensive, family relations are altered, and the adolescent begins to encounter many new demands and expectations in social situations. Adolescents may begin dating, working with others in a part-time job, or spending time with peers without adult supervision. (Coleman and Hendry, 1990)

According to this conventional picture, young people are 'at risk' not only because they are afforded a new independence (relational activity without adult supervision) but also because they are at a stage in life where they are emotionally and psychologically vulnerable: prey to peer pressures, delinquent cultures, unwanted pregnancies, conflicting relational intensities, and all whilst undergoing physical, emotional and cognitive changes. It is as if adolescence were a period of 'melt-down' – a crucial phase where the once 'solid' child is recast, via a period of flux, into a new adult solid.

Adolescence, then, represents what could be called a cultural 'hot spot'. It is presented as a region requiring careful supervision – yet at exactly the point when, we are told, direct adult supervision is becoming increasingly inappropriate. The interest in this 'life stage' is very much concerned with the management and regulation of what people will 'make of themselves' – but what is required is the installation of forms of *self*-regulation and *self*-management. This implies a set of ideals towards which young people can propel themselves – yet at exactly the historical point where 'adult' agreement on legitimate relationship ideals and end states is lacking and distinctly problematic. The last 40 years, for example, have witnessed a decline in the authority of religious legitimations concerning relationship organisation, and a general loosening of traditional morality and associated legislation around issues that bear directly upon relationships such as adultery, divorce, extra- and pre-marital sex, abortion and homosexuality. This situation, coupled with the value pluralism proper to contemporary urban multiculturalism, troubles the notion of a consensual 'ideal blueprint' for the conducting of intimate relationships.

These two points of crisis (the 'problem' of adolescence and the 'problem' of how to arrive at and legitimate human ideals in a climate of pluralism) are 'gaps' which have been filled by the human and social sciences. It is clearly thanks to the human and social sciences that we even have documentation on such matters as the changing norms around sexual activity for young people. A number of surveys, for example, have indicated an increase in the numbers of young people who are sexually active. A study conducted with 2,000 15–19 year olds in Britain found that while 20% of boys and 12% of girls were sexually active in the early 1960s, this figure had increased by the late 1970s to over 50% of 16–19 year olds (Farrell, 1978). Survey data from the US support these general trends, with one study reporting that in the early 1980s about 44% of 16 year old women had had sexual intercourse as compared with 7% in the early 1950s (Brooks-Gunn et al., 1986). Recent estimates across several Western nations suggest that about 60% of 18 year olds are sexually active and that the age for first sexual experience is decreasing, although it is important to take into consideration the variation within gender and ethnic groups (Ford and Morgan, 1989; Hofferth and Hayes, 1987; Rosenthal et al., 1990).

This descriptive task of establishing such statistical trends is often accompanied by a prescriptive concern with what is usually presented as the 'problem' of young people's sexual relationships. Because the legitimation for this is scientific in nature (rather than religious or normative) these problems are rarely presented as 'moral' concerns but as issues of practicality and health. Hence the focus is on problematic consequences such as teenage pregnancies, young mothering, teenage abortions and sexually transmitted diseases. Therefore typically moral judgements of right and wrong are replaced with naturalistic judgements of healthy and unhealthy, adaptive and maladaptive, with the legitimating idea being that the trained scientist makes their judgement with the benefit of objective knowledge about human nature.

> In the context of societal concerns about the care and cost of teenage pregnancies, it is essential that we understand the dynamics underlying this 'maladaptive' behaviour on the part of many adolescents, as well as the outcomes of that behaviour. (Moore and Rosenthal, 1993: 145)

Some social scientists have questioned the 'factuality' and interpretation of such statistics. For example, the notion of an 'epidemic' of teenage pregnancies has been contested on the basis that while in the US and Britain there was an increase in teenage birth rates up until the 1970s, there has been a subsequent reduction through the 1980s and into the 1990s (Furstenberg et al., 1989). Instead, they point to the trend in the increasing number of babies born outside marriage. Viewed within the current social and political context in Britain (particularly the widely publicised Conservative Party concerns and policy interventions around single parenting) it has been suggested that social scientists researching young people's relationships cannot avoid engaging with a politically charged agenda where distinctions between 'fact' and 'value' become particularly problematic (Doherty, 1995; Phoenix, 1991).

The scientific literature sometimes implies certain values, but at other times makes explicit the end states considered to indicate the markers of 'healthy', 'well-adjusted' development. One ideal especially associated with the 'successful' transition from 'childhood' to 'adulthood' is that of independence. This might seem paradoxical since relationships appear to have more to do with interdependence than independence. The point with this ideal, however, is that what is prescribed is not so much the form that relationships should take but the manner in which they are undertaken. Many 'types' of relationship are potentially acceptable, as long as the individuals involved are capable of autonomous and independent thought and behaviour – as long as they 'know themselves'. Hence relationships usually become cast as a vehicle for, and an index of, 'self-development'.

This ideal is equally present in the large numbers of magazines directed specifically at a readership of young people (mostly young women). A steady flow of advice on 'healthy relationships' is offered, stressing the importance of openly developing and retaining one's individuality and that of one's partner. Only then is a 'mature' togetherness seen as possible. The 'texts' of both popular culture and science, then, can be seen to combine to represent young people today as facing new identity-centred problems around personal relationships, particularly romantic ones. These 'texts' have played their part in recent years in shifting the guidelines for relationship conduct from those provided by the Church, the family or the community to a 'liberal individualistic' ethos whereby relationships are organised according to a trajectory of self-development based on the individual's 'feelings'. In this light, where advice and guidelines for conduct are sought, they are increasingly found in popular cultural resources such as magazines, television chat shows, soap operas and self-help manuals, and it is not insignificant that all of the sites of advice are supervened in some form by the 'psychological expert'. So what is wrong with the presentation of independence as a natural ideal applicable to all young people (as if they were themselves a singular category with a single discoverable nature)? Consider the following social scientific description of adolescence:

> becoming independent from parents can also involve leaving home . . . with the increasing emphasis on autonomy, teenagers are likely to move out of home, to share a house with friends, to move in with a girlfriend or boyfriend, and, over a number of years, may even have several cohabiting relationships before getting married. (Newman and Murray, 1983)

This quote presents 'independence' as a universal category with a singular meaning. The use of the category 'young people' veils diversity by assuming a heterosexual, white, middle class, European norm. Also there is no mention of the changing socio-economic context in Britain (mirrored in many other Western countries) whereby the combined impact of high unemployment, recession and changes in the labour markets has resulted in fewer 16 year olds leaving school to begin work and thus more young people remaining financially dependent on their families (OPCS, 1995; Roberts, 1995; Yates, 1994). The mapping of the goals of independence and autonomy onto an abstract and idealised 'young person' distracts attention from social inequalities which make independence an unattainable goal for many young people.

Working with a conceptualisation of young people which fails to engage with concrete specificities is problematic in various ways, which we will illustrate by drawing on material from 36 group discussions carried out with 146 16–18 year old women and men from diverse ethnic backgrounds, living and attending college in the East End of London.

Considerable variation emerged in the ideas and values expressed around friends and lovers in the discussion groups. In some cases differing gendered expectations and norms emerged, whereas in other instances a concern for religious and cultural values and beliefs as upheld by parents, family and/or community shaped the patterning of relationships.

Some young people raised the issue of parental involvement regarding friendship formation, as illustrated by this young Asian woman:

> I think with me, most of my friends have normally been Asians 'cos in second year school there was no white girls in our class or coloured girls. If my peer groups was white girls 'n coloured girls then maybe I would have had more of a conflict with my parents . . . because they think they're influencing you.

This quote shows that we cannot assume that all friendships are chosen autonomously by young people. Indeed, parental intervention, particularly around issues of 'colour', seemed normative. Below a young African-Caribbean cites 'colour' as playing a part in the way he is treated by friends' parents, and a young white woman discusses the difficulty in sustaining a relationship with 'a person of a different colour':

> What I find trouble with is their [friends'] parents, people's parents, 'cos I'm tanned. That always goes against me all the time and I have to prove myself to them and their parents.

> Yes, because if I wanted to go out with a person of a different colour my parents won't allow it, so it's a parents' problem most of the time.

The interlinking impact of ethnicity and gender on the ways interactions between males and females are viewed is voiced explicitly in the following extract, where a young Asian woman contrasts the negative consequences for Asian female/male interactions with the 'naturalness' of black and white female/male interactions:

> Everyone sees it for white and black people to talk with as many boys as they like and muck about with as many boys as they like and wear whatever kind of clothes they like and it's no problem. But if an Asian does it she's a slut or a slag straight away and I think that's so sad.

Gender and ethnicity emerged as playing a central role in the varying ways in which young women and men 'made sense' of sex, lovers and the possibility and organisation of intimate relationships. In the extract below a young Asian woman makes it clear that the 'advice' offered in magazines about intimate and sexual relations with men has little or no relevance to her life:

> Things like, you know: 'I want to have sex with my boyfriend but I can't tell my mother about it', and they say: 'Go and talk to your mother'. To me, I can't relate to that because I am Asian and I could never talk to my mum about sex.

Others were critical of what they saw as the consistently negative and stereotypical portrayal of their ethnic and cultural values in the magazines:

> If they do have an Asian person or something, it's like 'Oh yeah', I'm being brought into an arranged marriage or something negative.

> It's never positive, so you know, everyone goes around with this stereotype . . . They've got the idea that Western culture is the way.

In other instances, as illustrated below, young women self-defined as 'Asian' and 'British' shared views as to the different *gendered* meanings of sexual activity:

> Yeah, but boys see it like, I pull this girl, but girls are like 'Oh, I meet this really handsome guy and we're going out with each other' and they're sort of romantic about it, whereas boys they're more like, 'Oh, I pulled her, man.'

> Well Richard, he's so, he says 'Kylie I love you and I'd do anything for you', like he buys me flowers he buys me chocolate every time he comes round, and I say 'You can't buy love . . . it's something that comes naturally'. I say to him, 'There's no need to keep on telling me every five minutes that you love me 'cos it's not going to make me believe that you love me' . . . I think sometimes boys only say they love you to get you in bed.

In both the above extracts young women site sex in the context of a romantic relationship, whereas young men take sex to be a conquest. These varying meanings of sexual relationship are concealed by research which simply notes trends in the age of young people engaging in sexual activity. Additionally, some young Asian men talked about their role in regulating their sisters' relationships:

> From my point of view I've never let my sister go out with someone and have a relationship and then break it off and stuff. They get married and then they have the relationship.

Far from being a natural part of adolescence, for some young people the consequences of sex outside marriage are disgrace and shame on the family. In these respects the theorising of adolescence with the focus on 'getting to know the opposite sex' and the prioritising of romantic relationships exclude many Asian young people.

Finally, both the psychological and popular cultural literatures assume a heterosexual norm. The development of homosexual relationships has received scant attention. It has been suggested that views towards homosexuality have become more liberal and that the expression of different sexual preferences is now more accepted, with around 3% of young people identifying as homosexual during adolescence (Remafedi et al., 1992). However, the strongly anti-homosexual views expressed by some young people in our study would indicate the dangers facing a young person who declares their homosexuality. What is evident, again, is that choice of sexual 'lifestyle' is not always taken as being 'up to the individual' but may be a matter for culture and religion to proscribe.

Conclusion

Critical interrogation of the lives of young people in Britain today reveals the importance of contextual issues like gender, ethnicity and sexuality for the organisation of relationships in contemporary culture. There is no universal category of young people with a singular meaning and their relationships are to be read in the contexts of peer, family and community life.

Note

We would like to acknowledge the research assistance of Wayland Gilley and Helen Lee and the students and staff at the sixth form colleges in Newham, Tower Hamlets and Hackney who gave up their time to participate in the group discussions.

References

Brooks-Gunn, J., Warren, M.P., Samelson, M. and Fox, R. (1986) 'Physical similarity of and disclosure of menarcheal status to friends effects of age and pubertal status, *Journal of Early Adolescence*, 6: 3–14.

Coleman, J. and Hendry, L. (1990) *The Nature of Adolescence*, London: Routledge.

Doherty, S. (1995) 'Single mothers: a critical issue', *Feminism and Psychology*, 5: 105–11.

Farrell, C. (1978) *My Mother Said: the Way Young People Learned about Sex and Birth Control*, London: Routledge.

Ford, N. and Morgan, K. (1989) 'Heterosexual lifestyles of young people in an English city', *Journal of Population and Social Studies*, 1: 167–85.

Furstenberg, F., Brooks-Gunn, J. and Chase-Lansdale, L. (1989) *Adolescent Mothers in Later Life*, Cambridge: Cambridge University Press.

Hofferth, S.L. and Hayes, C.D. (eds) (1987) *Risking the Future: Adolescent Sexuality, Pregnancy and Childbearing. Vol. 2: Working Papers and Statistical Appendices*, Washington, DC: National Academy of Sciences.

Moore, S. and Rosenthal, D. (1993) *Sexuality in Adolescence*, London: Routledge.

Newman, B.A. and Murray, CI. (1983) 'Identity and family relations in early adolescence', *Journal of Adolescence*, 3: 293–303.

OPCS (1995) 'Labour Force Survey', cited in *Unemployment Unit Youth Aid 1995 Briefing*, London: Office of Population Censuses and Surveys.

Phoenix, A. (1991) *Young Mothers?*, Cambridge: Polity Press.

Remafedi, G., Resnick, M., Blum, R. and Harris, L. (1992) 'Demography of sexual orientation in adolescents', *Paediatrics*, 89: 714–21.

Roberts, K. (1995) *Youth and Employment In Modern Britain*, Oxford: Oxford University Press.

Rosenthal, D.A., Moore, S.M. and Brumen, I. (1990) 'Ethnic group differences in adolescents' responses to AIDS', *Australian Journal of Social Issues*, 25: 220–39.

Yates, J. (ed.) (1994) *School Leavers' Destinations 1993*, London: Association of County Councils.

21
Young People and Family Life: Apocalypse Now or Business as Usual?

Brian Dimmock

In 1989, Prime Minister Margaret Thatcher elaborated on her famous speech in which she claimed there is 'no such thing as society, only family life' (Abbott and Wallace, 1989), arguing that:

> The family and its maintenance really is the most important thing not only in your personal life but in the life of any community, because this is the unit on which the whole nation is built. (Margaret Thatcher, interviewed by Julie Cockcroft, *Daily Mail*, May 1989)

Where does this leave people who through choice, or circumstance, do not have family life at the centre of their identity? And what exactly did Mrs Thatcher mean by the family? Is hers an inclusive idea with a broad understanding of the range of domestic living arrangements in the UK, or one which excludes any non-nuclear form of collective living? If we do not live in such a family, does this in some way exclude us from the 'community' or even the 'nation'?

It is probable that Mrs Thatcher's beliefs about the importance of the family are held, to a greater or lesser extent, by most mainstream political parties and perhaps a majority of the population, even if they disagree with her views about the non-existence of 'society'. Some of the imagined features of a 'normal family' might be as follows:

1   It comprises two married adults, a male and a female, neither of whom has been married before, and who have an exclusive, mutually satisfying sexual relationship with each other.
2   They have broadly similar educational achievements and they share the same class, ethnic and religious background.
3   They married in their 20s or early 30s, and any age gap between them is not too great (men can be 5 to 10 years older). They will have between two and four children, biologically theirs, evenly spaced, which are 'planned and wanted', without any serious physical or learning impairments.
4   The family will be separately housed and the husband will be in full-time work of a nature which will enable him to 'spend time with his family'. While the children are young the wife may work, as long as it does not detract from her role as wife and mother.
5   They are likely to have at least one set of surviving parents who are active

grandparents to their grandchildren, and they are not dependent in any way on state benefits.

Although this list could be augmented and debated in terms of detail, any such list will be broadly similar. Yet the curious thing is that in 1992, according to the British Household Panel Survey, 11% of British households comprised people living alone, 10% were lone parents, and a further 34% were married couples either without children or with no dependent children. In addition, nearly 5% of households were described as 'other'. Even those who were married with dependent children (40%) would include people who had remarried and had stepchildren (Buck et al., 1994). They conclude that: 'the declining proportion of people who live in traditional family arrangements is almost part of the received wisdom.' And it is not just in the UK that this is happening, as such trends are common throughout the European Union. For example, by 1991, 26.7% of EU households were single person households and as high as 34.4% in Denmark (Ditch et al., 1996).

Despite the facts, or more likely because of the facts, politicians and religious leaders continue to promote the 'normal family' as essential to good order and civilisation. Why is this, and, more to the point, how does it affect those young people for whom family life (even 'normal' family life) is not beneficial, or who are excluded from this form of living?

The family and the problems of youth

One relatively straightforward answer is that those who promote the importance of family life do so because they believe that it provides the economic, psychological and spiritual/moral underpinnings required to prepare children and young people for adult life, work, and the continuation of good order and civilisation; many would add that such a life is either 'natural', ordained by God, or both. Some see religious morality as an essential component of good order in society. The decline in religious belief in white British society is thus closely linked with the decline of the family and the breakdown of society. One of the difficulties faced by such arguments is that the requirements for 'normal' or 'natural' family life continually change, and are always contested, either within or between political and religious orthodoxies. For example, the widely accepted definition of the word 'family' in the eighteenth century included 'the body of persons who live in one house or under one head, including parents, children, servants etc.'.

Griffin (1993) argues that the family is promoted as part of a way of organising and controlling the way society thinks and acts toward the economic, sexual and political behaviour of the young. She also sees it as a way of disguising class, 'race' and gender differences in terms of who benefits from the continuation of the ideological norm of the family. In general it is argued that the promotion of 'the normal family' benefits white, middle aged, heterosexual, middle class males the most. The more any individual deviates from this collection of characteristics, the more likely it is that the 'normal family' will be less than ideal. This is not to say that white middle class men always benefit, or that family life does not suit some, or even most, young black women. However, for some young people the idea of normal family life not only constrains choices, but, more importantly, constrains the very ways in which they think about themselves, their experiences and the choices open to them. If you cannot or do not wish to aspire to such a future, you are condemned to be 'other' than normal.

One of the possible purposes of the promotion of the 'normal family' is to create an explanation for, and a solution to, several categories of problems which are seen as 'the problems of youth'. For example, youth unemployment is caused by young people lacking qualifications, which is in turn caused by such things as truancy. Young people truant because they lack the parental discipline of normal family life. Thus, the solution is to remind parents of their responsibilities to ensure their children go to school, if necessary by making them accountable in law through the courts. The family is thus the cause of the problem and the site for its solution. Similarly, young women are sexually permissive and irresponsible when they lack the moral guidance and protection of two parents working together to protect and monitor their daughters' behaviour. The solution is to make it more difficult for young women to get outside advice and resources to sustain adult sexual relationships or to form any kind of family unit other than one which conforms to 'normal family life'. This is done by restricting access to housing, benefits, or child care, at a time of high levels of youth unemployment.

The problem with the ideal of the 'normal family' for young people is not that it puts forward arguments for a certain way of life, or a particular set of beliefs, but that it excludes some young people whose experience falls short of this ideal, or for whom it is culturally inappropriate or politically oppressive. For those who do aspire to it, it may prove unreachable for some, or profoundly disappointing for others. Despite the current concern about the uncertain future for marriage and the family, statistics suggest the majority today still seek a union of two people – 80% wanting children – ideally for many years. Is this evidence for the death of the family, or evidence which suggests that this aspiration requires better circumstances if it is to be achieved and sustained? In current political debate there are two opposed explanations for the fact that the British rate of divorce is the highest in Europe, and for the high percentage of lone parent families. One is that the morals of the nation declined owing to the alleged sexual revolution of the 1960s, which was nurtured and continued by its deluded converts and by a social security and housing system which encourages irresponsible behaviour in young women. The other is that many families in the UK have to struggle to bring up children in relative poverty and in a social security system which traps them and provides no help or incentive to behave differently. It is doubtful whether either of the two explanations gets close to understanding such a complex issue on its own, and the current debate has a depressing circularity about it. Data which compare European countries (Ditch et al., 1996) again suggest that although there are marked differences in divorce and lone parent rates, the trajectory of change is common throughout the EU. They argue that

> economic independence [for women] is associated with increased relationship breakdown, which not only interrupts child bearing but makes it even more risky and more important for women to remain in the labour market, given the high risks of poverty for lone parents.

Is the family in decline?

At a time of change we often look to the past for guidance, and the current debate about family life is replete with references to the past. If we do this we must take account of the fact that we are not comparing like with like. For example, the widely held belief that the nineteenth century was a golden age of happy extended families must be put alongside the reality that very few working class people lived long enough to sit in a rocking-chair by the fire, helping their children to cope with a growing family of happy grandchildren (Gittins, 1985; Hareven, 1993). Myths serve a social purpose, but must never substitute for debate about hard reality. There are so many myths about the family that it is difficult to navigate a path that recognises the reality of change without exaggerating or distorting its significance. Lévi-Strauss (1969) has argued that family relationships are the natural territory of myth, for this is where biology and culture come face to face. In order to put this into some historical context, research into sixteenth century English marriage (Schofield and Wrigley, 1981) and seventeenth century Europe (Laslett, 1977) show remarriage rates of 25–30%, mostly following the death of a spouse (not dissimilar to current rates caused largely by divorce). In those days, 'till death us do part' probably implied, on average, 10–12 years' wedded bliss!

A further difficulty in making comparisons is that in former centuries there were different types of marriage (Stone, 1995). These included customary unions, clandestine marriages, fleet marriages, concubinage etc. Equally, there were several different ways of ending marriage, including desertion and elopement, wife sale, separation by private deed, judicial separation, the doctrine of nullity and Parliamentary divorce. It is more likely that current debate is influenced by the widely held belief that family life between the end of the Second World War and the early to mid 1960s was a period when the nuclear family flourished, in contrast to trends in the 1970s and 1980s. This may be true, but equally, such a period of relative stability may prove to be the exception rather than the rule when a longer time frame is used for comparison (Seccombe, 1993; Weeks, 1981). In time, we may look upon the early post-war years as an untypical period for family life, and the current period of change as more typical of the history of family life in the nineteenth and twentieth centuries.

Family change and young people

There is a bewildering amount of data about families which can prove more or less what you want it to prove. While politicians, religious leaders and pundits debate the exact nature of the end of civilisation as we know it, most other folk get on with the business of birth, death and all the bits in between. As the next generation of young people enter adulthood, what do we know about their circumstances, and the likely course they will take with respect to family life? We can divide this into two parts, the families from which they are coming (family of origin) and the families which they might form.

Young people and their families of origin

It should be stressed that the figures below apply to the population as a whole, and that there may be important sub-groups, for example particular minority ethnic groups, with quite different patterns of family life. There may also be variations according both to class and region of the UK. Suffice it to say that these statistics should be treated with the same degree of scepticism as those quoted by anyone for any purpose.

For the current generation of young people, the majority will approach adulthood living with their birth parents. Currently some 25% of children under the age of 16 experience their parents' divorce. Considerable numbers of children and young people live in lone parent households (for part or all of their childhood), 90% of which are headed by women, arising because the woman either has never married, or has separated or divorced, or has been widowed (Haskey, 1991). Of those fathers who no longer live with their children, half do not maintain contact following separation and divorce, although many who don't keep in touch would like to do so but feel prevented by circumstances (Simpson et al., 1995). Secondary analysis of the National Child Development Study data by Kiernan (1992) has suggested that young people leave lone parent households and stepfamily households at an earlier age than those living in 'nuclear' families, from first marriages and have first children earlier, have lower educational attainment and have worse employment prospects.

The General Household Survey 1991 (Bridgewood and Savage, 1993) indicates that 8% of families with dependent children headed by a married or cohabiting couple contain at least one stepchild. In over half these stepfamilies at least one more child has been born since the couple started to live together. This suggests that there will be an estimated 2.5 to 3 million children growing up in a full-time or part-time stepfamily over the next 10 years (Batchelor et al., 1994).

For those who are working with young people, careful consideration has to be given to the extent to which there might be particular circumstances which make their clients differ from the averages above. For example, young people accommodated by the local authority under the Children Act 1989 are more likely to come from lone parent households or stepfamilies than the population at large, and to return to changed family circumstances (for example a new parental partner or additional siblings, half-siblings or step-siblings) (Farmer and Parker, 1991). Such categories, while relevant to professionals, may have different meanings in different communities. In Carl Hylton's (1995) study of services for minority ethnic group families in transition he summarises some of the issues which arise. For example, people of African origin living in the UK will probably not recognise the concept of stepfamily, and African-Caribbeans would only consider it when the family is confronted by state officials where different surnames of siblings may be questioned. Within the Chinese language there is an absence of 'never married' parenthood.

Young people and the families of the future

Assuming current trends continue, only 70% of young women will be married by the time they are 30 (far lower than in previous generations). The average age to marry has risen to 29 for men and 27 for women, although there are considerable class, ethnic and regional variations (Kiernan, 1992). This is explained, in part, by the increased rate of cohabitation. Child bearing is getting put off until later and, for one in five women, will not happen at all. The general figure for divorce is one in three marriages, although the rate for breakdowns of cohabitation is much higher. Second marriages/relationships may last longer than the ones they replace, although there are no British figures for this. In France, 60% of second marriages last longer than the ones they replaced, and this may well be the case in the UK (Villeneuve-Gokalp, 1995).

As for divorce, 50% happens in the first 10 years of marriage, and is particularly high following the birth of a child (Kiernan, 1995). There has been a recent drop in the number of divorces and the popularity of marriage is in decline: the number in 1994 was the lowest for 50 years. At the same time, cohabitation is increasing, with 7 out of 10 couples living together for at least two years before marrying. A minority cohabit 'permanently'. One in three children are born 'out of wedlock', although half of these are registered in the name of two parents.

Implications for young people

Clearly, the expectations of young people are going to be formed, in part, by what is happening now, and by their own experiences of family life. This would suggest that for heterosexual young people they are likely to cohabit for at least two years, have children in their late twenties and probably stay with the same partner they marry. Those who don't will probably repartner and/or remarry. At least 10% of young women will experience a period as a lone parent. For gay and lesbian young people there is some evidence of the development of 'families of choice' in the sense of developing community networks that function as families (Weeks, personal communication based on current research on gay and lesbian households as part of the ESRC Programme 'Households and Population Change').

For disadvantaged young people, they are more likely to leave home early, marry earlier and have their first child at an earlier age. The younger the marriage, the higher the chance of divorce. The message would appear to be to 'get a life' before you get a marriage partner. Of Northern European countries, Britain invests least and has the smallest proportion of young people in post-16 education. Children who leave home early owing to family difficulties fare less well than others with respect to education, which is a critical factor in life chances for the young (Kiernan, 1992).

Apocalypse now, or business as usual?

As we approach the year 2000 it is tempting for those of all political persuasions to use the type of information above to justify anything from fining parents whose children truant, to arguing for the end of heterosexual marriage. For a country which has, during this century, sent two generations to war, both of which involved mass slaughter and destruction on an unprecedented scale, and experienced a continuous cycle of boom and slump, we should not underestimate our ability to deal with social change of whatever magnitude.

Those of us who are concerned about the future of young people need to choose where and how we focus our energies. Is it on attempting to force back the current tide of social change with respect to family life, making it financially impossible to survive unless living in a nuclear family? Or should we look more at how we enable young people to become tomorrow's parents, supporting them in whatever form of domestic living arrangements appears to work best for them and their children? The Children Act 1989 contains much that has the potential to move our focus from the rights of adults to the needs and rights of children and young people. Other pieces of legislation, particularly those relating to social security, have made life considerably more difficult. Some of our European neighbours are concerned less with the distinction between married and unmarried parents, and more with ensuring that the next generation of children get good housing, good education and good health care, and the freedom afforded by safe and reliable public transport (Danish IMC, 1992). Is this a matter of individual responsibility or of social responsibility, or a deal between the individual and society which combines both? The cause of those who advocate traditional family life, and those who advocate diversity and tolerance, may both be served by a challenge to Mrs Thatcher's assertion that there is no such thing as society. For those who live and flourish in 'normal families', what is there to fear from a wider acceptance of different lifestyles, particularly among the young? Indeed, it may be that the very circumstances brought about by Conservative policies in the 1980s and 1990s (that is, relatively high youth unemployment and job insecurity) will continue to encourage non-nuclear forms of domestic living. Whatever one's views of the moral arguments, appeals to 'go back to basics', whatever they are, do not appear to make any difference. At the end of the day, the form of family life adopted may have more to do with economics than with morality.

References

Abbott, P. and Wallace, C. (1989) 'The family', in P. Brown and R. Sparks (eds), *Beyond Thatcherism: Social Policy, Politics and Society*, Milton Keynes: Open University Press.

Batchelor, J., Dimmock, B. and Smith, D. (1994) *Understanding Stepfamilies: What Can Be Learned from Callers to the Stepfamily Telephone Counselling Service?*, London: Stepfamily Publications.

Bridgewood, A. and Savage, D. (1993) *General Household Survey, 1991*, Series GHS no. 22, London: HMSO.

Buck, N., Gershuny, D., Rose, D. and Scott, J. (1994) *Changing Households: the British Household Panel Survey 1990–1992*, London: ESRC.

Danish IMC (1992) *Children and Young People Growing Up in Denmark: Growing Up in the 1990s*, Inter-Ministerial Committee on Children in Denmark, Denmark: The Ministry of Social Affairs.

Ditch, J., Barnes, H., Bradshaw, J., Commaille, J. and Eardley, T. (1996) *A Synthesis of National Family Policies 1994*, York: European Observatory on National Family Policies, University of York.

Farmer, E. and Parker, R. (1991) *Trials and Tribulations: Returning Children from Local Authority Care to their Families*, London: HMSO.

Gittins, D. (1985) *The Family in Question*, London: Macmillan.

Griffin, C. (1993) *Representations of Youth: the Study of Youth and Adolescence in Britain and America*, Cambridge: Polity Press.

Hareven, T. (1993) 'Family and generational relations in the later years: a historical perspective', in L. Burton (ed.), *Families and Caring*, New York: Baywood.

Haskey, J. (1991) 'Estimated numbers and demographic characteristics of one-parent families in Great Britain', *Population Trends*, no. 65: 35–47.

Hylton, C. (1995) *Coping with Change: Family Transitions in Multi-Cultural Communities*, London: Stepfamily Publications.

Kiernan, K. (1992) 'The impact of family disruption in childhood on transitions in young adult life', *Population Studies*, 46 (3): 51–82.

Kiernan, K. (1995) 'Transitions to parenthood: young mothers, young fathers – associated factors and later life experiences', research paper, London School of Economics.

Laslett, P. (1977) *Family Life and Illicit Love in Earlier Generations*, Cambridge: Cambridge University Press.

Lévi-Strauss, P. (1969) *Elementary Structures of Kinship*, Boston: Beacon Press.

Schofield, R. and Wrigley, E. (1981) *The Population History of England, 1541–1871: A Reconstruction*, London: Edward Arnold.

Seccombe, W. (1993) *Weathering the Storm: Working Class Families from the Industrial Revolution to the Fertility Decline*, London: Verso.

Simpson, B., McCarthy, P. and Walker, J. (1995) *Being There: Fathers after Divorce*, London: Relate Centre for Family Studies.

Stone, L. (1995) *Uncertain Unions and Broken Lives*, Oxford: Oxford University Press.

Villeneuve-Gokalp (1995) 'De la famille d'origine à la famille recomposée', in M. Meulders-Klein and I. Thery (eds), *Les Récompositions familiales aujourd'hui*, Paris: Nathan.

Weeks, J. (1981) *Sex, Politics and Society*, London: Longman.

22
Young Disabled People

Sally French and John Swain

We intend to examine the realisation of identity by young disabled people, not just as adults, but as disabled adults. This we will do by focusing on factors which shape their identity and considering ways in which disabled people can become more assertive and take more control of their lives.

Young disabled people grow up in a disabling environment where they face numerous physical and social barriers on a daily basis. These may include inability to take part in leisure pursuits, hostile attitudes or avoidance from other children, patronising behaviour from adults and exclusion from mainstream school. The formative people in their early lives are not usually disabled themselves and may unwittingly pass on stereotyped ideas about disability which affect adversely the young person's self-image and self-confidence. Such ideas may include the inability of disabled people to work, to become parents, or to have satisfying sexual relationships.

It is not surprising that young disabled people internalise the views of the wider society for, as Morris points out:

> Most of the people we have dealings with, including our most intimate relationships, are not like us. It is therefore very difficult for us to recognise and challenge the values and judgements that are applied to us and our lives. Our ideas about disability and about ourselves are generally formed by those who are not disabled. (1991: 37)

Some factors shaping the identity of young disabled people

The media

The media and charity advertising have played a large part in promoting inaccurate and unhelpful stereotypes of disabled people who are frequently depicted as evil, pathetic or heroic or, more often than not, are simply absent. Rieser explains:

> In nearly every programme that we see, every book that we read, every paper that we pick up, every comic that we saw as children we are absent except when we are used in what we call a stereotyped way, not as we are, but as society has grown to think disabled people should be treated and portrayed. (1995: 5)

The way that disability is depicted in the media can have a large impact on how young disabled people view themselves. One image almost guaranteed to lower their self-esteem is the way in which disabled people are frequently 'saved' or 'redeemed' by non-disabled people (Pointon, 1995: 17).

Education

The lives of young disabled people have been, and to some extent still are, characterised by exclusion and segregation which, in its turn, has had a impact on the way they view themselves. Nowhere has this been more extreme than in the system of special education. The rights and wrongs of disabled children attending special or mainstream schools has raged throughout this century. Disabled people have, in recent times, expressed their own opinions on the education they have received, with many finding the experience bleak, oppressive and woefully inadequate in both academic and social terms (French, 1996). Davies recalls the misery of being torn from his family, together with the pleasure of seeing his school friends again:

> The journey from Liverpool to London, where I would change trains for Kent took somewhere in the region of seven hours. The whole day was extended agony which was only relieved when I met one of my school friends. (1993: 36)

Most of the young people interviewed by Straughair and Fawcitt (1992) felt that special schools disadvantaged them in terms of their personal development and their ability to interact with non-disabled people. Those who had experienced both systems all preferred to be in mainstream schools.

There is, however, little agreement overall among disabled people on the type of schooling they prefer. This is probably because special and mainstream schools are very variable and the experience itself is extremely diverse, providing, for example, the means to an education and the chance to make friends and to develop socially. Wade and Moore (1993) found that a substantial number of disabled children in mainstream schools viewed themselves negatively and felt inadequate beside their non-disabled peers.

Some disabled people feel very positive about certain aspects of their special school experience, mainly in terms of the opportunity it gave them to develop alongside similarly disabled children and the freedom from day-to-day barriers it provided. Sullivan explains:

> It was a liberating experience. It taught me how to like myself, to take pride in myself, and most of all to be sensitive to the needs of others. (1992: 173–4)

It would seem that special and mainstream school both have the potential to affect positively or negatively the identity of young disabled people.

Attitudes and behaviour of others

Many young disabled people find themselves forced by their parents, teachers, professionals and society generally to behave in a certain way which Sutherland (1981) termed *the disabled role*. The disabled role requires young disabled people to strive for 'independence' and 'normality' (at whatever cost to themselves), to 'accept' their situation and to deny that they are disabled.

Striving for physical independence is rarely in the best interests of young disabled people. Morris (1989) found that many of the women with spinal cord injuries she interviewed chose to rely on personal assistance so that they could concentrate on other things, such as community work or political activity. Disabled people define independence, not in physical terms, but in terms of control.

Closely associated with the concept of independence is that of normality. The pressures placed upon young disabled people to appear 'normal' can give rise to enormous inefficiency and stress, yet many disabled people are well into adulthood before they realise what is happening or before they find the courage to abandon such attempts. The pressure to be 'normal' is often at the expense of the disabled person's needs and rights. Morris (1991) believes that the assumption that disabled people want to be 'normal', rather than just as they are, is one of the most oppressive experiences to which they are subjected.

If disabled people dare to challenge the stereotypes people have of them, or refuse to play the disabled role, they are likely to be confronted with unpleasant reactions. To protect themselves from this, disabled people learn from their earliest childhood to deny or minimise their impairments and the difficulties they encounter. Denial of impairment and disability can also be practised by the young disabled person's family. A young woman Straughair and Fawcitt interviewed recalled:

> We would go into town together and if I was wearing my wrist splints and we met any of my mother's friends she would tell them I had fallen over and sprained my wrist. (1992: 32)

To deny that a person is disabled deprives him or her of the help and support which is needed and rejects a central aspect of the disabled person's identity.

Young disabled people have been socialised from an early age into believing that the rights of non-disabled people do not apply to them. Most disabled people spend a great deal of time and energy both playing the role and attempting to reverse their conditioning. The growing cultural identity of disabled people, and the disability movement, have put forward new and radical interpretations of disability which offer disabled people affirmation and support as they redefine their situation.

Supporting the voices of young disabled people

The control that young disabled people have in their lives needs to be understood within the social and historical context both of childhood and of disability. The dominant ideology, particularly in the 1980s and 1990s, has emphasised the rights of the 'consumer', 'client' or 'service user' to have choice. The market orientation and minimalist intervention of state policies put the onus on individuals in terms of rights and, of course, responsibilities to compete for their share of scarce resources and services. It is in this context that such terms as 'self-advocacy' and 'empowerment' have gained easy currency.

This trend towards taking account of the wishes and feelings of clients can, to an extent at least, be found in recent developments in services for children (Davie and Galloway, 1996). The principle of listening to children is embodied, for instance, in the Children Act 1989. Developments are piecemeal, however, and there is little evidence, for instance, of equivalent trends in education:

> Children have few rights at school. They have no right to see their personal files until they are 16 and even then few schools seem to make the facility available so they have little opportunity to challenge what others have said about them. (Whitney, 1993: 40)

Young people under 18 are generally excluded from formal participation in educational decision-making, and this is compounded for young disabled people by the dominance of individual models of disability. Oliver suggests that young disabled people:

> see themselves as pitiful because they are socialised into accepting disability as a tragedy personal to them. This occurs because teachers like other professionals also hold to this view of disability, curriculum materials portray disabled people (if they appear at all) as pathetic victims or arch villains. (1990: 92)

The individual model of voice in decision-making has been easily incorporated into and reinforced by the individual models of disability which are readily apparent in the terminology of 'assessing needs' and 'individual programmes'. In the broader social and historical context, the voice of the individual young disabled person may be recognised but it competes against all the barriers he or she faces in being both young and disabled.

The past 20 years or so, however, have also seen the growth of the collective voice of disabled people in this country and internationally. In organisational terms the disability movement has been established through the growth of many small organisations throughout the world, run and controlled by disabled people themselves. Umbrella organisations have been founded in more recent years, including the *British Council of Organisations of Disabled People* and *Disabled People's International*, both in 1981.

In ideological terms, the movement has developed and promoted a social model, in which disability is understood as a social rather than an individual condition. Disabled people have shifted the focus to the barriers faced in a society geared by and for non-disabled people. These barriers pervade every aspect of the physical and social environment: attitudes, institutions, language and culture, organisation and delivery of services, and the power relations and structures of which society is constituted. In terms of activity, the movement is diverse, but in recent times the focus has been on securing anti-discrimination legislation in Britain.

An important element in the struggle of disabled people for equality and social justice is the recent emergence of the disability arts which can be viewed as part of the disability movement. Disability arts have the power to communicate the distinctive history, skills, customs, lifestyles, experiences, and concerns of disabled people, which many believe constitute a distinctive 'disability culture'.

The contrast of individual and collective voices is particularly apparent in ideas and practices relating to the integration of young disabled people in mainstream schools. A say for an individual young disabled person would, in theory, involve inclusion in placement decisions and in determining the necessary support and facilities for integration. Indeed, the principle of involving the child, wherever possible, in such decisions is apparent in the *Code of Practice* (Department for Education, 1994). A say for the collective voice of disabled people, however, would involve the recognition of disability culture, the inclusion of the representative voice of disabled people in formal educational decision-making and the promotion of a social model of disability as integral to the processes, relationships and content of education.

The context for supporting the voice of young disabled people, then, is one of considerable barriers but is also, in the wake of the burgeoning disability movement, a context for developing strategies and possibilities. There have been many developments in this direction, often under the umbrella terms of 'empowerment' and 'partnership'. Williams conveys the 'new foundation for professional practice' as follows:

> It removes power from them and hands it over to the client, and locates their base of power with their clients rather than with their professional body. (1993: 12)

The shift of power can be seen, at least in principle, in 'alternative approaches' (Greasley, 1995) to individual planning with people with learning difficulties. These approaches place greater emphasis on the principles of self-advocacy and a greater role being played by the person in planning his or her own future. There are also a number of examples of pupil involvement in the system of learning and school organisation. Sweeney (1995), for instance, uses drama in an empowering approach drawing on non-verbal communication and the development of self-expression through empathy.

The notion of empowerment is, however, deeply problematic. A damning critique comes from Gomm:

> Those people who say they are in the business of empowering rarely seem to be giving up their own power; they are usually giving up someone else's and they may actually be increasing their own. (1993: 137)

In the above examples of supporting the voice of young disabled people, empowerment is seen largely as an individual rather than a collective process. Oliver (1993) argues that, for disabled people, it is more realistic to see empowerment as a collective process.

Examples of strategies to support the collective voice of young disabled people are, however, difficult to find. 'Moving On' was a series of courses and follow-up days in the early 1990s for young people with learning difficulties and with physical impairments run by Skills for People, Newcastle upon Tyne. The courses have been planned, presented and evaluated by young people themselves in teams drawn from schools and colleges in the area. The overall aim has been to help young people to speak up for themselves. Topics covered have included 'rights and responsibilities', 'making choices' and 'listening'.

The recorded evaluations of the planning teams emphasise the importance of collective identity and voice:

> Planning it ourselves is important. It is our own and the teachers do not plan it for us.

> We made our own rules. We sorted out our own problems . . . instead of getting someone to do it for us like in school.

This has provided the context for personal empowerment:

> I know now that we all have our opinions and decisions that we have to make. That is why speaking up for yourself is important.

> There was one time when I would not have been able to go into the office and ask for my money, but I do now.

Conclusion

Ultimately it has to be asked whether would-be supporters of the voice of young disabled people, notwithstanding their good intentions, prepare them for life as disabled adults who are conscious of their identity as disabled people, and for the struggle for full participative citizenship in our society. Though it is questionable whether the collective voice of disabled people is supported by individualised strategies, it would seem that individual young disabled people are empowered by experiences of contributing to, and articulating their own views within, a collective voice.

Disability is now recognised by disabled people as a civil rights issue, and the stigma attached to disability, which has served as such a powerful disincentive to 'coming out', has been eroded. Young disabled people are, therefore, growing up in a society where conventional ideas about what constitutes disability are being challenged. The disability movement has made great progress in recent years in putting across their ideas about disability and bringing about change. This has been helped by a greater emphasis in society generally on civil rights and citizenship. Young disabled people do, however, remain relatively unexposed to the social model of disability. It is a challenge to the disability movement to reach young disabled people and ensure that they develop a strong and positive identity.

Note

The authors wish to thank Trish Webb of Skills for People.

References

Davie, R. and Galloway, D. (eds) (1996) *Listening to Children in Education*, London: David Fulton.

Davies, C. (1993) *Life Times: a Mutual Biography of Disabled People*, Farnham: Understanding Disability Educational Trust.

Department for Education (1994) *Code of Practice on the Identification and Assessment of Special Educational Needs*, London: DfE.

French, S. (1996) 'Out of sight, out of mind: the experiences and effect of a "special" residential school', in J. Morris (ed.), *Encounters with Strangers*, London: Women's Press.

Gomm R. (1993) 'issues of power in health and welfare', in J. Walmsley, J. Reynolds, P. Shakespeare and R. Woolfe (eds), *Health, Welfare and Practice: Reflecting on Roles and Relationships*, London: Sage and Open University Press.

Greasley P. (1995) 'individual planning with adults who have learning difficulties: key issues – key sources', *Disability and Society*, 10 (3): 353–63.

Morris, J. (1989) *Able Lives*, London: Women's Press.

Morris, J. (1991) *Pride against Prejudice*, London: Women's Press.

Oliver, M. (1990) *The Politics of Disablement*, London: Macmillan.

Oliver, M. (1993) *Disability, Citizenship and Empowerment*, Workbook 2 of course K665 *The Disabling Society*, Milton Keynes: Open University Press.

Pointon, A. (1995) 'How it is on film and television', in R. Rieser (ed.), *Invisible Children*, Report of the Joint Conference on Children, Images and Disability, London: Save the Children and Integration Alliance.

Rieser, R. (1995) 'The history of disabling imagery', in R. Rieser (ed.), *Invisible Children*, Report of the Joint Conference on Children, Images and Disability, London: Save the Children and Integration Alliance.

Straughair, S. and Fawcitt, S. (1992) *The Road towards Independence: the Experiences of Young People with Arthritis in the 1990s*, London: Arthritis Care.

Sullivan, S. (1992) 'My school experience', in R. Rieser and M. Mason (eds), *Disability Equality in the Classroom: a Human Rights Issue*, 2nd edn, London: Disability Equality in Education.

Sutherland, A.T. (1981) *Disabled We Stand*, London: Souvenir.

Sweeney, T. (1995) 'Curriculum matters: using drama to extend the involvement of children with special needs', in P. Garner and S. Sandow (eds), *Advocacy, Self-Advocacy and Special Needs*, London: David Fulton.

Wade, B. and Moore, M. (1993) *Experiencing Special Education: What Young People with Special Educational Needs Can Tell Us*, Buckingham: Open University Press.

Whitney, B. (1993) *The Children Act and Schools*, London: Kogan Page.

Williams, C. (1993) *No Hiding Place: Empowerment and Recovery for our Troubled Communities*, San Francisco: Harper.

23
The Mistreatment of Young People

Brian Corby

This chapter will consider how young people are mistreated in a variety of settings and circumstances: in their own homes, while in substitute care and custody, on the streets and in schools. Until recently it has been relatively unusual to focus on mistreatment of young people. They have been more frequently portrayed as threats to others and themselves and as being in need of control both for their own good and for that of society. As we shall see, this prevailing perception of young people and their needs has helped to create the conditions in some settings in which mistreatment can occur.

Defining the terms: young people

It is difficult to define precisely the notion of a young person (see Coleman, 1993). Physiologically (using the onset of puberty as the defining feature) the ground is constantly shifting, and adolescence for many can start as early as the age of 10 or 11. If economic and social dependence is used as a defining characteristic of a young person, this too is a moveable feast. Particularly over the last two decades, the opportunities for young people to achieve independence have been severely limited by changes in social security law, and shifts in thinking about their employability (Jones and Wallace, 1992). For the purposes of this chapter, therefore, young people will be taken to be those between the ages of 10 and 21.

Defining the terms: mistreatment

Defining child mistreatment or abuse is also highly problematical (Corby, 2000). There is much debate over the merits and demerits of broad and narrow definitions. Professionals in the child protection field tend to adopt narrow 'operational' definitions relating particularly to minimal levels of parental care acceptable to society. Their concerns are focused largely on physical abuse, neglect and sexual and emotional abuse within the family and in substitute care. Many academics take a broader view – they emphasise the quality of life that children and young people should be entitled to and locate the responsibility for enabling them to achieve this firmly with governments and social institutions. Gil (1975) is a good example of this school of thought. He defines child abuse as:

> inflicted gaps or deficits between circumstances of living which would facilitate the optimal development of children to which they should be entitled and their actual circumstances, irrespective of the sources or the agents of the deficit.

The extent of the problem

The examples of mistreatment found in the following sections are drawn first from the experiences of young people included in narrower definitions of abuse (that is, those mistreated within their families or while in substitute care) and then from those young people to whom the broader definitions of mistreatment apply (those who are homeless, or in custody or who are bullied by their peers in schools). It should be stressed, however, that we could widen our scope even further to include all young people who are disadvantaged by poverty and unemployment (see Gordon et al., 2000), including those from minority ethnic groups (Modood et al., 1997) and those with impairments (Westcott and Jones, 1999). Indeed, it could be argued that all young people are potentially subject to mistreatment as a result of a combination of power differentials between them and adults, and of the effects of state policies which arguably seem designed to control them rather than facilitate their progress to adulthood.

Mistreatment of young people within families

Physical abuse and neglect

Physical abuse and neglect within the family are largely associated in the public mind with younger children and infants. The cases of Maria Colwell, aged 7 (Department of Health and Social Security, 1974), Jasmine Beckford, aged 4 (Brent, 1985), and most recently Victoria Climbie, aged 8 (Laming, 2003), provide the prevailing images of children who are abused. Such cases create particularly strong feelings in us because children of these ages are so dependent and reliant on their parents. It is often forgotten, however, that older children (or young persons) are also subject to these forms of abuse. For example, Stephen Menheniott was 19 years old when he was killed by his father (Department of Health and Social Security, 1978). He had spent most of his life in residential institutions. Despite the fact that his father had convictions for neglect and ill-treatment of his children and had been acquitted on an incest charge, he was nevertheless returned to his 'care' at the age of 15. The underlying (and false) assumption of the authorities which made this decision was that he was not likely to be at great risk because of his age. In England just under a third of children on child protection registers and about a quarter of children registered under the categories of physical abuse and neglect are aged 10 and over (Department of Health, 2003a).

However, physical abuse of adolescents by their parents is far more extensive than that denoted by official statistics. In a study by Straus and Kantor (1994), 50% of a large sample of American adults reported that they had been physically punished by their parents more than once during their teenage years. While there may be disputes about how much of this punishment represents mistreatment, the authors believe that corporal punishment of adolescents is a risk factor for depression, suicide, alcohol abuse, and for physical abuse of children and physical assaults on female partners when they reach adulthood. Other studies (Wade, 2002) have demonstrated the links between physical assaults of adolescents and running away from home which, as we shall see in a later section, can lead on to other forms of mistreatment and risk. It should be noted that there are different patterns of physical abuse of adolescents in that for some such abuse is an extension of the mistreatment they have suffered throughout childhood whereas for others abuse starts in adolescence. The former are more at risk of the severe consequences listed above (see Rees and Stein, 1997).

The legality of parental violence   A major barrier to tackling physical abuse within the family is the fact that at the time of writing, the use of 'reasonable chastisement' of children and young people by their parents is legally sanctioned in the United Kingdom. This remains the situation despite the fact that physical punishment of children by their parents is illegal in 11 countries – Austria, Croatia, Cyprus, Finland, Germany, Israel, Latvia, Norway, Sweden, Denmark and Iceland, and well on the way to being banned in two others – Belgium and Italy (see www.endcorporalpunishment.org). In 1999 the European Court of Human Rights found that the judgement of an English court in the case of a 9 year old boy who was beaten with a garden cane by his step-father was not in accordance with the rights of the child. Although in response to this ruling the British government issued a consultation paper about whether and how to change current legislation (Department of Health, 2000), it has made it clear that a complete ban on parents' rights to hit their children is not on the agenda. There is now much evidence to suggest that banning physical punishment of children and young people by their parents would in all likelihood help to reduce the incidence of intra-familial physical abuse (see Freeman, 1988) and also lead to a general reduction in violence in society (Leach, 1999).

Sexual abuse

Forty per cent of registrations for sexual abuse involve young people aged between 10 and 16, with girls being nearly twice as likely to be registered as boys (Department of Health, 2003a). The most common age for the onset of sexual abuse within the family is between the ages of 8 and 12 (Finkelhor, 1986) though it is often only reported several years later. Prevalence studies suggest that 1 in 10 children experience sexual abuse (involving physical contact) at some time during their childhood (Cawson et al., 2003). Estimates of how much sexual abuse is intra-familial vary. Kelly et al. (1991) found that 1% of their sample had been sexually abused by fathers or father substitutes. Russell (1984) in her San Francisco study reported a rate of 4.5% abuse by fathers. Whatever the exact figures, it is clear that considerable numbers of young people (with girls being more at risk than boys) experience intra-familial sexual mistreatment, the consequences of which can in the more severe cases be devastating in terms of future mental health and social adjustment (Beitchman et al., 1992).

Dealing with the problem   There is now much greater awareness among social work and psychiatric professionals of the sexual abuse of young people. Behaviours that were previously seen as typical of the turbulence of adolescence such as acting out, aggression, self-harm, defiance, running away and sexual precocity are now more likely to be considered as potential symptoms of sexual abuse or mistreatment. However, there is still much work to be done in this field. There are still major difficulties in securing the prosecution of alleged abusers and follow-up therapeutic services for abused young people are still in limited supply (see Corby, 1998). On the positive side, changes in legislation and procedures mean that young people are now entitled to have a greater say in the way in which investigations are carried out (they can for instance refuse to be medically examined if they wish). In addition, they are less likely to be removed from the family home following allegations provided they have the support of the non-abusing parent.

The mistreatment of children in substitute care

Institutional abuse

There are approximately 59,700 children and young people in local authority care in England (Department of Health, 2003b). Over 34,000 children and young persons live in foster-homes. Most of these are at the younger end of the age range. There are just 8,500 children and young people living in residential settings administered by social services and education departments, voluntary and private agencies and the health service. Approximately 8,000 of these are young people over the age of 10 years, many of whom have been in care for long periods and have limited contacts with parents and relatives.

Our focus will be on young people in residential care and the ways in which they are exposed to mistreatment, though one should not assume that young people in foster-homes are by any means free from risk – indeed some studies suggest that they are more at risk (see Hobbs et al., 1999). However, particularly in the 1990s the spotlight of attention has been firmly fixed on the mistreatment of children in residential settings. There have been several inquiries into what is now commonly termed institutional abuse, including the Pindown (Staffordshire County Council, 1991), Beck (Leicestershire County Council, 1993) and North Wales inquiries (Waterhouse, 2000).

Two main patterns of institutional abuse have emerged (see Wardhaugh and Wilding, 1995). The first (Beck, North Wales) is that in which individuals in authority sexually abuse relatively powerless young people. The second (Pindown) is where a policy goal approved by an establishment is later judged to be abusive. The main response to the first of these types of abuse has been to introduce tighter checks on applicants for residential care posts and better complaints and whistleblowing processes. In addition the scandals of the 1990s have led to greater awareness of the existence of abuse and to the likelihood that young people making allegations will be taken seriously. The 'discovery' of the second type of abuse, that was found in the Pindown report, has raised more general concerns about the aims of residential care and the methods used to control children. The authors of this report were unequivocal that the regime was abusive:

> Pindown, in our view, falls decisively outside anything that could properly be considered as good child care practice. It was in all manifestations intrinsically unethical, unprofessional and unacceptable. (Staffordshire County Council, 1991)

While what happened in Staffordshire was probably an extreme case, it is likely that similar things were happening in other parts of the country at this time. In the dozen or so years since the Pindown inquiry there have been considerable changes in residential care of children. The number of children in care establishments and the size of establishments have both reduced and there have been changes in inspection procedures. A 1998 study of care homes found that regimes were still variable, but that young people generally felt safe from abuse by staff. They felt that the most likely source of abuse was other residents (Department of Health, 1998). In general terms there is greater awareness of the rights of children and young people following the passing of the 1989 Children Act and advice/advocacy groups for children and young people in care have increased in number. Nevertheless, two key problems continue to exist: the low qualification rate for residential social workers and the lack of clear guidance about acceptable forms of control and restraint.

Children in custody

The fact of children being in custody is here considered as mistreatment in itself by virtue of the fact that it is a punitive rather than care-based means of dealing with the problems of young offenders. Clearly such a view is disputable but incarceration of young people is a practice which goes against the principles of the United Nations Convention on the Rights of the Child to which Britain is a signatory. The problem has worsened in recent years. While some progress was made towards decarceration of young people throughout the 1980s there has been a reversal of this trend since 1993 when James Bulger was killed by two Liverpool children. This event prompted the passing of the Criminal Justice and Public Disorder Act in 1994 which established Secure Training Centres for 12 to 14 year olds and doubled the maximum sentence for 15 to 17 year olds in Young Offenders Institutions. Between 1993 and 1998 the numbers of 15 to 17 year olds in custody more than doubled. Another key issue in this field is the fact that large numbers of young people either serve sentences or are on remand in adult prisons (see Goldson, 2002).

Mistreatment on the streets – homeless young people

Runaways

The extent of the problem of young runaways has increased dramatically over the past ten years. In 1995, the Children's Society reported that 43,000 young people run away each year, and that 30% of these stay away from home over 24 hours (Thompson, 1995). In 2002 it was estimated that 77,000 children and young people had run away during that year (Social Exclusion Unit, 2002). The reasons why young people leave home in abrupt and seemingly premature ways vary. For about 80% the issue is conflict with parents. Many may well have been physically or sexually abused by members of their families. Young people such as these are particularly at risk because of low self-esteem and expectations. Homelessness and crime are outcomes for many.

The increase in runaway behaviour can also be linked to high levels of unemployment among young people since the mid 1980s, exacerbated by stringent government policy in relation to income support. As a result 16 and 17 year olds have been forced into greater dependence on their parents. It is now almost impossible for young people of this age who are in conflict with their parents to live independently. There are some opportunities for achieving independent living situations in that local authority social services departments have a responsibility to provide accommodation for 16 and 17 year olds whose welfare might otherwise be 'seriously prejudiced' (see Section 20(3) of the 1989 Children Act). Also local authority housing departments may accept young people as homeless and in priority need under Section 59 of the 1985 Housing Act. However, much depends on these departments' interpretation of the law, and there is little evidence of this legislation being effectively used at the present time.

Young people leaving care

Ironically, many homeless young people have been discharged (or run away) from local authority care. Young people may legally remain in local authority care until the age of 18, but in practice the majority are discharged from care at 16 and 17 (Biehal et al., 1992). Despite efforts to improve the chances of young people moving successfully into independent living by the development of leaving care schemes, it is clear from research that the odds are heavily stacked against young people in this situation (Biehal et al., 1995). Many are particularly vulnerable because of their poor experiences within their own families or in residential settings (or both), and lack the emotional strength to live independently. Financially many find it hard to cope. Broad (1994) found that levels of unemployment were much higher among 16 year olds who had left care than among their peers who had not. In addition far fewer of the care leavers were in further education. Biehal et al. (1992) found that a quarter of the young women in her leaving care sample were either pregnant or mothers. The disadvantages, therefore, that care leavers face are considerable and it is little wonder that they figure so largely among the young homeless. Legislation has been passed to try and tackle this problem more fully in the form of the Children (Leaving Care) Act 2000. This reinforces the already existing duty of local authorities to continue supporting children who have been in their care through to the age of 21 (and in the case of those in further and higher education beyond 21 until they have completed their courses). It adds new requirements on local authorities to provide care leavers with a personal adviser to help in the planning of careers and to give material and in some cases cash assistance. It is too early yet to know how effective these measures will prove in helping care leavers to live independently. It is sobering to think that the average leaving home age for the population as a whole is 23.

Mistreatment of young people in schools

In this final section, the focus shifts to the mistreatment of children in school looking at the issues of discipline, exclusion and bullying.

Discipline

The issue of discipline is all-pervasive in secondary schools. Children and young people are generally expected to follow school rules unquestioningly – indeed accepting school discipline is seen as an important method of preparing young people for adulthood. All disciplinary measures in schools are at the discretion of headteachers in consultation with governors. These powers are remarkably unfettered. There are very few limitations or requirements except that any measures must be generally known within the school. The main restriction is that since 1987 corporal punishment has been prohibited in state schools and since 1998 in independent schools. The Elton Report (Department of Education and Science, 1989) was commissioned to inquire into the issue of discipline in schools following concerns about what was considered to be a growth in classroom violence and made several recommendations. One of these was the development of whole school approaches to the issue of behaviour that involved parents, teachers and young people. Until recently the notion of young people being involved in determining rules in schools has been almost non-existent. The development of School Councils has been a positive step to involve young people more fully in the running of their schools. A study in Essex found that approximately 75% of schools had developed such councils and that half of these felt that they had provided significant benefits to behaviour and attitudes of pupils (see www.schoolscouncils.org.Essex). While such developments are a welcome move towards increasing the participation of young people in the running of their schools, it remains to be seen how far it will extend and what its limits will be.

School exclusions

All schools have the right under the Education Act 1986 to suspend or exclude children and young people from schools. The authority to take this course of action rests with head teachers. Appeals against permanent exclusions or expulsions may be made either to local education authorities or to school governing bodies. School exclusions escalated from under 3000 in 1990–1 to 10,000 in 1993–4, a rise seen by some as symptomatic of increasing indiscipline in schools and by others as an indication of a more intolerant approach to behaviour problems by head teachers and teaching staff. By 1997 there were over 12,000 exclusions. There has been some reduction in these numbers following central government intervention – in 2001 the number had reduced to just over 9,000. Nevertheless these relatively high numbers are still worrying particularly in view of the fact that it is extremely difficult to place excluded children in other schools and compensatory education facilities are often inadequate.

Bullying

Another type of mistreatment of young people in schools (in this case by other young people) is that of bullying. While this form of activity has a long history, it is only relatively recently that it has been seriously researched. A study of schools in Sheffield (Smith and Sharp, 1994) found that 10% of secondary school children were bullied 'sometimes' (4% of whom said they were bullied every week). Around 6% admitted to bullying others 'sometimes'. Bullying of boys tends to involve more physical assaults and that of girls more verbal insults often linked to their sexuality. There is also evidence of a good deal of racist bullying (see Macdonald, 1990). In extreme circumstances bullying can lead to killing and suicide. A clear message emerging from research is the need for schools to develop transparent policies and principles about bullying and to involve their pupils closely in the process. School mentoring schemes and the development of anti-bullying programmes in many areas have led to some improvement at least in terms of awareness and acceptance of the problem (see Rigby, 2002).

Concluding comments

The mistreatment of young people is far more widespread than has generally been appreciated. As noted in the Introduction this is largely because young people have been seen as more of a threat to others than as vulnerable in themselves. There is some evidence that this attitude is changing. There is greater awareness that young people are subject to abuse in their own homes and also while living away from home in residential homes and schools. There is greater awareness also that young runaways are particularly at risk and improved measures are being taken to tackle these problems especially in the case of those who have been in local authority care. In schools there is more awareness of the need to improve pupil participation, to tackle bullying and to work with young people to improve their behaviour and educational achievements rather than resort to exclusion. There is an acceptance by the present government that young people from more disadvantaged backgrounds suffered badly for most of the 1980s and 1990s from unemployment, poverty and alienation. The Connexions Service which was set up in 2001 has been established to try and remedy some of these problems entitling every 13 to 19 year old to have a personal adviser. How effective this will prove to be is still an open question. The emphasis of this new service is on helping young people make best and most effective use of available opportunities. It is notable that little has been done to improve the economic situation of over 16 year olds in terms of income support.

The trend to greater sensitivity to the needs of young people is not a consistent one. There remain some areas such as youth custody in particular where their situation has actually worsened over the past few years. It is clear therefore, that despite some progress over the past six years or so, young people remain at risk of mistreatment from adults and, therefore, society. The main reason for this is the fact that they are subordinates in power relationships. The way forward to ensuring an end to mistreatment therefore, is to place much greater emphasis on developing young people's rights. The justification for this approach is both ethical (self-evident) and practical, in order to avoid alienation of future generations. It is also important to note that within any cohort of young people there are those who are particularly at risk from adults in their own homes, in institutions or on the streets. Such young people (frequently from the most deprived sections of society), may themselves in turn abuse others (Boswell, 1995); they may suffer long-term psychological and psychiatric consequences (Carmen et al., 1984), or inflict harm on themselves. Again there are strong ethical and practical reasons for addressing these particular problems by providing adequate protection and treatment, and above all emphasising the rights of these young people to be as fully involved as possible in these processes.

References

Beitchman, J., Zucker, K., Hood, J., DaCosta, G., Akman, D. and Cassavia, E. (1992) 'A review of the long-term effects of child sexual abuse', *Child Abuse and Neglect*, 16: 101–18.

Biehal, N., Clayden, J., Stein, M. and Wade, J. (1992) *Prepared for Living? A Survey of Young People Leaving the Care of Three Local Authorities*, London: National Children's Bureau.

Biehal, N., Clayden, J., Stein, M. and Wade, J. (1995) *Moving On: Young People and Leaving Care Schemes*, London: HMSO.

Boswell, G. (1995) *Violent Victims*, London: The Prince's Trust.

Brent (1985) *A Child in Trust: The Report of the Panel of Inquiry into the Circumstances Surrounding the Death of Jasmine Beckford*, London: London Borough of Brent.

Broad, B. (1994) *Leaving Care in the 1990s*, Westerham: Royal Philanthropic Society.

Carmen, E., Rieker, P. and Mills, T. (1984) 'Victims of violence and psychiatric illness', *American Journal of Psychiatry*, 141: 378–83.

Cawson, P., Wattam, C., Brooker, S. and Kelly, G. (2003) *Child Maltreatment in the United Kingdom: A Study of Prevalence of Abuse and Neglect*, London: NSPCC.

Coleman, J. (1993) 'Understanding adolescence today: a review', *Children and Society*, 7: 137–147.

Corby, B. (1998) *Managing Child Sexual Abuse Cases*, London: Jessica Kingsley.

Corby, B. (2000) *Child Abuse – Towards a Knowledge Base*, 2nd edition, Buckingham: Open University Press.

Department of Education and Science (1989) *Discipline in Schools*, London: HMSO.

Department of Health and Social Security (1974) *Report of the Committee of Inquiry into the Care and Supervision Provided in Relation to Maria Colwell*, London: HMSO.

Department of Health and Social Security (1978) *Report of the Social Work Service into Certain Aspects of the Management of the Case of Stephen Menheniott*, London: HMSO.

Department of Health (1998) *Caring for Children Away from Home: Messages from Research*, Chichester: Wiley.

Department of Health (2000) *Protecting Children, Supporting Parents: A Consultation Document on the Physical Punishment of Children*, London: DoH.

Department of Health (2003a) *Referrals, Assessments and Children and Young Persons on Child Protection Registers in England Year Ending 31st March 2002*, London: DoH.

Department of Health (2003b) *Children Looked after by Local Authorities in England Year Ending 31st. March 2002*, London: DoH.

Finkelhor, D. (1986) *A Sourcebook on Child Sexual Abuse*, Newbury Park, CA: Sage.

Freeman, M. (1988) 'Time to stop hitting our children', *Childright*, 51: 5–8.

Gil, D. (1975) 'Unravelling child abuse', *American Journal of Orthopsychiatry*, 45: 346–56.

Goldson, B. (2002) 'Children , crime and the State', in Goldson, B., Lavalette, M. and McKechnie, J. (eds) *Children, Welfare and the State*, London: Sage.

Gordon, D., Adelman, L., Ashworth, K., Bradshaw, J., Levitas, R., Middleton, S., Pantazis, C., Patsios, D., Payne, S., Townsend, P. and Williams, J. (2000) *Poverty and Social Exclusion in Britain*, York: Joseph Rowntree Foundation.

Hobbs, G., Hobbs, C. and Wynne, J. (1999) 'Abuse of children in foster and residential care', *Child Abuse and Neglect*, 12: 1239–52.

Jones, G. and Wallace, C. (1992) *Youth, Family and Citizenship*, Buckingham: Open University Press.

Kelly, L., Regan, L. and Burton, S. (1991) *An Exploratory Study of the Prevalence of Sexual Abuse in a Sample of 16–21 Year Olds*, London: Polytechnic of North London Child Abuse Studies Unit.

Laming, Lord (2003) *The Victoria Climbie Inquiry*, London: The Stationery Office.

Leach, P. (1999) *The Physical Punishment of Children: Some Input from Recent Research*, London: NSPCC.

Leicestershire County Council (1993) *The Leicestershire Inquiry 1992*, Leicester: Leicester County Council.

Macdonald, I. (1990) *Murder in the Playground: the Burnage Report*, London: Longsight Press.

Modood, T., Berthoud, R., Lakey, J., Nazroo, J., Smith, P., Virdee, S. and Beishon, S. (1997) *Ethnic Minorities in Britain: Diversity and Disadvantage: Fourth National Survey of Ethnic Minorities*. London: Policy Studies Institute.

Rees, G. and Stein, M. (1997) 'Abuse of adolescents', *Children and Society*, 11: 63–70.

Rigby, K.(2002) *New Perspectives on Bullying*, London: Jessica Kingsley.

Russell, D. (1984) *Sexual Exploitation: Rape, Child Sexual Abuse and Workplace Harassment*, London: Sage.

Smith, P. and Sharp, S. (1994) *School Bullying: Insights and Perspectives*, London: Routledge.

Social Exclusion Unit (2002) *Young Runaways*, London: Social Exclusion Unit.

Staffordshire County Council (1991) *The Pindown Experience and the Protection of Children*, Stafford: Staffordshire County Council.

Straus, M. and Kantor, G. (1994) 'Corporal punishment of adolescents by parents: a risk factor in the epidemiology of depression, suicide, alcohol abuse, child abuse and wife beating', *Adolescence*, 29: 543–61.

Thompson, A. (1995) 'Running out of time', *Community Care*, 7–13 December: 14–15.

Wade, J. (2002) *Missing Out: Young Runaways in Scotland*, York: Social Work Research and Development Unit, University of York.

Wardhaugh, J. and Wilding, P. (1995) 'Towards an explanation of the corruption of care', *Critical Social Policy*, 44: 4–31.

Waterhouse, Sir R. (2000) *Lost in Care: Report of the Tribunal of Inquiry into the Abuse of Children in Care in the Former County Council areas of Gwynedd and Clwyd since 1974*, HC 201, London: The Stationery Office.

Westcott, H. and Jones, D. (1999) 'The abuse of disabled children', *Journal of Child Psychology and Psychiatry*, 40: 497-506.

www. endcorporalpunishment.org

www.schoolcouncils.org

24
The Dilemmas of Intervention

Sarah Banks

This chapter explores some of the dilemmas faced by practitioners in their work with young people. On a daily basis workers have to decide whether and when to intervene in young people's lives and what action to take. Much of the time decisions are made quickly and almost without thinking. This chapter focuses on the dilemmas that arise when particularly difficult decisions have to be made or when the worker faces a new situation not encountered before. The dilemmas faced by workers in the caring or welfare field often involve moral or ethical choices. It is these kinds of dilemmas that are the focus of this chapter.

Dilemmas

A dilemma is usually defined as a choice between two equally unwelcome alternative courses of action. For example, a youth worker might have to make a choice between banning from the youth club a young person whose behaviour is difficult (which means the young person will feel rejected and may get into further trouble) or allowing the young person to stay (which means disturbance for the other members of the club). This is a dilemma if the worker finds both courses of action equally unwelcome and therefore finds it difficult to decide what choice to make. It is important to recognise that a particular situation may be a dilemma for one person and not for another. Another youth worker may have a firm rule that disruptive behaviour will not be tolerated in the club, therefore the choice of action is straightforward: the young person should be banned. Nevertheless, there are certain kinds of situations that workers often experience as constituting dilemmas. These frequently involve conflicts between the interests, rights or needs of different people or groups of people; or between doing what the worker thinks is in the best interest of young people and what the young people would choose for themselves. These dilemmas involve moral or ethical choices; that is, they relate to how we should act in relation to others – what is regarded as good or bad, right or wrong.

There are other kinds of dilemmas which might be termed technical or practical dilemmas. For example, I may have the choice of replacing the roof on my house using a cheap contractor who offers no guarantees (with the danger of further trouble in the future) or using a much more expensive roofer who offers a guarantee (but this means using all my savings). Trying to resolve the dilemma might involve technical matters such as weighing up the quality of work done, materials and durability against the relative cost. Choosing a roof may not always be purely a technical matter, however. If I am a youth worker deciding what sort of roof to recommend for a youth centre, then the interests of others are also involved. I would need to consider what else the money could be used for, and how many people would benefit in the long and short term. In the role of youth worker I have certain public responsibilities and have to be accountable for my actions to my employers, to the management committee and to the young people of the area. This example demonstrates that many decisions and actions have ethical implications and there is often no clear boundary between the ethical and the technical. A situation in itself (choosing a roof) may be simply a technical decision devoid of ethical content, or it may have ethical implications, depending on the context of the situation and how the people involved regard it.

Work with young people

There are two features of work with young people that influence the kinds of ethical dilemmas that arise. The first relates to the fact that the work is with young people. In defining the work as with young people, we are already defining the people we are working with in a certain way – as not adults. Young people have fewer rights to make their own decisions in our society or the family or social groups of which they are a part. They tend to be regarded as vulnerable and therefore in need of special protection. They are also in a process of growing up and may need to learn how to participate fully in society and how to make responsible choices. Issues about the limits to individual freedom, the protection of the vulnerable and the enhancement of participation in decision-making are not unique to work with young people, but they do have particular relevance (Franklin, 1995; Lansdown, 1995). Young people with disabilities, or who are black, female, lesbian or gay, for example, face additional forms of discrimination and oppression (see Jeffs and Smith, 1990).

Many of the difficult choices faced by workers are about weighing up the need to protect or control young people as against respecting their rights to self-determination. Workers also have to decide when and how it is appropriate to challenge discriminatory behaviour and institutional structures. How workers make these choices depends upon many factors, but an important one is the role they perceive themselves as having in relation to young people: are they primarily carers, controllers, educators or advocates? Most workers have to fulfil all these roles to varying degrees, but some jobs may have a greater focus on one approach than others. This relates to the second feature of work with young people that influences the kinds of ethical dilemmas that arise, namely, the very fact that it is *work*. Questions of young people's rights and how they are treated are issues for people in the role of parents, relatives, neighbours, bus drivers or shopkeepers. But there are specific duties and responsibilities that attach to the role of a worker with young people and contribute to some of the ethical dilemmas in the work. Workers are practitioners with particular values, skills and responsibilities relating to the job they have to do. Sometimes practitioners are referred to as 'professionals' – a term that emphasises the special expertise and duties attaching to the role they are playing. However, this term is often defined in a rather narrow way, including only members of those occupational groups that make a public pledge to be trustworthy and/or have codes of ethics, specialised knowledge and registers of qualified practitioners, for example (Koehn, 1994: 56; Banks, 1995: 67–9). This could exclude many unqualified child care workers, play workers, youth workers and voluntary workers with young people. I will use the broader term 'practitioner' to refer to those who work with young people on a voluntary or paid basis in an insitutitional or agency setting. Some practitioners may be professionally qualified and identify themselves as belonging to a particular professional or occupational group, such as social work, play work or youth and community work. Other practitioners may not have undertaken professional education or training, and will see themselves more as workers for a particular agency or project. Nevertheless, all practitioners take on a defined role in relation to the young people they are working with and the agencies for which they work. Some of the dilemmas that arise relate to the fact that workers have to take account of not only the rights, needs and interests of the young people they are working with, but also the rules of the agency and any legal requirements.

How and why do ethical dilemmas arise in work with young people?

Some of the reasons why particular kinds of dilemmas arise in work with young people relate to the following.

Conflicting principles underpin the work

Most occupational groups in the caring or welfare field have statements of values or ethical principles which underpin their work. Sometimes these may be contained in a formal code of ethics, as is the case with social work, nursing and counselling, for example (see Watson, 1985; Thompson et al., 1994; Bond, 1993). In other cases, such as youth and community work, a statement may be produced by the body responsible for professional education and training (see National Youth Agency, 1993). Although there are variations between different occupations in emphasis and terminology, such statements generally contain principles relating to the promotion of:

1   the self-determination or freedom to choose of the individual service user;
2   the welfare of the individual user;
3   the public good;
4   social justice or equality of opportunity.

It is not difficult to think of situations where several of these principles conflict. For example, a 14 year old girl who has spent some time in local authority care argues that she wishes to return to live with her mother who has both neglected and physically abused her in the past. The girl says she is fully aware of the situation, believes she can handle it, and wishes to give the relationship with her mother another chance. The dilemma for the worker is between respecting the girl's right to make her own informed choices, and a concern for the girl's welfare.

The power of the practitioner

Practitioners have a certain level of expertise and knowledge which may not be shared or even fully understood by the people who use their services. This gives them power over the service user. Questions inevitably arise as to when it is appropriate to act in a 'parentalist' way towards young people (assuming the practitioner knows better than the young people what is in their best interests). There is also potential for exploitation. This is especially so in work with young people who traditionally are denied many of the rights of adults. Practitioners may also have powers attaching to their particular role in an agency, ranging from the legal powers of a youth justice worker to the powers of a youth worker to ban a young person from a centre.

Multiple roles of the worker

Workers with young people are often employed as part of state provision and services. There is some degree of societal ambivalence towards the role of the welfare state in supporting people who are in need. Some practitioners, especially social workers, find they have both care and control functions. Others, such as youth workers, may also have an informal educational role. This leads to role conflicts. For example, a youth worker may have to decide whether to ban a young person from a youth centre for bringing alcohol into the premises and disrupting the evening's session. The youth worker knows that the rules state no alcohol is allowed, but he wants to carry on working with this young man who is experiencing severe difficulties in his home and school life. This is an example of conflict between the worker's roles as a controller and an educator.

Conflict between personal, professional, agency and societal values

People who take on the jobs of, for example, social workers, youth workers or play workers will inevitably experience tensions between different sets of values. For example, they will have their own personal set of moral principles; there may be a particular set of principles relating to the profession (for example, a code of ethics); the agency they work for will have rules and procedures underpinned by moral principles; and there will be certain principles underpinning societal norms and laws. For example, a worker in a youth advice and counselling project is told by her agency that a limit must be put on the number of counselling sessions offered to each young person. This is due to increased use of the service and the lack of resources to employ more staff. The worker believes the number of sessions offered will be insufficient to meet the needs of many users, contrary to standards of professional practice, and has expressed this opinion to her manager to no avail. She has to decide whether simply to accept and implement the new agency policy, or to protest. This is a case of conflict between agency and professional values.

Ethical dilemmas in practice

In the literature relating to ethical dilemmas in medicine, nursing, social work and counselling, and in discussions with community, youth and social workers, the most frequently cited examples of dilemmas can be categorised as follows.

Self-determination (or autonomy) of the service user versus what the professional considers to be in the best interests of the user

Gillon (1985: 111) describes this as 'one of the commonest categories of medico-moral problems'. It is, in fact, also the dilemma most frequently described by other practitioners in the welfare and caring field. This type of dilemma includes the very common situations where the professional has to decide whether to tell the truth to a service user, or where a decision may have to be made whether to breach confidentiality in the user's best interests. If a young woman tells a youth worker about bullying at school but asks the worker not to tell anyone, does the worker respect the young woman's request even if the worker believes talking to parents or teachers would be in the young person's best interests?

The rights or welfare of an individual user versus the rights or welfare of other people

This is also a very common type of dilemma. For example, Bond (1993: 198–201) discusses a situation where a counsellor has to decide whether to breach the confidence of an HIV-positive person because he was putting his partner at risk. A social worker may have to choose whether to offer a very expensive package of care to a young disabled person wishing to stay at home, or to go for a cheaper residential alternative in the interests of rationing scarce resources amongst other people.

Conflicting value systems

These kinds of dilemmas often relate to the question of whether practitioners should challenge an agency, a colleague or a user whose views are contrary to their own and which appear to be harmful or oppressive. They include the dilemma of when to 'blow the whistle' on colleagues who are thought to be

Table 24.1 *Models of ethical decision-making*

Thompson et al.: nursing	Bond: counselling	Rhodes: social work
1 Assessment (a) What is the nature of the situation? (b) What are the needs of the service user? (c) What resources are available? (d) What moral principles are relevant?	1 Brief description of dilemma 2 Whose dilemma is it anyway? (Is it the client's, the counsellor's or both?) 3 Consider all available ethical principles and guidelines 4 Identify all possible courses of action 5 Select the best course of action 6 Evaluate the outcome	1 What is the client's point of view? 2 What is my perspective as a worker? 3 How should I handle differences between my client's and my own views? 4 What choice is required? 5 What are the alternative courses of action? 6 What positions do these alternatives represent and what arguments can be made for each? 7 Is the solution I reach consistent with my goals as a human services worker?
2 Planning (a) Examination of past experience (b) Anticipation of likely consequences of alternative courses of action (c) Choice of means to achieve goal (d) Formulating plan of action		
3 Implementation (a) Being confident, decisive and courageous in carrying through action plan (b) Implementing effectively and efficiently		
4 Evaluation (a) Judging how well each stage in process went (b) Considering if consequences are better or worse than anticipated (c) Learning from experience for similar situations in the future		

acting unprofessionally. Rhodes (1986: 145–50) gives the example of a social worker who takes a young woman's case over from a colleague and discovers that the colleague is an alcoholic, has made sexual advances to this service user and has frequently missed appointments with her. Should this worker betray her colleague and report him to the line manager? A youth worker may be working with a neighbourhood youth action group, the members of which frequently express racist views. The group is very new and members are lacking confidence. How does the worker challenge this racism without undermining the group's confidence?

Resolving dilemmas

Practitioners will seek to resolve dilemmas such as those described above as satisfactorily as possible by making a decision about what to do. It is in the nature of a dilemma that it is a choice between two unwelcome alternatives. In resolving a dilemma a practitioner has to decide which alternative is less unwelcome than the other. Whatever course of action is chosen, it will still be unwelcome. As MacNiven comments, a classic moral dilemma 'puts us in a no-win situation' (1993: 9). Practitioners have to accept this and be prepared to take some responsibility for the outcomes of their actions, whilst not feeling overwhelmed by unnecessary guilt. This requires an understanding of how and why ethical dilemmas arise in professional practice, an ability to hold tensions, conflicts and contradictions and an ability to make critical and informed decisions.

Several texts on ethical issues in the welfare professions see resolving ethical dilemmas as similar to general problem-solving. Thompson et al. (1994: 184–8) offer a model based on the nursing process. Bond (1993: 190–5) develops a six-stage process for ethical problem-solving in counselling derived from American sources in pyschotherapy and group work. Rhodes (1986: 50–5) offers a model for ethical analysis which entails a systematic list of questions designed to broaden the possibility of creative solutions to ethical problems in social work. Details of these models are given in Table 24.1.

Whilst these models are slightly different, they are all ways of encouraging practitioners systematically to analyse the nature of the dilemmas they face and possible courses of action. All three models cover what Thompson et al. call the assessment and planning stages. Both Thompson et al. and Bond think it important to consider what ethical principles are relevant. In fact, Bond uses the codes of ethics and practice for counsellors extensively as a source of guidance for practitioners about how to act. Rhodes, on the other hand, focuses her key questions very much on clarifying and understanding the service user's point of view and acknowledging differences between this and the practitioner's perspective. She also asks whether the solution reached is consistent with the practitioner's goals as a human services worker. Rhodes's model concentrates on the assessment of the situation and planning action stages. Thompson et al. include implementation and evaluation. Their inclusion under evaluation of 'learning from experience' is particularly important, as is the fact that they include 'judging how well each stage of the process went' as well as evaluating the outcomes. In deciding which model of decision-making to adopt, the practitioner might use that of Thompson et al. as a framework, whilst adding in important additional elements from those of Bond and Rhodes. For example, Bond's question 'whose dilemma is it anyway?' is a very useful one to ask. Sometimes the dilemma belongs to the service user and is nothing to do with the practitioner.

These models do not necessarily reflect what we actually do when we make ethical decisions. Most decisions in our professional practice may be made quickly, almost intuitively, with very little explicit reflection or analysis at all. The models provide an artificial framework within which we can study more systematically what we are doing, both to clarify for ourselves how we actually work, and to help in thinking through very tough and unusual ethical dilemmas. As Thompson et al. point out:

> We do not normally reflect critically on what we are doing when we make decisions, particularly those decisions which embody and express established moral values, unless faced with a crisis. In this sense a 'crisis' may be interpreted as a situation which demands a decision or where the nature of the circumstances challenges or forces us to reflect on what we are doing or challenges us to give a clear explanation of our reasons for deciding and acting as we do. (1994: 172)

Conclusions

There is not always a clear right or wrong answer to ethical dilemmas in work with young people. Practitioners will approach them differently in the light of experience, how they view the particular situation and their own internalised sets of personal and professional values. However, the aim of reflective practitioners must be continually to question and review the ethical dilemmas experienced in the work, to engage in debate and discussion with colleagues, to be able and prepared to justify their decisions and actions and to take responsibility. This entails being conscious of their own values and priorities in the work, being aware of how these may differ from and conflict with those of others and being prepared either to justify and defend their views or to change or modify them.

Note

Some of the material in this chapter was developed for the YMCA George Williams College for the Professional Studies module of the BA in Informal and Community Education. I am grateful to the college for allowing me to draw on this material.

References

Banks, S. (1995) *Ethics and Values In Social Work*, Basingstoke: Macmillan.

Bond, T. (1993) *Standards and Ethics in Counselling in Action*, London: Sage.

Franklin, B. (1995) 'The case for children's rights: a progress report', in B. Franklin (ed.), *The Handbook of Children's Rights: Comparative Policy and Practice*, London: Routledge, pp. 3–22.

Gillon, R. (1985) 'Autonomy and consent', in M. Lockwood (ed.), *Moral Dilemmas in Modern Medicine*, Oxford: Oxford University Press, pp. 111–25.

Jeffs, T. and Smith, M. (eds) (1990) *Young People, Inequality and Youth Work*, London: Macmillan.

Koehn, D. (1994) *The Ground of Professional Ethics*, London: Routledge.

Lansdown, G. (1995) 'Children's rights to participation and protection: a critique', in C. Cloke and M. Davies (eds), *Participation and Empowerment In Child Protection*, London: Pitman, pp. 19–38.

MacNiven, D. (1993) *Creative Morality*, London: Routledge.

National Youth Agency (1993) *Guidelines to Endorsement of Initial Training for Youth and Community Work*, Leicester: NYA.

Rhodes, M. (1986) *Ethical Dilemmas in Social Work Practice*, London: Routledge.

Thompson, I., Melia, K. and Boyd, K. (1994) *Nursing Ethics*, 3rd edn, Edinburgh: Churchill Livingstone.

Watson, D. (ed.) (1985) *A Code of Ethics for Social Work: the Second Step*, London: Routledge.

25
You're the Last Person I'd Talk To

John Coleman, Liza Catan and Catherine Dennison

This chapter concerns communication between young people and the adults they come into contact with in the course of their daily lives. Here we concentrate on the issues that arise when adolescents negotiate with teachers, social workers, doctors and others. Of course adults in their professional capacity have considerable power and influence over young people. It is for this reason that we need first to look at the general context of relationships between the two groups. Communication never occurs in a vacuum, so in order to make sense of this subject we need to consider the position of adolescents in society today, and to look in particular at the difficulties confronting the young in making the transition to adulthood.

Understanding adolescence

Adolescence is best understood as a complex transition between the states of childhood dependence and adult independence. Transitions are never easy, but there are some unique characteristics of this transition which make it an unusually problematic one. In the first place the beginning and the end of the transition are not clearly defined. None of us is really clear when adolescence begins, and there is even less clarity about the moment when adulthood is achieved. Perhaps it is at 16 – the legal 'age of consent' – or at 18 – the age when we can vote. Yet different elements of adulthood are permitted at different ages, thus creating confusion for all concerned (Coleman and Warren-Adamson, 1992).

A further point is that there are in fact a number of different transitions which occur during adolescence, all of which contribute to the overall process of reaching maturity. Thus there is the transition from one sort of school to another, the transition from education to work or training, the transition to independent living, and so on. Of course all these are experienced differently depending on social background, on ethnic origin, on gender, and on living circumstances. It is important to recognise that the overall transition from child to adult is accomplished through multiple smaller transitions all of which may potentially be stressful or difficult in themselves (Coleman, 1992; Heaven, 1994).

A third issue is that adolesence is both beginning earlier and ending later in industrialised countries today. As for the beginning, it is clear that puberty is gradually occurring at a younger age. Girls as young as 10 may have started their periods, while many boys at 11 will already have commenced the growth spurt.

At the other end evidence shows clearly that the age of leaving home has, over the last two decades, become later and later. Similarly the entry into the labour market has been delayed, so that more and more young men and women find themselves on training schemes or in further education, rather than in paid employment. The implications of all this are important, for if the beginning and ending of a transition are ill-defined, and at the same time the transition is experienced as taking longer and longer, then a high degree of uncertainty and ambiguity is created (Chisholm et al., 1990; Coleman, 1995). It should be no surprise to us that it is exactly these feelings which are experienced by so many of the young people in Britain today.

Status ambiguity

Status ambiguity is an appropriate term to outline the position of adolescents in our society, as it is used to describe a situation where the individual's rights or roles or responsibilities are not clearly defined. This can lead to a high degree of uncertainty and confusion, not just on the part of the young person, but for many adults as well. Within the legal framework young people are allowed to do different things at different ages. The well-known Gillick case failed to clarify matters, and, as recent research has shown (Moore and Rosenthal, 1995), the majority of teenagers are still convinced that a doctor will breach confidentiality and tell their parents if they seek medical advice under the age of 16. The Children Act 1989 is well intentioned in respect of the rights of young people, for it made a serious attempt to clarify and extend the protection of the law to minors in a number of important areas. While this has been successful in some respects, especially in the realm of family law, there are many areas where the situation has hardly improved at all, for example the position of young people being accommodated or looked after by local authority social services departments.

Power and equality

The question of status ambiguity is a key one because of what it tells us about the balance of power in the relationships between adults and young people. If the individual's status is ambiguous, and if his or her rights are not clearly defined, then inevitably he or she will lack the power to influence events and to take control of his or her life. The experience of powerlessness is a common one for adolescents, and its significance cannot be overestimated. For some it may lead to feelings of hopelessness and despair. Others may be unable to make use of their skills and capabilities, settling for an easy but unfulfilling option; yet others may become angry and resentful (Rutter and Smith, 1995).

These issues may not at first sight appear especially relevant to the topic of communication but, as we shall see, they are indeed an essential context. Effective communication can only take place if both parties believe in their ability to be heard. Where power is unequally shared, and where one participant is aware of his or her relative powerlessness or where they fail to acknowledge the power of their position, then communication inevitably suffers. It is to this that we now turn.

The nature of communication

There is a large literature on the nature of communication, and what makes for good communication between people. There are certain requirements of good communication that need to be observed if adults and young people are to get through to each other (Sypher and Applegate, 1984). Three elements may be mentioned here:

1　the necessity for both participants to be genuinely involved in the communication, that is to listen to each other;
2　the importance of each showing respect for the other's point of view;
3　a willingness on both sides for there to be give and take in the rhythm of the conversation; that is that each must give way to the other at certain times, and there must be relative equality in the time allocated for each person in the overall communication.

As will be immediately apparent, these conditions are not always fulfilled in the interactions that occur between the two generations. All too often exactly the opposite takes place, with one or more of these principles being violated. Such situations have obvious consequences. We need also therefore to outline briefly some of the reasons why communication between adults and young people is likely to fail. Again three reasons may be given:

1　where one person pursues their own agenda without taking account of the needs or requirements of the other;
2　if one party is unwilling to listen to what the other has to say;
3　where one party – usually the adult – is perceived as being patronising or sarcastic by the other.

Because teenagers will bring to any interaction with adults their own previous experiences, particularly those with parents and teachers, it is important to say something about this. Research which looks at young people's views on communication with adults makes it clear that, by and large, they have little confidence that they will be listened to or that their opinions will be respected. One of the most common findings is that adolescents do not feel that their views are taken seriously by adults. One of the things they most wish for is for adults to show them some respect, to listen to them, and to treat what they have to say as a legitimate contribution to any discussion or conversation. These conclusions are especially pertinent, since we know also from research that adolescents need adults (Noller and Callan, 1991). In spite of appearances to the contrary, young people remain dependent on the adults around them for advice and guidance. They continue to need adults for support, for good quality information, for encouragement, and for endorsement of their hopes, goals and aspirations. From our own research (Catan et al., 1996) it is clear that when young people face significant interactions with professional adults in their lives, whether these are social workers, housing officers, counsellors, or police officers, they do have high expectations. In spite of past experiences they continue to believe that adults will treat them well, and will show respect for their views and opinions. Disappointment is therefore all that much more difficult to cope with, and leads to strong feelings of resentment and frustration.

Some experiences of young people

These examples are taken from our own study (Catan et al., 1996), in which we have been exploring communication among a wide range of young people. In the first example both effective and ineffective communication is illustrated. It concerns a young man of 16 who is taking a GNVQ course. First he recounts an incident where a community nurse, working with his severely disabled mother, presses him to see a social worker about his own needs.

> Because my mum thinks it would help me to have someone to talk to, which I don't have. But I don't have much time [he works nine hours a week on top of his school work]. I just listened to her – this nurse – and she went on pressurising me. No. I don't think I will go and see this person.

Next the same young man tells of a good communication experience where appropriate help with a practical basis was offered. A social worker visited the family to talk through the implications of the mother's increasing disability due to multiple sclerosis.

> She [the social worker] was very helpful. She listened to our views, and got to know us a bit. She told us about the help my mum would get when she came home – people to clean up and bathe her, do the shopping and the like. She'll come back and see us from time to time. She made a nice atmosphere. My family often fights when we're together, but then with her things were said that no-one took to heart. There was no pressure. It was mellow.

A different example was given by a 15 year old young man, still at secondary school, who was stopped by a police officer on his way home one night.

> I was walking home and he pulled me over about a stolen motorbike. He asked me all sorts of questions, but I was not involved. I knew nothing about it. It went well and I felt OK afterwards because like he didn't pressure me and he didn't say it was me and he spoke very politely and so did I speak politely too.

Finally we give an example from a situation where communication would be difficult at the best of times. A young man of 16 has left home, and been living rough for a few months. He has at last been found B&B accommodation by the local housing officer. After three weeks his benefit cheque has finally come through. However no sooner had he cashed it and was on the way to the supermarket to buy some food when the money was stolen from him. He returned to the benefit office to fill in a claim to have the loss made good. He was told to wait, and after two hours the benefits officer appears.

> She come back and said 'We can't accept your claim.' I says 'I don't have no money. What am I going to do? I can't help getting my bag stolen. I've got to do something. I don't have any family around here.' But she just went 'There's nothing I can do.' So I got cross and said 'You just take the piss' and I walked out.

What can we learn from this material? As we have indicated, many of the principles of good and bad communication are illustrated here. Where the young person feels that his or her viewpoint is not being acknowledged, or where someone else's agenda is being imposed, then the outcome is likely to be negative. The reader may note the number of times the word 'pressure' is used by adolescents to indicate an unwelcome attempt by adults to force upon them views that are seen as alien or inappropriate. On the other hand the adolescent perceives the communication as being valuable or positive when the adult is prepared to listen and to take seriously what the young person has to say. To be treated politely, to be respected, to be accepted as someone who has a legitimate opinion: these are the essential prerequisites, as far as the teenager is concerned, if he or she is to be able to communicate openly with an adult.

Communication: some contentious issues

Anyone who claims that communication with teenagers is a simple matter of getting the principles right could reasonably be accused of over-simplifying things (McConnon, 1990). The fact is that there is a range of factors which play their part in determining whether adults and young people get through to each other or not. Let us now look at some of these factors. First, adolescents themselves may be angry, depressed or simply uninterested in making contact with adults (Coleman, 1987). However hard a social worker or teacher may try, and however skilful they may be, there are times when it will not be possible to establish communication with the young person. There may be a wide variety of reasons for this. The young person may be in a phase of needing privacy, of not being free enough or open enough to be able to share something important with that adult. Alternatively the young man or woman may recently have had a bad experience with another adult, and may still be angry or upset about the way they were treated. Of course some individuals are poor communicators: they may be shy, lacking in self-confidence, or simply unable to articulate their thoughts and feelings. All these are possibilities, and it is important to bear in mind that communication is a two-way street: both sides have to be willing to play their part.

A second factor that has to be taken into account is the context in which the communication is taking place. No one is going to be able to talk as openly and freely in a busy social services office, or in a noisy youth club, as they are in a quiet room. The setting of the communication does have an effect on what can be said, especially if one or other individual is feeling uncertain or tentative about the subject matter. A good example of this comes from work on young people's attitudes to their doctors. Recent research shows that adolescents are hesitant to attend their local GP's surgery, particularly if they are seeking contraceptive advice. They believe that they may be recognised by someone in their community, who may then inform their parents. They also feel uncertain about the sort of reception they will receive from the doctor. Thus communication in a setting of this sort is doomed before it starts, since the young person has to deal with a very personal issue, and has no trust in the adults involved. The lesson from this is that services for young people will never be truly effective unless the needs of the clients are fully taken into account.

A third issue to be considered is that there are many different types of communication. In the present context it is worthwhile to remember that, for example, seeking help because of an emotional problem will not be the same as having a discussion about the relative merits of two local schools. In the first instance a much higher degree of trust will be needed before the young person is able to express his or her feelings and to share the problem with an adult. Thus a sensitive adult will seek to create a suitable context if personal or private matters are to be discussed. This is especially important for young people, who may feel awkward and embarrassed when talking to adults about such things.

Finally it needs to be emphasised that communication skills can be learnt. To some extent, therefore, adults have a responsibility to look for ways in which young people can be empowered through the development of such skills. We have in mind here those who might be disadvantaged in their relationships with adults – those being looked after by a local authority, for example – who need more than most to be able to articulate their needs and to express in front of professional adults their views and opinions. Communication is not a mystery. All of us can improve our abilities in this realm, and it would be encouraging to see those in the field of education taking this seriously as a subject for study.

What can adults do to make communication with young people easier?

Let us now outline a few strategies that professionals might consider to assist the process of communication.

1   Try and remember what it is like to be in a position where you have little or no power. Keep in mind the effect this is likely to have on an individual's feelings and on their ability to express themselves clearly. In your dealings with young people, work hard to see things from their point of view.

2   Learn something more about communication, and about its many facets. While in this chapter we have concentrated on verbal communication, we should not lose sight of the fact that non-verbal communication is important too. The messages we send through our gestures, our body posture, our eye contact and so on all have an impact. Indeed in situations where adolescents are anxious and uncertain, and where words do not come easily, these non-verbal cues can assume an even greater significance than we realise.

3   The context or setting in which you meet a young person also has a significance for communication. If you want to maximise the possibility of effective communication between you, then pay attention not only to what is said but also to where the interaction is located.

4   Communication is a skill, and we can all improve our skills! You can do this by thinking carefully about how you plan and manage your interactions with young people. You can pay careful attention to the messages you send – both verbal and non-verbal – in the course of your contacts with teenagers. You can bear in mind that they too will have an agenda, so ask yourself if you are really listening to what the adolescent wants to say. Lastly, never sit someone down and say 'Talk.' It just won't work. Communication is a delicate process, a process which has to be nurtured. The more nurturance we are prepared to give it, the more rewarding it will be.

Inequality in communciation

As a conclusion to this chapter, let us consider some of the issues which arise as a result of the inequality which exists between adults and young people. Such inequality has a number of effects in the context of communication. In the first place, if the adolescent perceives the relationship as unequal then his or her expectations of the communication are bound to be affected. He or she may start out with the assumption that his/her views will not be given a fair hearing, and may as a result give up before the conversation has even got going.

Inequality may be manifested by the context of the communication, or by the way the interaction is initiated. A young person may be 'instructed' to come to the teacher's office, or may be 'asked' to go and see the social worker. Such messages are fundamental in creating a frame for the interaction, and inevitably have a profound effect on what actually happens between adult and teenager.

In addition to the context and the imbalance of power in the relationship there is also the question of how adult power is exercised. Thus adults may use their power to override the young person's viewpoint, or to 'tune out' anything which they do not want to hear. Adults can bully ('now just listen to me'), they can pull rank or status ('I'm older than you, so I know better'), or they can use emotional blackmail ('Look at all the things I've done for you'). Not all adults behave like this. Young people will have had positive experiences with adults who have not misused their power in interactions, and have genuinely tried to listen on an equal basis. However it is surprising how difficult it is for adults to give up the power they hold over children and young people.

In trying to understand our communication behaviour it is essential that we recognise the effects of the inequality between the generations. Effective communication involves the creation of a relatively equal interaction, with give and take between both participants. Effective and positive communication between adults and adolescents can take place, but one essential prerequisite is an acknowledgement that young people might need some framework of support to be able to start with a sense of equality.

References

Catan, L., Coleman, J. and Dennison, C. (1996) 'Getting through: effective communication' in *Adolescence: Research Project Funded by the BT Forum*, Brighton: Trust for the Study of Adolescence.

Chisholm, L., Buchner, P. and Brown, P. (1990) *Childhood, Youth and Social Change*, London: Falmer Press.

Coleman, J. (ed.) (1987) *Working with Troubled Adolescents*, London: Academic Press.

Coleman, J. (ed.) (1992) *The School Years*, London: Routledge.

Coleman, J. (1995) 'Adolescence', in P. Bryant and A. Colman (eds), *Developmental Psychology*, London: Longman.

Coleman, J. and Warren-Adamson, C. (eds) (1992) *Youth Policy in the 1990s: the Way Forward*, London: Routledge.

Heaven, P. (1994) *Contemporary Adolescence*, London: Macmillan.

McConnon, S. (1990) *Interpersonal Communication: a Personal Skills Course for Young People*, Walton-on-Thames: Nelson.

Moore, S. and Rosenthal, D. (1995) *Sexuality in Adolescence*, London: Routledge.

Noller, P. and Callan, V. (1991) *The Adolescent in the Family*, London: Routledge.

Rutter, M. and Smith, D. (eds) (1995) *Psychosocial Disorders in Young People*, Chichester: Wiley.

Sypher, H. and Applegate, J. (1984) *Communication between Children and Adults*, London: Sage.

26

Working with Young People in Residential Settings

Adrian Ward

This chapter looks at what happens in residential settings for children and young people, and at the difference between what actually happens in many places and what can happen if things are planned and managed properly. I will begin by looking at the current state of residential care for young people in the UK, and at some of the factors that seem to make for good quality practice. I will then focus on the theme of power, and especially on the sense of powerlessness which is sometimes experienced both by the young people in residential care and by the staff working with them. Finally I shall give some examples of ways in which staff may be able to engage in constructive and supportive work with young people. My argument is that the task facing residential staff is to work *with* young people in a very active sense, using skills of listening and reflecting, and aiming to engage directly and wholeheartedly with them, in order to make the most of all the opportunities for communication which arise in everyday life in these settings.

The current state of residential care

The term 'residential care' is used to cover a very wide range of settings including children's homes, boarding schools, and secure units. It also covers a range of young people including those from minority ethnic groups, those with emotional and behavioural difficulties, learning difficulties and physical and other impairments. Some residential care is long-term, but more often it is relatively short-term, covering periods ranging from a few days to a few months. There is also 'respite care', an arrangement through which some children regularly spend brief periods in residential care to give them and their families a break from each other. For the purposes of this chapter, residential care can also be thought of as including fostering, since this involves young people being looked after for periods of time by people other than their parents. Many of the skills required to work with young people in residential care apply to those who are fostered.

The broad scope of residential care can make it difficult to generalise, especially when we think also of the different functions which the care setting may be expected to carry out (Berridge and Brodie, 1998). This ranges from assessment to rehabilitation (Rose, 2002), and from 'looking after' a child during a brief family crisis through to the specialised work of the therapeutic communities, in which the whole work of the care setting is geared towards promoting an ethos of psychotherapeutic treatment for some of the most emotionally-damaged young people (Ward et al., 2003). Yet it can be argued that from the young person's point of view, all residential care has a core element in common, in that it consists of their being looked after away from home by people who are not their parents or other family members.

Given this simple core element in all residential care, it is an unhappy indicator of the value society places on children that residential care has always been a relatively low status service, even in comparison with other branches of social care, with staff often feeling underpaid and undervalued. Efforts to achieve good quality practice are frequently undermined by lack of training and supervisory support (Baldwin, 1990).

The status of this work has been further undermined in recent years. Clear evidence of repressive and/or abusive regimes in several highly-publicised court cases in the early 1990s led to a number of official reports cataloguing the evidence of bad practice and prescribing ways in which better practice could be planned and delivered (for example, Utting, 1997; Waterhouse, 2000). Although the Utting Report led to the Quality Protects/Children First initiative that aims to improve outcomes for children and young people in public care, it can be argued that the cumulative effect of these reports was to further undermine the status of residential care (Corby et al., 2001). Increasingly, it was seen by senior staff in social service departments as the very worst option for young people – even though research evidence clearly indicated that for many young people it was actually the preferred option in some circumstances (Berridge, 1994).

There is risk of a 'vicious circle' operating here. If residential care is seen as something inherently harmful to be avoided as far as possible and perhaps to be dispensed with altogether, then not enough priority will be given to improving its quality. The service will then deteriorate further, and staff may become more demoralised and even less able to offer the quality of service they wish to.

It is true that there are many problems in the achievement of good quality residential care. A national inspection of residential child care in the early 1990s found that:

> There were considerable variations in the quality of care provided. In some homes standards were high and children very well cared for, in others Inspectors were concerned about the quality of accommodation, lack of facilities and the general level of care provided. (Social Services Inspectorate, 1993: iv)

However, the national inspection did find many residential units in which young people felt valued and supported in everyday life. Young people talked positively about receiving help in their development and in the resolution of the challenges facing them. Some described feeling respected and encouraged by their keyworkers, and valued the support of living in a group in which they could talk with other young people.

The contrast between the low professional status of residential care and the high value some young people place on the service may seem puzzling. But it can be better understood by asking: 'What makes for high quality residential care?' The evidence from the Inspections is quite clear on this point: a key finding of the inspection teams was that in those units where there was felt to be a high quality of staff relationships with children,

> the effectiveness of staff in those homes . . . was based on clear leadership, organised and consistent ways of working, and clarity of purpose. (Social Services Inspectorate, 1993: 31)

Whereas on the other hand,

> In those homes where poor practice was observed there was a general lack of awareness on the part of external managers to the difficulties staff were presented with and therefore concerns were not being well represented to senior managers. (1993: 32)

In other words, staff are more likely to achieve positive and constructive relationships with young people where they are clear and in agreement about roles and responsibilities, and where their work is managed in a positive and constructive way. These findings were given further support in the Department of Health's overview of a number of research studies (DoH, 1998). This included several 'outcome' studies that looked at the impact on young people's lives of their time in residential care. They reported that

> outcomes tend to be better where objectives are clear, where they can be implemented, and where they are in accord with one another . . . than where they lack clarity, are unattainable or contradictory or undermined by other parts of the personal social services (1998: 48)

The findings from both research and inspections therefore point clearly to the importance of good management (both internal and external) and of a clear sense of purpose in the residential care and treatment of children.

At the same time as these various inquiry reports were published in the early 1990s, residential care was also starting to be strongly influenced by the requirements of the Children Act 1989, and the legally-binding Guidance which accompanied it. Volume 4 of the Guidance (Department of Health, 1991) set out detailed guidelines for the management and delivery of residential services. These guidelines were largely constructive and positive in their impact, especially as they required much greater clarity of purpose than before. But they also created some difficulties for residential staff in attempting to formalise aspects of practice which had previously been managed in a much more informal way. The guidance also required staff to pay more formal attention to the views of the young people about their experiences in residential care, and this too can be difficult for staff to work with. Quite understandably, young people have strong things to say about their experiences, such as this comment made to an inspection team:

> There is nowhere to be on your own, and that does my head in. The rules change in this place depending on which staff are on. (Social Services Inspectorate, 1993)

Views such as these clearly reflect some of the unhappier situations young people may experience in residential care, and convey a strong sense of powerlessness, and inability to influence the system or the staff who work within it. It is this sense of powerlessness, and the young people's need for real and positive communication with their carers, which underpins the approach described below.

Power, care and 'working *with*' young people

The painful reality of young people's situation in residential care, then, is that at times they can feel extremely powerless. For many of these young people, important decisions about their present and future life have been taken without their being properly involved and consulted. For example, they may have been required to move away from their previous setting without giving their consent. However unsatisfactory that previous setting was at that time, it was at least a known and familiar place. Additional lack of power can be experienced if young people have encountered discrimination and exclusion through being black, disabled, lesbian or gay or combinations of these and their other social identities. They may be disaffected from and mistrust adult society and be emotionally vulnerable and volatile as a result of loss or other trauma experienced prior to coming into care (Anglin, 2003).

Young people in this complex situation will understandably be prone to feeling 'got at' and misunderstood in everyday situations. They are likely to express strong feelings about instances of unfairness often in relation to apparently minor incidents which can arise in the course of everyday living together. Young people may feel that at least *these* incidents can be brought back under their own control, even if the larger scale aspects of powerlessness are completely beyond their influence. This may help to explain the explosions of strong feeling about apparently trivial events in residential settings. It can also indicate, as we shall see later, how important it may be for staff to 'read' and respond to messages of despair or frustration which can underlie such explosions.

Paradoxically, many residential staff also describe themselves as powerless. They may feel powerless in relation to their voice as a worker in the child care system and feel they lack influence over key decisions in young people's lives or other aspects of their work. They may also feel powerless in relation to their everyday interactions with the young people where they feel they have insufficient authority to control young people whose behaviour is difficult and challenging. In reality this is not such a paradox, because both groups are powerless, but in relative terms. There can be 'relative powerlessness' just as there is 'relative poverty'. A person living on a subsistence level of state benefits in the UK can be living in genuine poverty even though their actual income is far higher than that of another person living in poverty in a developing country. So both the young people and the staff in a residential setting can feel they lack power, even though the staff member will always hold more actual power than the young person does, and probably in more areas of her or his life. For a closer analysis of power and empowerment in residential care see Frost et al. (1999).

Nevertheless, judging from the reported views of some young people, and from some inspection reports, it appears that staff can deal with their own frustration by exceeding or abusing the power they do have. Typically they may disregard or undermine young people's views and wishes and pay insufficient attention to their needs and rights. In these situations, staff can appear to be taking revenge for their own sense of powerlessness upon the next least powerful group available – the young people themselves. It is therefore important that those working in residential care are trained, supported and managed to recognise and deal with their own sense of powerlessness, and to respond more constructively to the young people's needs. In other words, they need professional management in order to develop and focus on their professional task.

The professional task in question can be summed up as 'working *with*' the young people: getting alongside them, understanding their needs, and acting appropriately in collaboration with them. This will involve:

1   developing an everyday atmosphere of trust and respect, in which communication is encouraged and taken seriously;
2   finding ways of identifying and responding to opportunities for communication as and when they arise;
3   trying to work collaboratively with the young people, rather than 'talking down' to them or over-riding their wishes; and
4   trying to help them resolve difficulties and disputes which may arise and to restore in them a sense of personal power and influence, without infringing other people's rights.

Staff therefore need to demonstrate that they are willing to listen and take the young people's views and feelings seriously, even though they may not always be able to act upon them in the way young people would like.

But such communication is not always easy and it may be hard at times for young people to articulate their views in ways they would like to, or in ways that might gain them the most sympathetic response. For example, if young people are not used to being taken seriously, or heard at all, they may feel they have to shout or display their feelings physically in order to get their message across. Others may have given up hope that anyone will listen and be extremely reluctant to say *anything* personal. This can leave staff with the frustrating task of trying to guess what they may be feeling or thinking. It can be difficult to 'work with' young people in the collaborative sense described above, especially where staff are not adequately prepared and supported for such work. Yet this frustration should not be a barrier to aiming high. The final section of this chapter describes two approaches that have been tried in some residential units.

Ways of working *with* young people

Despite the difficulties identified above, residential care actually provides many opportunities to work *with* young people. Two ways in which such opportunities can be identified and used are through an 'opportunity led' approach, and a system of regular group or 'community meetings'.

Daily life: opportunity led work

We saw in the previous section how difficulties in communication may lead to things going seriously wrong between young people in residential care and those trying to work with them, and how some of these difficulties can arise over the handling of apparently minor everyday events. Since much of the work with young people in residential settings happens in these informal everyday encounters, it is important that staff should have some way of planning for and thinking about this. I have called this 'opportunity led' work (Ward, 1993), in order to draw attention to the many opportunities for communication that can arise in this context, and have proposed a simple framework for thinking about what's involved (Ward et al., 2003). The framework is based on an analysis of the process involved, from *Assessment* and *Decision-making* through to *Action* and eventually to *Closure*, and traces the skills required of the worker from the beginning to the end of a piece of work.

An example of opportunity led work is when a worker notices a young person looking sad, confused or angry, and turns this observation into an opportunity to help the young person express his or her feelings. Part of the skill required for this mode of work lies in careful and reflective observation, and coupled with this will be the ability to assess people and situations. Thus, in the *Assessment* phase, the worker might notice the young person avoiding contact with peers. Through a combination of observation and assessment she might judge that he[1] may be feeling anxious about an impending visit home to his family or may just be tired and not wanting to socialise. This assessment will inform the *Decision-making phase*, in which the worker decides between a range of methods through which she might try to establish contact with the young person. In this case she might need to choose between a direct approach (such as asking him how he is feeling) and a more indirect one, for example, just 'getting alongside' the young person and being willing to talk about everyday trivia. She may just wait in the hope that *he* will decide that he has an opportunity to talk about his worries. The worker needs to have a range of methods at her fingertips to deal with how the situation may turn out. This is sensitive work, and requires tact and strategic thinking on her part. The decision-making phase is therefore crucial. It is in the *Action* phase that the worker actually tries out her plan, in this case either asking the question or getting alongside. She then watches for the young person's response before making another judgement as to how to follow it up. This phase may become quite prolonged through a sustained conversation or 'on the spot counselling', or it may come to nothing and she may need to withdraw and wait for another opportunity to arise. In the meantime, the residential context means the worker is also having to keep an eye on what is happening with all the other young people and with her colleagues. This is demanding work! Finally, in the *Closure* phase, the piece of work has to be brought to an end so that people can get on with everyday life. It is especially important that things are left clear, and that as far as possible no 'loose ends' are left from whatever conversation has developed.

Even this brief account of opportunity led work reveals how complicated it can be. Yet these decisions and interventions often have to be completed within the space of a few seconds if the opportunity is actually to be seized. The opportunity led framework is one which can be applied to a wide range of situations, ranging from the one-to-one exchanges as described above to the more complicated patterns of interaction which arise between teams of staff and groups of young people. It can also be adapted to different settings, according to the communication and other skills of the young people involved. The aim of using this framework is to help workers to heighten their awareness of the range of opportunities for 'working with' which occur in everyday life, and to develop their repertoire of ways of spotting and using these opportunities. The framework is therefore best used when it has been rehearsed in a training context, in which staff themselves are encouraged to think about how they would want to respond to a range of situations (see Ward, 1995a). It has also been argued (Brown et al., 1998) that the whole 'culture' of a children's home can be evaluated from an analysis of the ways in which staff typically respond to the kinds of situations described here.

Community meetings

The opportunity led approach builds on events and comments that arise in everyday life, and looks for opportunities for communication. But it is also possible to plan for communication in a fuller and more predictable way. This is by guaranteeing to the young people that they will have *regular* time to come together as a group to share their thoughts, feelings and concerns, and to be listened to and responded to by the residential staff. This can be provided through what are known variously as house meetings, young people's meetings, or 'community meetings'. There are various approaches to this mode of working, and it will be important to adopt a model relevant to the particular setting. Meetings may be held on a fortnightly, weekly, or even a daily basis. The main aim will be for the voices of the young people to be heard, individually, sometimes collectively, by their peers, by the staff and perhaps others.

Getting such a system established can feel daunting for staff if they are not experienced in groupwork. Even if they are, a proposal to set up such a system may not always be received enthusiastically Both young people and staff may be concerned about what may emerge, whether what is said will actually be heard and taken seriously by others, and whether any action will result. My own experience (Ward, 1995b) in establishing regular community meetings in a children's home was that it was very difficult at first, for a number of reasons. People (both staff and children) were initially anxious at the prospect of sitting together in one room simply to talk to each other. Some people find talking in a large group quite intimidating at first, and others find the idea of talking to *anyone* about their own thoughts and feelings threatening. However, my experience was that, by starting with as simple as possible a format, and developing slowly, it was eventually possible to achieve a great deal through these meetings. Children and staff gradually found the confidence both to express their own views and to tolerate listening to others' that might be in conflict with their own. The message to those thinking of establishing such meetings in a residential setting can be summarised as follows. Start small; be ready to adapt your methods according to need; be totally reliable and consistent and finally, work as a team, and be sure of your support systems.

Both opportunity led work and community meetings are examples of ways of promoting communication between young people and the staff working with them. In both examples, what is called for on the part of the staff is some initiative, resilience, and willingness to listen and to take young people's thoughts and feelings seriously. Both of these approaches *can* be implemented without huge amounts of planning and policy making. In some settings versions of these approaches happen largely through the informal and intuitive efforts of committed individuals. However, it is always better where possible to aim to incorporate such methods into the agreed ways of working of a staff team, with the appropriate planning, support and monitoring. In this way, there is more chance that the approach will be used in a reliable and consistent way by all members of the team, rather than implemented by some and ignored or even undermined by others.

The examples given are not the only ways in which residential care practice needs to be improved. Other initiatives have developed out of new legislation, research, policy and practice. The Human Rights Act 1998 has built on the Children Act 1989 and influenced local authority willingness to involve young people directly in decisions about their well-being. Participation by young people is now expected and monitored, though recent evidence suggests there is still much work to be done (DoH SSI, 2002). The Children Act 1989 and the Quality Protects/Children First initiative have promoted and supported young people's contact with their families, following research that showed better outcomes leaving care when young people had strong and positive family and peer relationships (Biehal et al., 1995). Practical guidance has also emerged on what can work in maintaining contact (Chakrabarti and Hill, 2000; Ainsworth, 1997). A third area of change is the attention being paid to better educational outcomes for young people in public care. This follows reviews and studies that identified high levels of non-attendance, school exclusions, truancy and poor attainment amongst looked after children (Utting, 1997; Brodie, 2001). Joint guidance issued in 2000 requires local authorities to put a range of provisions in place such as individual personal education plans and advises that every school appoint a designated teacher for looked after children. In addition, young people leaving care should now all have personal advisors responsible for developing pathway plans to support their transition to independent adulthood.

Conclusion

This chapter began with an account of some of the difficulties that can arise in the residential care of children and young people, and showed how these difficulties were highlighted in a national inspection of the services. The themes of power and powerlessness, and the central need for communication between young people and their carers were highlighted, and the rest of the chapter described two different approaches to promoting communication within residential settings. The remaining difficulty is that, despite some efforts at improvement and the introduction of Care Standards (Dept of Health, 2001), residential child care is still an undervalued and under-funded service. This is especially the case in respect of opportunities for professional development and training (Crimmens, 2000). The real challenge that still faces those responsible for the service is how to implement the models for improved practice now available. There are many good ideas around, but employers at both national and local level still have to face up to their responsibility for funding sufficient opportunities for staff training and development.

Note

For the sake of convenience, in this example I have used 'she' to refer to the worker and 'he' to refer to the young person.

References

Ainsworth, F. (1997) *Family Centred Group Care: Model Building*, Aldershot: Ashgate.
Anglin, J. (2003) *Pain, Normality and the Struggle for Congruence: Reinterpreting Residential Care for Children and Youth*, Binghamton, NY: Haworth Press.

Baldwin, N. (1991) *The Power to Care in Children's Homes. Experiences of Residential Workers*, Aldershot: Avebury.

Berridge, D. (1994) 'Foster and Residential Care Re-assessed', *Children and Society*, 8 (2): 132–50.

Berridge, D. and Brodie, I. (1998) *Children's Homes Revisited*, London: Jessica Kingsley.

Biehal, N., Clayden, J., Stein, M. and Wade, J. (1995) *Moving On: Young People and Leaving Care Schemes*, London: HMSO.

Brodie, I. (2001) *Children's Homes and School Exclusion: Redefining the Problem*, London: Jessica Kingsley.

Brown, E. Bullock, R., Hobson, C. and Little, M. (1998) *Making Residential Care Work: Structure and Culture in Children's Homes*, Aldershot: Ashgate.

Chakrabarti, M. and Hill, M. (eds) (2000) *Residential Child Care: International Perspectives on Links with Families and Peers*, London: Jessica Kingsley.

Corby, B., Doig, A. and Roberts, V. (2001) *Public Inquiries into Abuse of Children in Residential Care*, London: Jessica Kingsley.

Crimmens, D. (2000) 'Things can Only Get Better!' An Evaluation of Developments in the Training and Qualification of Residential Child Care Staff' in D. Crimmens and J. Pitts (eds) *Positive Residential Practice: Learning the lessons of the 1990s*. Lyme Regis, Russell House Publishing.

Department of Health (1991) *The Children Act Guidance and Regulations. Vol. 4: Residential Care*, London: HMSO.

Department of Health (1998) *Caring for Children away from Home: Messages from Research*, London: The Stationery Office.

Department of Health (2001) *Children's Homes: National Minimum Standards: Children's Homes Regulations* London : The Stationery Office.

Department of Health Social Services Inspectorate (2002) *Delivering Quality Children's Services: Inspection of Children's Service Summary*, http:www.doh.gov.uk/ssi/deliveringqualitycssummary.pdf

Frost, N., Mills, S. and Stein, M. (1999) *Understanding Residential Child Care*. Aldershot: Ashgate.

Rose, J. (2002) *Working with Young People in Secure Accommodation*, Hove: Brunner-Routledge.

Social Services Inspectorate (1993) *Corporate Parents: Inspection of Residential Child Care Services in 11 Local Authorities, November 1992–March 1993*, London: Department of Health.

Utting, Sir William. (1997) *People Like Us: The Report of the Review of the Safeguards for Children Living away from Home*, London: Department of Health and The Welsh Office.

Ward, A. (1993) *Working in Group Care: Social Work in Residential and Day Care Settings*, Birmingham: Venture Press.

Ward, A (1995a) 'Opportunity led work Part 1: the concept', *Social Work Education*, 14 (4): 89–105.

Ward, A. (1995b) 'Establishing Community Meetings in a Children's Home', *Groupwork*, 15 (1): 4–23.

Ward, A., Kasinski, K, Pooley, J., and Worthington, A. (eds) (2003) *Therapeutic Communities for Children and Young Peoples*, London: Jessica Kingsley.

Waterhouse, R. (2000) *Lost in Care: Report of the Tribunal of Inquiry into the Abuse of Children in Care in the Former County Council Areas of Gwynedd and Clwyd since 1974*, HC210. London: The Stationery Office.

27
The Management of Growing Up: Youth Work in Community Settings

Simon Bradford

Late modernity's enduring concern with the problem of young people (and young people's problems) has resulted in the massive expansion of youth work and other services for young people during the last 100 years.

In common with public sector services in general, professional youth work now operates in a social and institutional climate which has radically altered during the last few years. The background to this has been well rehearsed elsewhere, but includes growing inequality in general and amongst young people in particular (Williamson, 1993; Commission on Social Justice, 1994), fundamental changes to the fabric of the welfare state (George and Miller, 1994), and the wholesale 'managerialisation' of public services (Pollitt, 1993; Clarke et al., 1994). In this context youth work has faced difficult tasks. Increased demands on diminishing or reconfigured resources have meant that youth work has had to present itself carefully to survive. Its institutional location – the 'youth service' – has had a curious history, largely as a consequence of its somewhat confused legislative status. Historically part of a complex of education provisions and practices, youth work's position was recently confirmed by moves to mark out a distinct youth work pedagogy through a 'core curriculum'. Despite falling short of a 'national curriculum' as such, an agreed 'statement of purpose' for youth work has led to the *local* determination of curricula.

In this chapter it is suggested that long-standing tensions in youth work are particularly acute at present. The chapter outlines a discernible sharpening of the tension between the principle of 'universal' youth work provision, and a focused approach on young people 'at risk'. In doing this, it is suggested that the latter may accord with current political priorities, but should by no means be seen as a permanent shift in the direction of youth work.

Justifying youth work

Youth work has its roots in nineteenth century attempts to render the working-class 'governable by reason' (Donald, 1992: 23), seeking to mould the character and conduct of working class youth (Gillis, 1974; Springhall, 1977; Smith, 1988). The notion of adolescence, shaped by the new science of psychology, formed a relatively stable underlying discourse which has justified youth work to the present time (Rose, 1985; Jones and Wallace, 1992; Griffin, 1993). Nineteenth century fears and fascination with the 'perishing and dangerous classes of children and young offenders' also have their contemporary expression in concerns about the so-called 'underclass' (Murray, 1990).

Despite having achieved some recognition as one of the 'caring professions' (Abbott and Wallace, 1990), youth work has remained an ambiguous practice or set of practices, pushed in different directions at different times by different interests. It appears to be infinitely fluid, flexible, and mobile. It has a capacity to work in diverse settings, and to shift its identity in response to varying conceptions of 'youth need', either self-defined or specified by others. In one guise, for example, youth work appears to be aimed at the careful management of young people's leisure time, with youth workers organising a range of activities with and for young people: sports, arts, and drama in youth clubs, centres, and projects. Elsewhere, youth workers touch on the therapeutic domain through their work in counselling, advice, and information services. In yet another incarnation, youth workers may be seen in an explicitly 'educational' role, helping young people to understand matters connected with health, sexuality, personal and social relationships, race, or gender. Underlying all of these activities is a professional commitment to *voluntary* and *participatory* relationships between youth workers and young people. Youth workers argue that it is the intimacy of these relationships, freely chosen by young people, which leads to their potency.

As well as being a strength, youth work's protean nature is also a weakness. Youth work has never been able to colonise a distinct territory of its own, and youth workers have often been forced to occupy the spaces left by other institutions: social work, schooling, or leisure, for example. Perhaps because of its flexibility, youth work has recently become increasingly deployed in 'youth justice work', and work with young people variously considered to be 'at risk'. This raises the seemingly intractable dilemma (for youth workers, at least) of whether they are 'agents of social control', or informal educators seeking to provide a universal service to young people (Jeffs and Smith, 1994). The main problem in this apparently inexhaustible debate is that the concept of social control inadequately discriminates between the multiple interventions and initiatives which attempt to enact the administration of human conduct in modern societies (Rose and Miller, 1988: 172). Youth work should be seen as part of a network of institutions and practices whose task has been to ensure the stability, harmony, growth, and care of populations – to contribute to the 'government' of modern societies (Foucault, 1991: 102). The concept of government in this sense denotes a characteristically modern and liberal form of political authority and rule which is neither necessarily repressive, nor prohibitive. Rather, governmental power is intended to operate quietly and efficiently in managing and regulating populations, often through the 'technical' expertise of professionals: social workers, health visitors, and youth workers, for example. Their contemporary role is to encourage individuals to exercise their own responsibility and freedom – in effect, to 'govern' themselves.

Discourses of social education

The term 'social education' has provided youth work with a discursive, though changing, centre of gravity since the 1960s. The Thompson Committee's 1982 report on the future of the youth service confirmed that its specific task is 'to provide social education' as a universal service to all young people who might benefit from it (Department of Education and Science, 1982: 122). Although something of a movable feast, it is possible to discern 'liberal' and 'radical' genres of social education. These embody different perceptions of young people and their needs, and their emergence is loosely associated with particular historical periods. However it should not be assumed that one of these has supplanted the other, and current youth work ideologies embrace different combinations of both.

Liberal accounts of social education emphasise the (abstract) individual, and his or her relations with others. In this essentially humanist and 'person-centred' perspective, social education seeks to enable the individual (young person) to become more conscious of and better understand 'self'.

By fostering an 'ethics of the self', liberal social education aims in part at least to develop an introspective, 'reflexive', and active self, able to appraise, evaluate, and work on its constitutive feelings, attitudes, and opinions. According to Davies and Gibson, social education should be initiated in the context of the personal relationships which young people form with others, enabling them to 'know first hand and feel personally how common interests and shared activities bring and keep people together and what causes them to drift apart' (1967: 13). Thus *experiential* and *participative* dimensions to social education emerge as its defining features. Typically, youth work activities are designed to maximise young people's participation in personal relationships, and to encourage them to reflect on and learn from these experiences.

An accommodation between individual desires, and the social responsibilities which individuals must bear, is one of social education's intended effects. As Davies and Gibson put it, 'truly helpful social education' must create a proper equilibrium between 'self-expression' and conformity. It should take account of the demand to be '"loyal", "responsible", "respectful", and especially "law-abiding"' (1967: 17). In this sense the concern is with the production of a particular kind of subjectivity, sensitive to social values and responsibilities, and simultaneously active in developing its own self-defined potential. This is of prime importance. Social education aims to ensure that individual young people learn to 'govern' themselves, to 'effect by their own means, various operations on their own bodies, souls, thoughts, and conduct . . . [and] transform themselves, modify themselves' (Miller, 1987: 206–7). As such, it is a practice compatible with the principles of liberal democracy in which the self-regulating and autonomous individual exercises choice, responsibility, and freedom in the pursuit of 'good citizenship'.

Davies and Gibson's account of social education is paradigmatic. Its dissemination through various reports and accounts over the years has given identity and meaning to youth work, although its individualistic stance and liberal outlook have been subject to considerable criticism (Butters, 1978; Smith, 1988). During the 1970s and 1980s, this mode of social education was apparently 'radicalised'. Newly emerging discourses and politics of gender, race, and disability became imprinted on youth work in a variety of ways. The abstract inhabitants of earlier discourses of social education became transformed into 'young women', 'young black people', 'disabled', or 'gay' young people. Youth workers (as social educators) came to see themselves as responding to a range of 'issues' which mapped out young people's lives, and thus structured the terrain of youth work. Young people, it seemed, could receive an appropriate response only if they were understood as being subject to and shaped by various social forces and factors: racism, sexism, disability, unemployment, poverty, and so on. Youth workers became concerned with 'empowering' young people, helping them to develop the skills, knowledge, and dispositions necessary to become society's active participants, rather than its passive victims. This process-oriented practice is further shaped by 'a belief in justice: all people have the same rights' (Karsh, c. 1984). It retains an individual focus, but introduces the 'political' background against which young people are illuminated.

In practice, different elements from the two modes of social education have meshed. Youth work has become a complex of sometimes ambiguous aims, techniques and initiatives drawing on both liberal and radical modes. Social education remains a debated theme, though with marked continuities: a focus on the problematic nature of young people's transition to adulthood, experience as the well-spring of learning, a concern with the relationship between the individual and the 'social', and the sometimes explicit, and at others implicit, aim of cultivating the autonomous and self-regulating individual.

From universal social education to work with 'at risk' young people

As part of a commitment to rendering public services more transparent and amenable to mechanisms of accountability, youth work and youth services have recently come under political scrutiny. The minister responsible challenged the service to specify its objectives (Howarth, 1989), signalling the increased political demand for a sharper focus for youth work, including the identification of specific young people to be targeted. However, following three national youth service conferences 'universalism' rather than 'targeted' provision appeared to be embodied in the following rather utopian youth service 'statement of purpose':

> to redress all forms of inequality and to ensure equality of opportunity for all young people to fulfil their potential as empowered individuals and members of groups and communities and to support young people in their transition to adulthood. (National Youth Agency, 1992: 21)

Drawing on earlier social education discourse, the statement goes on to indicate that youth work should be educational, participative, empowering, informal, responsive and based on *secure* relationships, and should provide information, advice and counselling to young people between the ages of 11 and 25, with those in the 13 to 19 age group being the priority (National Youth Agency, 1992).

Youth work has always had a rather troubled perception of its proper role with 'delinquent' or marginal young people. Whilst it has always voiced a commitment (arguably rhetorical) to this work, youth workers have simultaneously resisted being regarded as part of the formal 'justice' system. Like the Albemarle Committee in 1960 (Ministry of Education, 1960), the Thompson Committee promoted a view of youth work with 'at risk' young people (a term left unspecified) as part of the routine provision of a *universal* service. The youth service, Thompson suggested, should engage with 'at risk' young people as part of the process of

> following up *its proper concern for the personal development of all young people,* including those in difficulties, . . . young people at risk or in trouble. (Department of Education and Science, 1982: 51, my emphasis)

Interest in youth work with 'at risk' young people accords with current ministerial and political priorities. These attach great symbolic significance to various 'risk' populations: the so-called 'underclass', young single mothers, drug abusers, truants, young homeless, and of course young offenders. Some youth workers and youth services are being drawn into a substantial role with such 'at risk' groups. Inevitably, this has exacerbated the tension between the principle of universality, and 'targeted' work. For some commentators, this is part of a Faustian pact, in which short-term funding will be paid for by youth service's long-term marginalisation (Gutfreund, 1993: 15). However, various policy initiatives designed to encourage work with 'at risk' groups have been taken centrally as well as by local authorities and voluntary sector agencies.

Initiatives with 'at risk' young people

Much of the work organised around the concept of risk is aimed at young people considered to be at risk of *offending* – in other words, young people potentially (or actually) involved in criminal behaviour. Between 1992 and 1996, £10 million of DfE money has funded short-term community-based 'youth action schemes', which are emblematic of initiatives in this field. They are intended to contribute to the reduction of youth crime in urban areas by encouraging work with groups of 13–17 year olds 'at risk of drifting into crime' (Department for Education, 1993). Local authority youth services and their youth workers have been heavily involved in the schemes, and have brought together a range of statutory departments and voluntary agencies in collaborative work. Schemes have operated in a variety of ways and used a range of media with young people.

Drama and arts work in schools, detached work on the streets, residential experiences, mobile activity programmes, and information and counselling services are among the settings in which social education expertise is being deployed. Although crime reduction or diversion has been the principal rationale, work has been undertaken on various issues considered to place young people 'at risk'. This procrustean concept offers infinite scope for constituting a vast repertoire of behaviours and circumstances as part of its special territory. The organisers of one youth action scheme in the West Midlands included in their definition of young people 'at risk' of offending those who:

– are seen as experiencing the consequences of anxious and 'hostile' reactions of individuals/sections of the community to their specific behaviour or particular social issues;
– are being stereotyped, or have a reputation and stigma attached to them as a result of perceived or real manifestations of anti-social behaviour;
– are 'vulnerable' by virtue of their age, gender, or community identity. (Huskins, 1993: 21)

This scheme identified a further 32 'less formal' factors placing young people 'at risk'.

Four principal factors have justified the youth service's sharpening profile in this area of work, all of which should be regarded as ideological. The first of these is that this work is regarded as 'social education', and as such is part of the traditional fabric of youth work.

Secondly, like other 'welfaring' and educational practices, some youth work takes an approach (particularly toward 'difficult' young people) informed by the rationale that some young people are 'at risk' *rather than* simply 'dangerous'. This is a reworking of the idea (implicit in many early accounts of youth work) that *vulnerable* young people can all too easily become dangerous. By identifying their 'at risk' status (that is, their vulnerability), early *diversionary* or *preventive* intervention is thought possible. Rather than privileging characteristics which are thought to reside *in* individuals, the concept of 'risk' concentrates attention on abstract factors which constitute an individual as being 'at risk'. In constructing the 'at risk' individual – part of what Hacking refers to as a process of 'making up people' (1986: 222) – almost anything can be plausibly incorporated. The notion of risk offers limitless possibilities for identifying new sites for expert intervention in the social and material worlds (Castel, 1991: 289), powerfully justifying professional activity, of which the 'multi-agency' approach is an expression (Department for Education, 1993). The concept's utility lies in its capacity to render the entire domain in which the young person is located potentially knowable and amenable to the calculus of professional evaluation and intervention. As such it greatly facilitates the expansion of governmental activity.

Thirdly, arguments advanced from influential sources indicate that youth work approaches to crime and criminality are both efficient and effective, and offer 'value for money'. Janet Paraskeva, then Director of the National Youth Agency, argued that youth work is cost effective, and 'A little more money invested in youth work could save a lot more in community sentencing' (Paraskeva, 1992: 16).

A high profile report by the accountants Coopers Lybrand suggested that youth work offers a valuable means of 'crime diversion' (1994: 25). If Coopers Lybrand's calculation of youth work expenditure per young person is correct – they estimated £30 per annum for each potential participant in youth work, against a £2,300 short-term saving on each youth crime prevented (1994: 25) – this must surely be seen as offering a convincing justification (at least as far as its proponents are concerned) for youth work involvement in this area.

This work might also be thought to be more amenable to managerialist practices already flourishing in public services (Pollitt, 1993; Clarke et al., 1994). Arguably, targeted rather than universal provision provides the opportunity for the identification of clearer 'outcomes', as well as for the deployment of apparently unambiguous 'performance indicators' in measuring these. The Department for Education (1993) has pointed out that in evaluating youth action schemes, 'Outcomes are the key consideration'. Supporters of these initiatives have also claimed that youth work is *effective* in this context. Paraskeva has argued that 'at risk' young people need

> help in developing their communication skills, activities which are exciting, stimulating and challenging, and opportunities to take part in education or training programmes which enhance their understanding of themselves and give them a chance in the world. (1992: 16)

Almost simultaneously, the Assistant Commissioner of the Metropolitan Police concluded in a report on juvenile crime in the capital that youth provision had considerable potential in diverting young people from criminal activity (Winship, quoted in Young, 1992: 10). Academic support for youth work involvement in this field has focused on its potential in programmes of 'social crime prevention' (Pitts, 1992: 186; Smith and Paylor, 1994: 33).

The final element in the rationale for youth work involvement in this area is fundamentally pragmatic. At a time of diminishing budgets and uncertainty in the public services, a tangible and socially valued role for youth workers is important if they are to survive. Thus, Smith and Paylor have remarked that 'immediate political interest and more principled considerations' (1994: 33) should encourage youth workers to become increasingly involved in this work. A recent OFSTED report on the youth service suggests that there is

> a continuing debate concerning the proper target for resources . . . the question is whether the service should continue to be broad in scope to provide opportunities for all or whether parts of it should concentrate resources on those most in need, however defined. (1993: 1)

This tension between universal and targeted provision is particularly acute at a time when the actual numbers of young people participating might make youth service vulnerable. Indeed, the relatively small overall number of young people participating in youth service activities (Department for Education, 1995) already undermines the claim to be a 'universal' service.

Conclusions

Youth work's emergence as part of a range of initiatives (education, leisure provision, and social work, for example) designed to manage and regulate the exigencies of 'growing up' has been discussed in this chapter. The significance of notions of 'social education', social education's role in encouraging young people to govern their own experiences and conduct, and its deployment in dealing with contemporary concerns about young people, have been indicated. Some difficulties associated with the 'universal' provision of social education, and the political and practical utility of the concept of risk, have also been highlighted.

Youth work has been increasingly drawn into initiatives explicitly designed to manage specific groups of young people, particularly those thought to be 'at risk' of involvement in criminal activity. Four factors have justified this: an established tradition in this work; the general prevalence of the notion of 'risk' in welfare and education practices; the claim that youth work is effective and offers 'value for money'; and finally, pragmatic reasons associated with uncertainties surrounding publicly funded youth work, its limited contact with young people, and an ensuing need for youth work to demonstrate a socially valued role. It remains to be seen whether work with young people considered at risk of involvement in crime will provide this.

Youth work's history is predicated on the idea that young people (*qua* adolescents) are *essentially* vulnerable (and thus at risk). Young people are likely to remain a source of political and social concern, and no doubt new aspects of youth risk wait to be revealed or constructed. Youth work, in one form or another, will continue to offer a flexible means of contributing to the governance of young people.

References

Abbott, P. and Wallace, C. *(eds)* (1990) *The Sociology of the Caring Professions*, London: Falmer Press.

Butters, S. (1978) *Realities of Training: a Review of the Training of Adults who Volunteer to Work with Young People in the Youth and Community Service*, Leicester: National Youth Bureau.

Castel, R. (1991) 'From Dangerousness to Risk', in G. Burchell, C. Gordon and P. Miller (eds), *The Foucault Effect: Studies in Governmentality*, London: Harvester Wheatsheaf.

Clarke, J., Cochrane, A. and McLaughlin, E. (eds) (1994) *Managing Social Policy*, London: Sage.

Commission on Social Justice (1994) *Social Justice: Strategies for National Renewal*, the Report of the Commission on Social Justice, London: Vintage.

Coopers Lybrand (1994) *Preventive Strategy for Young People in Trouble*, London: ITV Telethon/Prince's Trust.

Davies, B. and Gibson, A. (1967) *The Social Education of the Adolescent*, London: University of London Press.

Department for Education (1993) *GEST, Youth Action Scheme, Arrangements for Evaluation and Reporting*, London: Youth Service Unit.

Department for Education, (1995) 'Young people's participation in the youth service', Statistical Bulletin 1/95

Department of Education and Science (1982) *Experience and Participation: Report of the Review Group on the Youth Service in England and Wales*, London: HMSO, Cmnd 8686.

Donald, J. (1992) *Sentimental Education, Schooling, Popular Culture and the Regulation of Liberty*, London: Verso.

Foucault, M. (1991) 'Governmentality', in G. Burchell, C. Gordon and P. Miller (eds), *The Foucault Effect: Studies in Governmentality*, London: Harvester Wheatsheaf.

George, V. and Miller, S. (1994) *Social Policy towards 2000: Squaring the Welfare Circle*, London: Routledge.

Gillis, J. (1974) *Youth and History*, New York: Academic Press.

Griffin, C. (1993) *Representations of Youth: the Study of Youth and Adolescence in Britain and America*, Oxford: Polity Press.

Gutfreund, R. (1993) 'Towards 2000: which direction for the youth service?', *Youth and Policy*, 41: 13–19.

Hacking, I. (1986) 'Making up people', in T. Heller (ed.), *Reconstructing Individualism: Autonomy, Individuality, and the Self in Western Thought*, Stanford: Stanford University Press.

Howarth, A. (1989) 'A core curriculum for the youth service?', Ministerial Address to the First Ministerial Conference with the Youth Service, 13–14 December 1989.

Huskins, J. (1993) *Youth Action Scheme, 6 Month Report*, Report to the Metropolitan Borough of Dudley on the GEST funded Youth Action Scheme.

Jeffs, T. and Smith, M. (1994) 'Young people, youth work, and a new authoritarianism', *Youth and Policy*, no. 46, Autumn.

Jones, G. and Wallace, C. (1992) *Youth, Family and Citizenship*, Buckingham: Open University Press.

Karsh, H. (*c*. 1984) 'Social education defined?', *ILEA Newsletter*, editorial.

Miller, P. (1987) *Domination and Power*, London: Routledge and Kegan Paul.

Ministry of Education (1960) *The Youth Service in England and Wales*, London: HMSO.

Murray, C. (1990) *The Emerging British Underclass*, London: EA.

National Youth Agency (1992) Background Papers to the Third Ministerial Conference for the Youth Service.

OFSTED (1993) *Youth Work Responses to Young People at Risk*, Report from the Office of Her Majesty's Chief Inspector of Schools, 395/93/NS, London: Office for Standards in Education.

Paraskeva, J. (1992) 'Keeping out of trouble', *Times Educational Supplement*, 21 October.

Pitts, J. (1992) 'Juvenile-justice policy in England and Wales', in J. Coleman and C. Warren-Adamson (eds), *Youth Policy In the 1990s: The Way Forward*, London: Routledge.

Pollitt, C. (1993) *Managerialism and the Public Services: Cuts or Cultural Changes in the 1990s?*, 2nd edn, Oxford: Blackwell.

Rose, N. (1985) *The Psychological Complex: Psychology, Politics and Society in England 1869–1939*, London: Routledge and Kegan Paul.

Rose, N. and Miller, P. (1988) 'The Tavistock programme: the government of subjectivity and social life', *Sociology*, 22 (2).

Smith, M. (1988) *Developing Youth Work*, Milton Keynes: Open University *Press*.

Smith, D. and Paylor, I. (1994) 'The youth service and crime prevention', *Social Action*, 2 (2).

Springhall, J. (1977) *Youth, Empire, and Society*, London: Croom Helm.

Williamson, H. (1993) 'Youth policy in the United Kingdom and the marginalisation of young people', *Youth and Policy*, no. 40.

Young, S. (1992) 'Strapped in and ready for a very bumpy ride', *Times Educational Supplement*, 13 November.

Index